Fortune
Strategy

FINANCIAL TIMES
Prentice Hall

In an increasingly competitive world, it is quality
of thinking that gives an edge – an idea that opens new
doors, a technique that solves a problem, or an insight
that simply helps make sense of it all.

We work with leading authors in the fields of
management and finance to bring cutting-edge thinking
and best learning practice to a global market.

Under a range of leading imprints, including
Financial Times Prentice Hall, we create world-class
print publications and electronic products giving
readers knowledge and understanding which can then
be applied, whether studying or at work.

To find out more about our business and professional
products, you can visit us at www.financialminds.com

For other Pearson Education publications, visit
www.pearsoned-ema.com

Pearson
Education

Fortune Strategy

Portfolio management for the new economy

Arun Abey, Clifford German
and Ean Higgins

An imprint of **Pearson Education**

London • New York • San Francisco • Toronto • Sydney • Tokyo • Singapore
Hong Kong • Cape Town • Madrid • Paris • Milan • Munich • Amsterdam

PEARSON EDUCATION LIMITED

Head Office:
Edinburgh Gate
Harlow CM20 2JE
Tel: +44 (0)1279 623623
Fax: +44 (0)1279 431059

London Office:
128 Long Acre, London WC2E 9AN
Tel: +44 (0)20 7447 2000
Fax: +44 (0)20 7240 5771
Website: www.financialminds.com

————————————

First published in Australia in 1995 by Allen & Unwin
Second edition published in Australia in 2000 by Allen & Unwin
This edition published in Great Britain in 2001

© Arun Abey, Clifford German and Ean Higgins 2001

The right of Arun Abey, Clifford German and Ean Higgins
to be identified as authors of this work has been asserted by them
in accordance with the Copyright, Designs and Patents Act 1988.

ISBN 0 273 63927 7

British Library Cataloguing in Publication Data
A CIP catalogue record for this book can be obtained from the British Library.

10 9 8 7 6 5 4 3 2 1

Typeset by Northern Phototypesetting Co Ltd, Bolton
Printed and bound in Great Britain by Bell & Bain Ltd, Glasgow

The Publishers' policy is to use paper manufactured from sustainable forests.

About the authors

Arun Abey (B.A. Hons, B.Ec., ASIA) took degrees in economics and Asian studies at the Australian National University in Canberra. After graduating with First Class Honours in 1979, he worked for the Department of Economics in the Research School of Pacific Studies at the Australian National University, and later for the Australian Bureau of Agricultural and Resource Economics. In 1983 he helped found ipac securities limited, a company specializing in investment portfolio research and management both for institutional and private clients. He has directed the company's expansion overseas into Europe, Asia and South Africa. The ipac group of companies, of which Abey is Executive Chairman, employs more than 400 professional staff globally. Abey is an associate of the Securities Institute of Australia, and regularly writes investment articles for the media and research journals.

Clifford German (M.A. Hons) learned Russian as a National Serviceman in the Royal Navy, then studied geography at Cambridge University. He taught geography at the University of Michigan and Wayne State University in Detroit and co-authored *An Economic Geography of the USSR* with Professor John Cole before joining the *Financial Times* in 1961. He has since worked for *The Times*, the *Daily Telegraph*, where he was Associate City Editor, and *Today*, where he was City Editor. From 1987 to 1994 he was City Editor of *The Scotsman* before joining the *Independent*, where he was Personal Finance Editor from 1995 to 1997. He has also written the Norwich Union *Guide to Mortgage Finance*, published by Penguin in 1988.

Ean Higgins (B.A. Hons, M.A.) studied international relations at the University of Sussex in England and the Australian National University. Between degrees, he worked for the United Nations Centre for Regional Development in Japan. He joined *The Australian Financial Review* in 1982, spending five years as a reporter and section editor covering a range of financial and political rounds. In 1984 he set up the *Financial Review's* bureau in Wellington and served for one year as the newspaper's first New Zealand staff correspondent. He later worked for the national investigative journal *The Times on Sunday* as a senior reporter, then joined *The Australian*, where his roles included Foreign News Editor. From 1996 to 1998 he was posted to London as *The Australian*'s Europe correspondent. He is currently a senior editor on the newspaper.

Contents

PART ONE

Concepts of investment

PART TWO

The asset classes

PART THREE

Theory into practice

Authors' note

The laws relating to taxation, social security benefits and the investment and handling of money are constantly changing and are often subject to the discretion of tax officials. Investment markets too are subject to frequent and significant change. While every reasonable care has been taken to ensure the accuracy of the material contained herein at the time of publication, neither the authors nor the publisher will bear responsibility or liability for any action taken by any person, persons or organization on the purported basis of anything contained in this book.

Without limiting the generality of the foregoing, no person, persons or organization should invest monies or take other action on reliance of the material contained herein but instead should satisfy themselves independently (whether by expert advice or otherwise) of the appropriateness of such action.

To our parents
Don Samson and Annapurni (in memoriam)
Reg and Jessie
Ben and Jean

Acknowledgements

The authors would like to thank everyone who helped them compile this book. They include the press offices of the Bank of England, the Inland Revenue, the Association of Unit Trusts and Investment Funds, the Association of Investment Trusts, the Council of Mortgage Lenders, the Bankers Association, the National Savings movement, and Proshare.

Special thanks are due to David Gaite, Geraldine Minords, Andrew Ford and other staff of ipac securities limited, who put enormous personal effort into assisting with research, mathematical modelling, editing and production.

Andrew Skirton, Chris Sutton, Alistair Harding-Smith and Hannah Skeates of Barclays Global Investors provided invaluable assistance with the collation of data and graphs.

Eric Browne of PricewaterhouseCoopers, John Battersby of KPMG, and Ian Brown of Deutsche Morgan Grenfell all provided valuable comments on the various tax sections. Other valuable comments were provided by independent adviser Michael Royde, property consultant Rodney Adams, Simon Cooke of Morgan Grenfell Property Management, Willie Slattery of Deutsche Morgan Grenfell, Mark Edwards of Royal and Sun Alliance, Paul Wright of Allied Dunbar, and Martin Dryden of Gartmore (Jersey). Their assistance has been invaluable.

For any errors of fact and interpretation the authors alone are responsible.

Arun Abey, Clifford German and Ean Higgins

List of figures

List of tables

Preface

Britons and their European neighbours begin the new millennium with more opportunities for wealth creation through investment markets than ever before. But simultaneously, there are more obstacles to succeeding in investment markets.

The UK has enjoyed a decade of economic revival and solid investment market performance. More and more Britons now own shares and show an interest in investment, and the media has responded with an avalanche of information.

Yet in spite of the current prosperity, an extraordinary level of uncertainty surrounds financial markets and the economy. And closer examination of the portfolios of the hundreds of thousands of new investors in the stock market shows most to be haphazard and badly flawed.

At one level, the doubt stemmed from the Asian economic crisis that ignited in 1997 and spread to other emerging markets. At another level was the huge bubble in information technology and dot com stocks that amazed the City of London around the turn of the century. New, untried technology companies with tiny profits such as Freeserve pushed Whitbread, one of the oldest established UK companies with annual profits more than 20 times greater, out of the prestigious FTSE index of the top 100 UK stocks. Then, in the middle of April in the year 2000, the dot coms were severely shaken by a plunge in high-tech stocks on most of the world's sharemarkets.

The heart of the uncertainty, however, is the fact that the new millennium marks an epochal change as we move from the Industrial to the Information Age. This era began more than 30 years ago as computer use began to spread. Its full realization today is associated with a rapid rate of technological change, deregulation, globalization and connectivity – that is, the effective linking of most human beings on the planet through computer networks. In turn, this trend is causing upheaval in society, politics and business.

There is little doubt that the Information Age is creating great new wealth and investment opportunities. The world's best minds, however, are struggling to understand fully how the world economy and financial markets work in this new era. Economists have long been derided for their inability to forecast the future. But now they are struggling to explain even the recent past, limited as they are by tools and models honed for the Industrial Age.

As recently as the mid-1990s, conventional models would have dismissed the possibility that even with higher interest rates, an over-valued currency and a declining industrial base, the UK could outperform its neighbours in the European Union. Equally incredible would have been the prospect that the US could experience sustained rapid growth with minuscule unemployment and not trigger inflation, and the US stock market could treble in price in less than five years.

The replacement of the Agrarian Age by the Industrial Age three centuries ago saw a similar mix of uncertainty and opportunity. Some saw only the destruction of the past and were fearful of change. Others, less myopic and less fearful, perceived the emerging opportunities and, using wit, skill and no doubt some luck, positioned themselves to benefit, sometimes handsomely.

It took societies well over a century to adapt economically, politically and culturally to the Industrial Age. While the pace of adaptation today is arguably much faster, we are still likely to face more than a decade of profound uncertainty. The challenge for investors will be to have the courage to seek the huge opportunities that are accompanying this change and to ditch the dogmas, prejudices and outdated models of the past.

Investors in the UK and Europe have never had a better opportunity to increase their stock of wealth. Deregulation of domestic and global financial markets has created an array of investment opportunities undreamt of only a generation ago. The average wage earner can simultaneously hold financial stakes in the Japanese car industry, California's Silicon Valley, Malaysian tin mines, the British short-term money market, and German government bonds. Through the development of managed investment funds, the outlay for such a portfolio can be as little as £500 or even £25–30 a month.

So far, few have moved to grasp these opportunities in a complete way. During the 1980s and 1990s, the privatization and listing of several great icons, such as British Telecom, Cable & Wireless, British Airways, British Gas, National Power, PowerGen and Railtrack, attracted a vast number of first-time investors in the stock market.

Unfortunately, far too many investors have so far not gone beyond this step. A survey by Proshare, the organization set up to promote share ownership, showed that at the end of 1998 almost half the 12 million shareholders in the UK held shares in only one company.

With the British government deciding against making it compulsory for individuals and their employers to contribute to private pension plans, it is vital that people develop a better understanding of how to develop more effective investment strategies.

A number of modern strategies are available to help investors get the most out of financial markets while managing risk. These approaches have not, however, been made generally available to the average investor. They were for many years confined to the universities where they were developed, and have more recently been taken up by major financial institutions.

This book explains investment strategy in practical terms that can be applied by the average person. It starts with the premise that there are great, easily accessible options for wealth creation. Everyone wants to get in on these opportunities: the question is how to do it without risking financial ruin.

In nine chapters, *Fortune Strategy* provides the basic knowledge and strategy to help ensure survival and prosperity in the fast-moving international investment scene of the third millennium. Where most investors go wrong is in failing to understand three key concepts: how wealth is created, how return is produced, and what constitutes risk. The dynamic nature of investment markets makes it dangerous to create and follow rigid 'investment laws'. There are, however, four enduring investment principles: quality, value, diversity and time. These apparently simple concepts are too often ignored or poorly executed.

Knowing how to apply these approaches in a changing environment provides a solid foundation for a successful strategy. By the end of the book, readers will know how to participate in genuinely productive investment and how to maximize returns for the level of risk they are comfortable with. They will have a sense of how to develop a strategy to capture the opportunities and deal with the uncertainties of the Information Age.

The first chapter aims to increase the reader's awareness of emerging wealth-creation opportunities, and how the evolution of a world securities market has made them accessible. Many investors lose money because they do not know how to measure return correctly. Chapter 2 shows how it should be assessed, taking into account inflation, tax, transaction costs and, where relevant, currency exchange. Most people take on far too much risk or, more precisely, accept excessive risk for the level of return they seek. Chapter 3 provides powerful insights from investment theory to discover how returns can be raised, without necessarily increasing risk, by constructing a portfolio of different assets.

The vast range of investments confronting would-be investors can often appear daunting. Most major investments, however, fall into one of four classes:

short-term interest-bearing investments (cash), long-term interest-bearing investments (bonds), the share market (equities), and property. An understanding of how these markets work is critical to successful investment. Chapters 4, 5 and 6 outline the mechanics, categories and characteristics of each asset class, and provide guidance on how to look 'behind the price' and assess their real worth.

One of the most important developments in the investment scene has been the proliferation of managed investment vehicles, including individual savings accounts, investment trusts, unit trusts and open-ended investment companies, insurance bonds and pension funds. Correctly used, these can give the private investor the chance to take part in the major investment markets around the world along with the large institutional investors. Chapter 7 explains how investment vehicles work, how to choose among them, and how to use them to put an overall strategy into practice.

Chapter 8 explains how to design an individual investment strategy and how to construct a portfolio to match it. It provides guidelines for defining needs and objectives, setting priorities where trade-offs exist, and tailoring the portfolio to maximize return for the investor's risk profile.

Chapter 9 concludes the book by explaining how to get started in investment, and how to manage the portfolio over time. It provides some useful tips to deal with the most excruciating questions of investment: when to buy, when to sell, and when to switch assets.

Many Britons seek an easy road to wealth. Unfortunately, much of their money is misdirected. The introduction of the National Lottery in 1994 has proved a huge financial success, raising £1.5 billion a year for good causes, not to mention £650 million in extra taxes and allowing the government to reduce its direct spending on the arts, sport and charities.

But the lottery has syphoned an estimated £5 billion a year out of the pockets of individuals who forlornly hope to become millionaires. If the average family were to invest sensibly the same amount they typically spend on gambling, and on the lottery in particular, they would be virtually assured of a big payout over time. A good strategy can secure prosperity through prudent investment and financial planning, without having to rely on the random drop of a pingpong ball.

PART ONE

Concepts of investment

CHAPTER 1

The wealth revolution

Summary

▨ The new millennium opens with an expanding revolution in the individual's ability to take part in wealth-creation opportunities around the world.

▨ As the pace of technological change picks up and new investment instruments develop, the potential for investors will be even greater.

▨ However, with these new opportunities come new and often greater risks, as investors learned during the emerging markets crisis of the late 1990s and the bursting of the 'dot com bubble' in April 2000.

▨ In this exciting but fluid environment, investors need to identify the factors driving this 'wealth revolution'. They need a framework to assess risk and opportunity, and they require tools to develop a strategy to generate sustainable wealth.

▨ Four principles provide the key to successful investment: being able to assess *quality*, being able to assess *value*, developing effective *diversification*, and allowing a strategy to work over *time*.

Introduction: crashing the rich man's party

As they enter the third millennium, investors in all advanced economies are storming onto a vibrant investment scene that was once the preserve of a small monied elite. The past two decades brought a revolution in the ownership of capital, which may prove to be the biggest agent of individual empowerment ever seen and comparable to the freedoms created by democracy. Twenty years ago fewer than one in ten adult Britons had a stake in the stock market. Now, more than a quarter own some shares, either through direct shareholdings or through managed investments such as unit trusts, and more than half have an indirect stake through their pension funds.

Interest in the stock market has led to the creation of thousands of investment clubs, where individuals met to pool their investment ideas and their cash, and play the market. Two years previously there had been just 350 clubs across the UK. By the start of the new millennium there were more than 5000 and new ones were opening up at a rate of 100 a week.

They included Dirty Harry's, an amateur investment club set up in November 1999 in a pub called the Harry in Leigh on Sea, Essex. The club's chairman, Mark Goodson, is a 30-something probate clerk in a solicitor's office; other members include printers, electricians and a company director. At their first meeting the members broke all the rules of prudent investment and staked the whole of their initial capital in six different companies, all in the high-tech sector. These included ARM Holdings, the best share performer in the index of 100 top shares in 1999, but three of their chosen companies had not yet made a profit. By the time the London market peaked at the end of the year, however, the value of their initial investment had risen by 84 per cent net of dealing costs in just seven weeks.

Not all investors fare quite so well, of course. In that year the information technology sector as a whole trebled, the electronics and mining sectors more than doubled, but 14 of the 39 individual sectors in the London stock market, including retail trade, food retailing, pharmaceuticals, water, electricity and insurance, and a host of famous names such as Marks and Spencer, Sainsbury, Lloyds TSB, SmithKline Beecham and Prudential, all ended the year lower than they had started. It is also worth noting that prices far outpaced the growth of earnings and dividends, so that out of a total return of almost 24 per cent in 1999, 21 per cent came from capital gains and less than 3 per cent before tax came from bankable dividends.

The big question remained: how would investors react when share prices fell, as experience and logic show they must from time to time? From 1996 onwards Alan Greenspan, the chairman of the US Federal Reserve Board, warned repeatedly that share prices were becoming overvalued. But investors ignored such warnings, anticipating a new era in investment opportunities, and a step-change in the relationships between the growth of the economy as a whole, and the respective claims of labour and capital. Other markets, including bonds, cash, unit trusts, investment trusts, insurance bonds and endowment policies, commercial and residential property, have also flourished.

On top of all this direct investment, the pensions industry has expanded at a colossal rate, pouring funds into investment markets. In the UK, more than half of all employees are covered by pension plans. They include company schemes, many of which promise pensions linked to final salaries, as well as a range of personal portable schemes which pay pensions based on the value at maturity of the assets in which they are invested.

Successive governments have brought in policies intended to encourage savers and investors to build up additional assets. The Conservative government of Margaret Thatcher abolished the surcharge on investment income and John Major's government brought in a basic rate of tax on interest and dividends at 20 per cent, slightly below the basic rate on earned income. The Conservatives also introduced a range of instruments which allowed investors to invest a limited amount each year in shares, bonds and cash deposits which would be exempt from both income tax and capital gains tax. These personal equity plans and tax-exempt special savings accounts were replaced in 1999 by individual savings accounts (ISAs) which can be used to invest in cash deposits, bonds and shares, in insurance-linked investments, or in a combination of all three.

The New Labour government has also taken steps to help owners of small businesses to protect their investments and reward themselves more effectively with share options and incentives. There are now more than 3 million self-employed people in Britain, and on average at least they are more prosperous than ever before.

A number of new share dealing operations have also set themselves up, offering individual investors a choice of low-cost 'execution-only' dealing services or boutique services offering access to professional advice and specialized research material. The increasing access to trading on the internet has also made it easier, quicker and cheaper to trade.

The growing coverage of investment issues in newspapers, specialist magazines and on television and radio has contributed to a more critical investing public. New investors come from all walks of life, but the average is becoming younger, more knowledgeable and more sophisticated. Stock exchange surveys show that experienced investors are diversifying by putting their money into a broader range of stocks. They are turning to online trading systems and dabbling in new instruments such as derivatives.

However, while there may be greater opportunities for investors to build wealth, there are also bigger traps. Where many investors go astray is in trying to seize on one-off investment opportunities. They lack an overall plan, and a solid theory to help them construct such a plan. Many 'investors' still think of stock market investment as yet another form of gambling and are always on the look-out for a quick speculative profit, based on 'hot tips' and 'inside information'. By the end of 1999 several thousand investors had become 'day traders', buying and selling shares and options and futures in the same trading day, although only 30 per cent were thought to be making money.

The astute investor adopts a long-term strategy, and relies on a solid framework to formulate it. This book focuses on how to develop such a strategy using a number of proven approaches. It endeavours to concentrate the investor's mind on the fundamental factors that lie behind investment markets. It develops the investor's ability to watch the big picture of world economic and political trends rather than be bogged down in minutiae and short-term fluctuations. It encourages investors to direct their investment strategy towards what they want in life, and inculcates a discipline in carrying out the strategy.

Among the tools that *Fortune Strategy* introduces to investors is portfolio theory.[1] Used wisely, this body of knowledge helps investors to achieve a better outcome from the balance between risk and return – in other words, to get the best return for their 'risk budget'. In its modern form, portfolio theory owes its origins to a now famous article by American academic Harry Markowitz, which appeared in the *Journal of Finance* in 1952.[2] Nearly four decades later, in 1990, Markowitz won the Nobel prize for his work on the theory, sharing the highest distinction in economics with other academics who had worked in the same field. One of the co-winners, William Sharpe, took the theory a step further to develop a model for how securities are priced in the market.

Portfolio theory's main premise is that, by knowing the characteristics of different types of investments, the investor can combine them to optimize the trade-off between risk and return. Portfolio theory can provide guidance on taking advantage of opportunities in different industries and economies around the world.

The theory is built in part on an intriguing paradox: two investments that are individually risky can, in combination, provide a safer overall investment if they tend to move in random or, better yet, opposite directions. *Fortune Strategy* outlines professional applications of portfolio theory used by fund managers, but presents the underlying concepts in a way that can be understood and applied without complex mathematics.

The investment community did considerable work in advancing the application of portfolio theory in the 1990s. This research coincided with a broader debate about the need for a 'new economic paradigm' to explain emerging trends in the global economy which do not always fit traditional economic analysis. Out of this process, many new insights have emerged to improve an investment approach based on portfolio theory, and these are canvassed here.

Many observers suggest that fundamental changes in political values in Western democracies, along with big changes in the world economy, are not just temporary phenomena but revolutionary developments. These changes, they suggest, call for dynamic new approaches to economic and investment analysis. This developing body of thought is described by one of its proponents, the American economist Horace Wood Brock, as 'the economics of uncertainty'.

A number of trends do indeed point to a new ball game which investors will have to learn to play. The emerging markets crisis of the late 1990s showed how world markets can still fall prey to dramatic movements of global capital, sparked, in some cases, by investment fund operators. Some of these operators command such huge war chests that they are prepared to take on national governments and international financial organizations.

The possibility of a sustained period of low inflation, and even a return to deflation, across the developed world would also require some major rethinking of investment strategy. Of the longer-term trends, changing demographics – and most notably an ageing population – are already starting to have a significant effect on investment markets.

In addition, increased accessibility to these markets is itself producing structural change. As more and more people become involved – particularly in the share market – and obtain more information, two key things happen. First, the potential benefit of purchasing shares is reduced, as more and more investors are prepared to pay higher prices for equities in relation to company earnings. All else being equal, such a trend will produce lower returns from that market, while the level of risk remains as high, or moves even higher. Second, the sheer volume of information available reduces the value of that information as a means of gaining an advantage. One of the most important rules of investment is that once an idea, no matter how good, is 'priced in' to the market, it ceases to have any value as a guide to investing.

This book is aimed at the intelligent person who wants to invest for the medium haul, rather than those seeking a quick, and often illusory, short cut to wealth. The strategy outlined in this book is designed to first preserve and then to increase wealth in terms of buying power over time, while managing risk.

Markets, tax laws and investment products change all the time, and it is essential to keep up with these changes. Readers are well advised to consult financial advisers, who can provide current information and specific guidance, before taking the plunge. *Fortune Strategy* gives a guide to investment concepts, the dynamics of investment markets and investment strategy. This knowledge is valuable in all situations, and investors can adapt it to suit their individual circumstances and the investment scene of the day.

A brief history of wealth

Films such as *Wall Street* and news footage of floor traders shouting their bids have promoted a vision of investment that combines glamour, intrigue and excitement. These elements, although present, reflect the public face of the investment industry rather than what lies behind it. Investment is really about taking a stake in the very fibre of an industry or economy in which people work, things are made, and goods and services are bought and sold.

It is therefore essential to understand the difference between opportunities for sustainable wealth creation, and speculative traps. Such knowledge helps the investor to assess which companies, industries and economies are advancing, which are stagnant, and which are dying. It also provides a basis for working out the value of a particular investment.

Essentially, wealth comes from production, at a profitable margin, of goods and services that people want to buy. Greater wealth requires continuously adding value to production, to make more goods and services, better and environmentally cleaner. The rate of increase in productivity is closely linked to the rate of investment and the application of advances in technology.

The good news is that the speed of technological advance, and hence the scope for wealth creation, has never been greater. Figure 1.1 illustrates this point and provides some strong insights into the comparative fate of nations.

In Britain, which led the industrial revolution, output per head doubled between 1780 and 1838. Before the industrial revolution, wealth came primarily from the land. Secondary wealth came from artisans and craftsmen, who owned their establishments as blacksmiths, tanners or leather workers and provided the labour themselves. The introduction of machines and factories changed the fundamentals by separating capital from labour. An entrepreneur who had the money to buy machines and employ workers to use them could create a product at several times the rate of individual craftsmen and reap the profits accordingly.

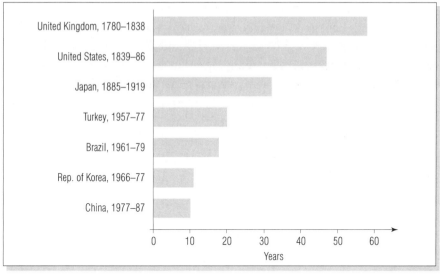

Source: World Bank

FIGURE 1.1 The wealth revolution: years taken for output per person to double

The use of machinery greatly improved output per head, and the development of railways and steamships made it possible to move goods in great quantities over long distances at much lower cost, which in turn encouraged trade, allowing producers to specialize where costs were lowest.

The increase of wealth in the 19th century owed a great deal to trade especially in manufactured goods which was also expanded by the abolition of tariffs, taxes, quotas and controls on exports and imports. Free trade opened up wider markets in the 19th century and brought wealth and power to colonial powers such as Britain and massive domestic markets such as the United States. The benefits were less obvious to nations without colonies of their own, to those with small home markets and limited resources, to countries mainly dependent on the export of raw materials, or to agrarian economies such as China which remained largely outside the world system. Even in the industrial economies wealth was largely concentrated in a small section of society. The excesses of 19th-century capitalism encouraged thinkers such as the eminent German sociologist Karl Marx to advocate a workers' revolution and ownership of the means of production, distribution and exchange by the state.

Progress remained resolutely slow and erratic. In the years leading up to the First World War the world economy was dominated by a handful of major industrialized powers led by the United States, which had overtaken the UK some time in the 1880s. Germany had caught up with the UK by 1914, with France, Japan and Russia still some way behind. Wealth was usually seen as a useful adjunct to military power. Economic policies were crude in the extreme. The leading national currencies were pegged to gold, and the money supply depended on the rate at which gold was being dug out of the ground. Periods of economic growth were also interrupted by cycles of recession. The First World War caused massive loss of life in Europe and left the losers, especially Germany, burdened by huge debts, while the Russian Revolution in 1917 brought to power an autocratic Marxist regime committed to state ownership of all major assets.

During the 1920s some governments, including the UK, tried to return to the Gold Standard in the belief that sound money was the only sure way of ensuring economic prosperity. The resulting deflation led to a slump in domestic demand and priced UK goods out of export markets. Other nations resorted to printing money, which created runaway inflation and led to the collapse of confidence in the currency. Almost all the independent nations imposed tariffs and quota restrictions on imports and subsidized their exports or deliberately manipulated their currencies in order to make their goods cheaper and more competitive abroad while pricing foreign goods out of domestic markets.

The stock market crash of 1929 and the ensuing Great Depression that lasted until 1933 made matters worse. Rival nations resorted to similar 'beggar-my-neighbour' policies which led to a downward spiral in world trade in the 1930s and chronic unemployment. Only re-armament appeared to offer a way of creating work.

The ensuing war caused even greater economic destruction as well as loss of life and left virtually the whole of Europe on the verge of bankruptcy. But the experience of the period since the end of the Second World War has been in stark contrast to the experiences of the period between the wars. The spectacular successes of the past 50 years have not been accidental. The Western world created a defensive alliance that has ensured that no major war has disrupted economic growth.

In an attempt to avoid a repetition of the mistakes which followed the First World War, the United States introduced the Marshall Plan, which between 1948 and 1952 provided Western Europe with what was then the massive sum of $13 billion to finance reconstruction.

The main trading nations also constructed a system of international co-operation which created a framework for economic recovery and an explosive growth in world trade, with all the resulting benefits in improved efficiency, increased mass production, and opportunities for harnessing improved technology. Even before the war had ended, representatives of 34 independent nations met at Bretton Woods to plan a programme of economic co-operation to encourage mass production, economic specialization and trade. The conference led to the creation of three international organizations. The International Monetary Fund (IMF) encouraged member countries to fix their exchange rates against the dollar and made loans available to them to buy time to introduce domestic economic policies designed to maintain the agreed exchange rate, and so avoid competing devaluations.

The World Bank used subscriptions and loans to finance development projects in member countries. Initially, the money went mainly to state bodies to finance the construction of large infrastructure projects such as dams, power stations and communications. Later the bank used additional subscriptions and its early profits to provide cheap loans to help finance education, public health and family planning programmes, and lent an increasing proportion of its money to emerging economies in Africa, Asia and Latin America.

The third body, the International Trade Organization, failed to get off the ground in 1946. But its intended role was taken over by the General Agreement on Tariffs and Trade (GATT). The agreement committed member states only to reduce and never to raise tariffs and other obstacles to trade, and to negotiate successive rounds of mutual reductions in trade barriers.

At the same time national governments gradually improved their methods of managing economies and maximizing the opportunities for wealth creation. Equally important, they gradually dismantled the extensive system of controls and regulations built up during and immediately after the war to allocate scarce resources. But the Soviet Union refused to take part in the Marshall Plan or the Bretton Woods system and forced the countries in Eastern Europe which fell into its sphere of influence to follow suit, while China also opted out of the system after the Communist revolution in 1949. Most of the under-developed economies in the so-called Third World, including Latin America and the countries of Africa and Asia which only gradually obtained their political independence in the post-war period, were too poor to participate fully in the Bretton Woods system.

In the Western world, the Bretton Woods system and the domestic economic policies based on the ideas of John Maynard Keynes which accompanied it led to an unprecedented surge in economic output and individual wealth. The United States opened its doors to foreign goods and was able to run a persistent deficit in its balance of trade because of its immense power and influence. Almost by accident the surplus dollars flowing out of the United States helped to create the so-called eurodollar market which grew up outside the control of the US authorities.

This growing pool of tax-free dollars was banked mainly in London, where it helped to finance international trade and investment. It also enabled the City of London to regain its place as an international financial centre. In time, smaller amounts of other currencies, including marks and yen, found their way into accounts with London banks, offering a growing choice of capital for borrowers and opportunities for investors.

Recessions were not eliminated entirely, but after the Great Depression it was 60 years before the major world economies again suffered a simultaneous slow-down in peacetime that lasted more than two years. World population doubled from 2 billion in 1945 to 4 billion in 1970, but world wealth multiplied tenfold in real terms to around $4 trillion. Over the same period, world trade grew even faster, encouraging specialization and mass-production and helping to reduce the cost of goods and services in all the developed economies.

In the advanced economies able to make the best use of constructive domestic policies and international co-operation, living standards rose sharply, creating mass demand for consumer goods, especially cars and consumer durables, television sets, washing machines and refrigerators, and increasingly expensive service industries such as tourism, banking and finance. Service industries multiplied and living standards rose sharply in North America, Western Europe, Australasia and Japan. These countries formed the Organization for Economic Cooperation and Development (OECD), the rich nations' club.

The benefits spread only gradually to an increasing number of 'developing' economies, especially in East Asia, which were able to import capital and employ cheap labour to supply goods such as textiles, plastics and metal goods to the developed economies at competitive prices.

By the early 1970s, however, Keynesian economic policies were increasingly under a cloud. Critics accused them of putting too much emphasis on stimulating growth at the expense of monetary stability, and playing into the hands of increasingly well-organized trade unions, which were determined to force up wages faster than the productivity needed to finance them.

Within a decade, Keynes's ideas had been replaced by 'monetarist' doctrines associated with Professor Milton Friedman and his supporters. They believed the only duty of governments was to manage the money supply through raising and lowering interest rates, reducing government borrowing, and balancing government budgets. They also developed policies designed to break the powers of trade unions.

At much the same time the Bretton Woods system began to break down. French President Charles de Gaulle resented the ability of the US to finance its foreign policies, including the war in Vietnam, and of US companies to finance expansion into European markets, using dollars borrowed back from leading banks.

France began to use its surplus dollars and demand payment in American gold at the fixed price of $35 an ounce. As other countries followed suit the American gold reserves were rapidly being depleted. In 1971, President Nixon was forced to abolish the convertibility of the dollar into gold and to devalue the dollar against gold by 15 per cent. Within two years the system of fixed exchange rates had broken down irreparably, although the member countries of the European Common Market tried with varying degrees of success to limit fluctuations between their currencies, efforts that led eventually to the creation of the single European currency in 1999.

The international trade and payments system was also hit, first by two successive oil shocks the first in 1973 when Arab members of OPEC imposed an oil embargo after the Arab–Israeli war, quadrupling the cost of the world's most important raw material, and again in 1979. Oil importing nations such as Japan, most of Western Europe (including at that time the UK), and many of the developing countries such as Korea, Taiwan and Brazil were forced to borrow massively from international banks.

Over the next decade many of the weaker economies defaulted on their debts, creating a world-wide banking crisis.

International co-operation helped the world economy escape from the oil crises, the 'debt crisis' and other shocks to the system in the next two decades. World leaders continue to meet regularly to review developments and try to co-ordinate economic strategies. The GATT was replaced in 1994 by the World Trade Organization which seeks to reduce remaining trade barriers and 'unfair' trading practices. But events have proved beyond reasonable doubt that individual governments, even the United States, the engine of post-war economic growth, could no longer resist the global power of speculators using the massive pools of money in international banks to force down the value of currencies of countries whose economic policies they disliked. The collapse of Communism has left market capitalism as the only effective basis for economic development. Competition, globalization, the deregulation of markets and further improvements in technology – in particular the development of computer-based technology – became the driving force for continued economic growth in the last quarter of the 20th century.

Globalization has its critics, especially among environmentalists, trade unions, and nationalists, who fear it will undermine traditional values. But the trend seems irreversible. The triumph of market forces has made it increasingly possible for international companies to supply world markets from a handful of locations worldwide. The remaining exchange controls on the movement of money from one currency to another and one economy to another were also rapidly dismantled. The free movement of capital created a massive pool of finance which enabled huge international companies like General Motors, Siemens and Philips to expand, cross frontiers and establish new businesses to take advantage of low local operating costs.

The globalization of big business was also encouraged by stock markets, especially in the English-speaking world, which allowed small and less efficient companies to be taken over by bigger rivals and led to the establishment of a hierarchy of truly international companies. International banks accelerated the trend by lending an ever-increasing proportion of their funds to international rather than national customers.

Competition from newly industrializing economies in Southern Europe, East and South Asia and Latin America, and the emphasis on strict anti-inflationary policies in the developed economies, have held down costs and increased demand for goods and services.

The increasing speed of development of new technologies and the rapid adoption of technology into economic output has had a marked effect on the industrial nations. Demand for many old technologies, supporting the 'rust-belt' industries such as coal, steel, ships and heavy machinery, has plunged, creating massive unemployment in traditional manufacturing regions. But the overall level of demand has been much more than made good by the emergence of new industries and services using computer-based technology and information rather than raw materials to generate massive increases in wealth.

The explosion of wealth in the Western world and increasingly in the newly industrializing economies exposed the inefficiencies and lack of innovation in the centrally planned economies, making a mockery of Nikita Khrushchev's boast in 1958 that the centrally planned economies would bury the West economically. Governments in the emerging nations of Asia, Latin America and even Africa have been forced to abandon state socialism and open their economies to market forces, in many cases under heavy pressure from the International Monetary Fund and the World Bank.

The combination of technology, globalization, and deregulation has led to a continuing boom in global wealth creation. Between 1970 and 2000, world population increased by 50 per cent to more than 6 billion, but world production quadrupled again. Living standards more than doubled in North America, trebled in Western Europe, quadrupled in Japan, and increased more than tenfold in new economic power centres especially, in East and South-East Asia. By 2000 these developing economies accounted for around 35 per cent of world gross domestic product (GDP) and 25 per cent of world trade.

Some developing countries have performed genuine miracles in improving the lot of their people. As recently as 1961, South Korea was a poor country, with a gross national product (GNP) per capita of little over $100. In 1962, however, its economy began to grow at an average annual rate of 8.4 per cent. Now, notwithstanding the financial crisis of the late 1990s, South Koreans have a standard of living on a par with, and in some cases surpassing, some European countries. Taiwan, Hong Kong and Singapore are also now developed economies, and the wealth-creating process has taken root in Malaysia and Thailand and seems set to establish itself throughout South and South-East Asia.

China and India, the two largest nations on Earth in population terms, are well established on the path to sustained economic growth, although they both still have huge rural populations which are poor and largely excluded from the process. In Latin America, Brazil, Mexico, Argentina and Chile have also taken the first steps to joining the developed world, although they too have large numbers of people in rural areas, and urban slums who have yet to see much benefit.

Several of the former Communist countries of Eastern Europe, notably Poland, the Czech Republic, Hungary, Slovenia and Estonia, have made good progress in adopting market economies, privatizing state companies, and opening their doors to foreign investment, and are already seeking to join the European Union. Slovakia, Lithuania, Romania, Bulgaria and Bosnia have been less successful, and Serbia, Ukraine, Belarus and especially Russia are struggling to come to terms with the commercial world. In Russia in particular output and living standards are well below what they were in the Communist era and the infant Moscow stock market remains one of the most volatile and speculative of all.

Much of Africa between the Sahara and South Africa has also failed to climb aboard the capitalist bandwagon. Its nations are mostly artificial creations of the colonial era, and most are small and lacking either in resources or in basic infra-structure or both. Standards of living, education and health are low, and commercial development lags far behind the rest of the world.

Economic development is not in fact either inevitable or guaranteed. It is interesting to contrast the fortunes of those countries that industrialized in the 19th century with those that missed the chance. In the 16th century, Spain and Portugal were regarded as wealthy because they had vast amounts of 'treasure' – especially gold and silver plundered from their colonies. Instead of industrializing, the Iberian nations used unsustainable resource exploitation to pay for imports. Spain and Portugal were left behind in the technological race, and were still classed by the OECD as 'underdeveloped' well into the 1960s.

The modern equivalent of 17th-century treasure is oil, which creates great wealth but little employment. Although some oil-rich countries including Kuwait, the Gulf States and Saudi Arabia have invested part of their surplus to generate dividend income, many have squandered their good fortune, and there is a real risk that in the 21st century many of the oil-rich economies will stagnate economically as Spain and Portugal did.

Some nations that did industrialize, but went soft, have been categorized by some economists as 'failed industrialized countries' or FICs.[3] Examples include Chile, Uruguay and especially Argentina, which just after the First World War ranked as one of the richest half dozen countries in the world. Its domestic markets quickly proved too small and isolated to sustain efficient industries and successive governments preferred to protect local industries, leaving the Argentine economy largely dependent on the exports of grain and livestock industries. A similar fate faced Australia and New Zealand in the 1970s before their governments realized the dangers and took conscious decisions to throw them open to competition.

Technological change: economies in the fast lane

The discussion so far shows how the rapid expansion of output and wealth over the past 30 years has been due in large measure to superior management of the domestic and international economy, globalization, the encouragement of free trade, and entrepreneurship. The critical element, however, has been technological change. Each subsequently industrializing country has been able to leapfrog much of the intermediate technology. In Britain in the 1780s, one agricultural advance involved the move from wooden to metal ploughshares. In China in the past 30 years, the move has been from a human or buffalo-drawn plough straight to the mechanized hand tractor. The pace of technological change had accelerated to the point where China could double its output per head in just ten years, from 1977 to 1987.

These examples show that a number of factors need to come together to create sustainable wealth. The United States has vast natural resources and a large internal market. But it has remained the powerhouse of the world economy through its ability to create and employ new technologies. Economists point to a flexible labour market, taxation and regulatory systems that encourage innovation and investment, a solid democratic and legal tradition, a generally good education system, and an entrepreneurial spirit, as supporting factors.

Abundant natural resources do not necessarily assure continued prosperity. In fact, wealth creation no longer depends primarily on physical resources. Singapore has used high-quality human resources, good planning, innovation and hard work to succeed without any 'natural' resources.

As the world entered the 21st century, the global economy was once again almost entirely heavily dependent on the US as the engine of growth. Some traditional industries, including many in manufacturing, were not doing well, having been affected by the downturn in Asia and low commodity prices. But US entrepreneurs had seized world leadership in a new wave of information technology, including the internet, and this was propelling the economy.

Information technology promises to create as big a leap forward in productivity as the coming of the railway, electrification and mass production methods did in their day, and to bring the same kinds of savings to service sectors, including banking and retailing, as automation did to manufacturing industry. New ways of operating should provide substantial benefits to consumers and new players at the expense of established service providers saddled with old-fashioned premises and expensive workforces.

Between 1992 and 1997, the information technology industry increased its share of US output from 0.8 per cent to more than 4 per cent, compared with 2.5 per cent in continental Europe. Observers said that spending was likely to remain high because new technology meant office equipment became obsolete every two or three years.[4] Indeed, many observers suggest the world may be in for a surge in technological growth, the like of which has never been seen in such a short period. In 1997, the McKinsey corporate strategy group conducted a study suggesting the big potential impact of this technology was in improving 'interaction' in the economy. Interaction covered the exchange of goods, services and ideas and accounted for more than 33 per cent of economic activity in the US.[5] It took form in sales calls, reports, memos, telephone calls, and so on.

Some observers have claimed that the 'IT revolution' had not, by the start of 1999, had any big, measurable impact on productivity, which in the UK has risen by around 2 per cent a year for the past two decades. However, there are a number of persuasive arguments that such an impact had begun in the US and may be about to occur in Europe and elsewhere.

In a review of the IT question, the US-based Strategic Economic Decisions (SED) group noted that the real value of many forms of information technology would occur as they all came together.[6] The full worth of a personal computer, for example, would occur when combined with complementary technologies so that the individual elements became more than the sum of the parts, SED suggested. These technologies included more powerful and inter-usable software programs, connective networks enabling communications with other PCs within the same company, and most recently the internet, enabling cheap, online global applications of all of these elements. SED also noted that interactive technologies such as the fax machine became worthwhile to an individual company only when enough other companies had fax machines – then the technology took off.

The most immediate effect of the IT revolution on investment markets was a speculative splurge in companies at the forefront of providing these technologies, such as internet services. Stock prices of such companies rose to absurd levels in early 2000 before, in some cases, crashing back down. The London market also experienced a frenzy of buying, especially by small investors looking for quick profits in IT stocks, which helped push daily turnover to an all-time record of more than 2 billion shares a day.

A more significant implication in the medium-term, however, is for companies using the new technologies: once their full impact on productivity takes effect, these companies will be able to produce wealth far more quickly.

As the new millennium opened, the US appeared to be the first major economy cashing in on this new technology dividend. Productivity was improving at nearly 5 per cent a year, and companies were reporting direct profit improvements from technological innovation. The Bloomberg news service reported how the Delphi Automotive Systems plant in Oak Creek, Wisconsin, could produce a catalytic converter in 36 seconds compared with 20 minutes a few years earlier. Clothing manufacturer Hampton Industries of Kinston, North Carolina, purchased new information systems for order entry, inventory control and distribution in 1998, and doubled earnings per share.[7]

While attention has focused on the IT revolution, other areas of techno-logical advance are also reaching a crescendo and starting to have an effect on investment markets. Advances include the cluster of activities around biotech-nology, genetic engineering, and medical research. Many of these technologies are controversial, such as genetically modified crops, while others, such as Viagra, have become overnight sensations.

As SED put it, the impact of the new technologies on the overall economy is 'like a giant 747 jet just beginning to taxi down the runway'. Sophisticated investors will be looking to get seats on board this jumbo, while choosing them carefully. They can do this because of a radical change in the ownership of capital, a trend that has run in parallel with the technological revolution.

Securitization: dividing up the capitalist riches

If there was a quiet revolution of the late 20th century, it was the transformation in the ownership of capital. Hand in hand with industrialization comes the need to amass capital to fund the purchase of large-scale plant and equipment and pay the workers to run it. Entrepreneurs need to attract money from a wide range of individuals and institutions and, over time, the ownership of companies and their borrowings has been divided into small units. This process, now known as securitization, has radically changed the distribution of ownership of the economy. Once, only a small section of society held a direct stake in wealth creation; now, most people do. It is worth looking briefly at how this came about.

The industrialization of the 18th and 19th centuries was justly called a revolution. It gave rise to a new class of capitalist, encouraged huge migrations, and created an urban working class, which formed the core of the union movement.

As Frenchman Paul Mantoux wrote in 1927:[8]

> The whole structure of the factory system is built up on the power furnished by machinery, together with an immense accumulation of human labour, supporting, at the top, the towering and ever-growing force of capital. Producers are divided into two classes. The first gives its labour and possesses nothing else, selling the strength of its arms and the hours of its life for a wage. The second commands capital, owns the factories, the raw materials, the machinery, and reaps the profits and dividends. At its head are great leaders, the captains of industry ... organizers, rulers, and conquerors.

While the industrial revolution eventually contributed to higher living standards, the rise was uneven. During periods of oversupply and recession, workers suffered lower wages or were tossed on the scrap heap of the unemployed. Such 'contradictions' led Marx to predict the ultimate collapse of capitalism.

There was, however, a crucial twist in the plot, which was only in its infancy when Marx wrote *Das Kapital* in 1867. This trend, the spreading out of capital, eroded the neat class structure of industrial capitalism. Instead of the means of production being owned by individual moguls or a small group or family, it became diffused among many shareholders and, eventually, accessible to the workers themselves. The concept of the *security* – a tradable parcel of equity or debt – developed.

Every business needs capital to buy stock and equipment. Many founders of the British cotton factories were self-made men, who used their savings or borrowed from friends and family. Initially, the sums of money were not enormous: a 40-spindle jenny could be bought for £6 in 1792. As time went on and the amount of machinery, the number of workers and the size of factories expanded, the need began for pooled capital. The development of the modern securities market stemmed from the need for massive infrastructure projects that required huge amounts of capital before they could produce any income. The best example is the financing of the railroads, canals and turnpikes in the United States in the 1800s. The banks of the time, and even state governments, were unable to finance these enterprises on their own. The promoters had to create units of capital that could be divided among a variety of investors.

The result was the large-scale distribution of two basic types of securities: bonds and shares. Bonds were units of company indebtedness that paid a fixed rate of interest. The colourful certificates issued by the Chinese and Russian railway companies in the early 1900s are a good example. Shares were units of equity in which the holder owned part of the company and shared in its profits. The need to set up a formal structure to acquire such diffused capital led to the first laws allowing three or more people to form a legal business entity – the beginning of the corporation.

As the holding of securities became more widespread, formal securities markets were established so that holders could trade their interests for cash. The London Stock Exchange traces its history back to the coffee houses which began operating in the 17th century. The Stock Exchange was incorporated in 1801. It abandoned its traditional structure, which separated brokers – who dealt only on behalf of clients – from jobbers – who acted as principals setting prices at which they would buy or sell stocks – only at the time of the 'Big Bang' in 1986. Since then the old system of trading based on buyers and sellers meeting physically on the trading floor of the Stock Exchange building has been entirely replaced by electronic trading carried out by specialist traders using prices quoted on electronic screens.

The London stock market trades shares in more than 2000 quoted British companies as well as several hundred smaller companies quoted on AIM, the alternative investment market established in 1994. On AIM the requirements to secure a listing are less strict, and risks as well as possible rewards are correspondingly greater. The OFEX market allows trading in shares in even smaller and more speculative companies providing the market can match buyers and sellers. The London market also trades shares in several hundred foreign companies which are applying in increasing numbers for a listing on the London market so that they can raise capital by issuing shares in the UK and also use their shares to finance takeover bids. In recent years, trading in the London market has averaged more than 100 000 trades daily.

In the United States, the New York Stock and Exchange Board opened in 1817, renting a second-floor room at 40 Wall Street. By 1857, it could claim 71 000 trades on a good day. By the end of the 20th century there were more than 5000 listed companies on the main New York Stock Exchange plus almost 5000 listed on Nasdaq, a specialized exchange mainly for high-tech companies established only in 1971.

European markets have lagged behind the three world leaders. The Tokyo stock market has suffered persistent weakness in the past decade, but remains one of the Big Three stock exchanges partly because of the traditionally greater importance of bank finance. Germany is now the largest single exchange in continental Europe, encouraged by the sheer size and wealth of the German economy and the merger of the regional stock exchanges to create a single centre based in Frankfurt. Plans are also well in hand to federate and eventually merge the stock markets in all member states of the European Union to create a single European stock exchange.

At the same time there are more than 50 smaller stock exchanges in countries as far apart as Mexico, Argentina, Ghana, Egypt, Israel, Russia, India and China where individual investors and institutions, domestic and foreign, can trade.

In the second half of the 20th century institutional investors, especially insurance companies, investment funds and pension funds grew to dominate the biggest stock exchanges, especially in New York and London, at the expense of individual shareholders. But private shareholders have begun to make a comeback, and the ownership of capital has become much more broadly spread over the past 20 years, to the point where most Britons have a direct or indirect stake. This trend reflects a number of factors: government policies encouraging the pension fund industry and investment generally, and expanding coverage and knowledge of investment markets. Another key element was the privatization of a wide range of public enterprises, including British Telecom, British Airways, rail services, and a range of gas and water utilities. These floats brought many first-time investors into the stock market, increasing their awareness of the market generally.

Figure 1.2 shows that 16.5 per cent of the UK stock market is now owned by individual investors, with a further 57.5 per cent owned indirectly through financial and non-financial companies (which include pension funds, insurance companies, banks and unit trusts). Table 1.1 shows that in the main countries of Europe, there is a similarly high private ownership of shares, either by individuals directly or through intermediaries. Italy, with almost 24 per cent of its stock market owned by the public sector, stands out in terms of government involvement in the stock market.

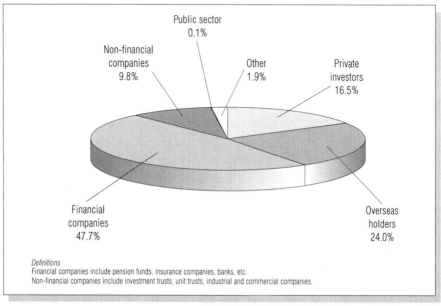

Definitions
Financial companies include pension funds, insurance companies, banks, etc.
Non-financial companies include investment trusts, unit trusts, industrial and commercial companies.

Sources: Office of National Statistics, Federation of European Stock Exchanges, 1997

FIGURE 1.2 Ownership of UK-listed equities

TABLE 1.1 Ownership of European-listed equities

Country	Private investors %	O/seas holders %	Financial cos %	Non-financial cos %	Public sector %	Other %
France	32.1	22.1	23.0	16.4	6.4	0
Spain	28.7	37.3	22.8	5.6	5.6	0
Italy	25.8	6.6	22.2	21.6	23.8	0
Germany	16.8	12.2	37.2	30.9	2.9	0
UK	16.5	24.0	47.7	9.8	0.1	1.9

Definitions
Financial companies include pension funds, insurance companies, banks, etc.
Non-financial companies include investment trusts, unit trusts, industrial and commercial companies.

Sources: Office of National Statistics, Federation of European Stock Exchanges, 1997

The process has, in a way, produced the revolution that Marx and his followers had in mind, but by different means. The Marxist goal was for the workers to seize the means of production. While in some countries such as Russia this process required a bloody insurrection, in North America, Western Europe, and Australasia it has been achieved through the spreading out of capital. Shrewd investors know that to get a share of the means of production today, they no longer need to storm the barricades – they have only to log onto an internet share-trading site.

The financial global village

While many new investors may take the wealth of opportunities available to them for granted, the breadth of the international investment scene is a comparatively new development. Today's freewheeling marketplace is the product of the lifting of government controls on financial markets around the world.

A parallel trend has been the development of true international financial markets, in which equities, bonds, and other securities can be traded in exchanges throughout the world, around the clock.

We now live in a financial global village. This trend has, to use a financial markets' euphemism, both upside and downside. The upside is that the average individual has a range of investment opportunities that would have been undreamed of a generation ago. With controls over who can trade what lifted, a vast range of financial services institutions now eagerly compete for customers across the gamut of products. With external controls lifted, investors can easily put their money into foreign markets, either via managed funds or direct trading. With derivatives – financial instruments which usually involve agreements to transact sales of currency and securities in the future – it is often possible to reduce the risk of offshore investment.

The level of competition, coupled with computer technology, has drastically reduced the cost of trading, with financial services now marketed in the same fashion as common consumer goods. Online trading is growing at an exponential rate. In the UK as the new millennium dawned a number of dealers were offering private investors credit to finance speculative investments, a phenomenon not seen since the early 1970s.

But investment in shares is not free of risk, especially in the short term. Markets have tended to rise further and faster than they fall but they can and do fall by 30–50 per cent in a downturn and individual shares can do even worse. Poor results or a profits warning can cut individual share prices by 10–30 per cent in a single day and falls (and rises) of 5 per cent a day can pass almost unnoticed in the media. The downside of globalization is that with the removal of so many internal and external barriers to international financial flows, money can move as fast as emotion. As a former chairman of Citibank, Walter Wriston, wrote:[9]

> The global marketplace is a reality. Money and ideas can and do move to any place on this planet in seconds and there is no longer any place to hide from the judgements of others.

An event anywhere can send international markets gyrating within seconds. A good example is the Iraqi invasion of Kuwait in 1990, which threatened a large chunk of world oil supplies. A series of panics wiped $1.1 trillion off stock values on world exchanges in Tokyo, New York and London within three weeks.

The way the markets moved had some traditional economic logic: the West runs on oil. More recent crises do not always fit this sort of rational analysis. Economists are still debating the financial crisis that started with the collapse of Asian markets in 1997 and spread to other emerging economies. The pace of events, and the huge swings in financial markets, went well beyond what traditional analysis could explain.

The ripples began in early 1997 with the collapse of South Korea's Hanbo Steel. The Thai currency, the baht, came under pressure and, in July, Thai authorities abandoned the policy of keeping the baht in a trading range linked to the US dollar. That move sparked a massive wave of capital outflow from Asia. The crisis drew attention to the warts that had previously been ignored in other economies. The Japanese stock market was sent reeling as the country's major banks said they would write off 'hundreds of billions of yen' of bad debts, often involving South-East Asian projects. In Indonesia, riots erupted against ethnic Chinese shop-owners, against Indonesian rule in East Timor, and against the nepotistic regime of President Suharto.

Phase two of the emerging markets crisis exploded in August 1998, when Russia gave up its defence of the rouble and defaulted on international debt repayments. Long-Term Capital Management, one of the most prominent US 'hedge' funds – pooled investment funds that specialize in sophisticated international financial manoeuvres – came to the brink of collapse, threatening an even greater crisis. The US Federal Reserve intervened to assemble a rescue package to shore it up.

Phase three began in early 1999, when the governor of Brazil's central bank resigned, and the currency was devalued. Soon afterwards Ecuador became the first country to default on international debts which had been rescheduled and guaranteed in US dollars.

The Russian default caused the capitalization of the world's stock markets to fall by more than $4 trillion – nearly four times that caused by the Gulf crisis nine years earlier. Equally remarkable though was the speed with which the subsequent recovery occurred. By the end of 1999, Asian economies such as South Korea and Thailand that had been forecast to experience continued falls in GDP in fact recorded increases of 10.7 per cent and 4.1 per cent respectively. And as a whole the index tracking the performance of the leading shares in emerging markets globally was up an astonishing 70 per cent in US dollars.

While the jury is still out on what this all means, a number of themes are emerging. One is that there is a big divergence between what could be called 'rational' market behaviour and what world markets actually do. Looking at the emerging economies with the benefit of hindsight, it is clear that international investors had allowed their expectations of the 'economic miracle' to get out of touch with reality.

Looking at the past 50 years, however, the miracle is a real one. Between 1991 and 1997, developing countries accounted for almost two-thirds of new output growth in the world economy. But there are speed limits, and the pace of investment in these economies exceeded what even fast-developing countries could productively absorb. In the late 1980s, capital flows to developing countries were running at about $40 billion per year. By 1996, the figure was around $300 billion. Over a similar period, the capitalization of stock markets in emerging economies more than trebled, from $613 billion to $2.1 trillion. Much of this investment was overly ambitious, and international banks lent money for projects that could not realistically provide the returns expected of them.

Some of the more shrewd observers note that the shakeout in the emerging markets may ultimately strengthen national institutions in the countries concerned. David Hale, a leading global economist, wrote in early 1999:[10]

> ... the odds are high that the current crisis will be viewed as a secular turning point. It will probably go down in the history books as the event which crushed the naïve investor optimism of the years immediately after the cold war while laying the foundation for the establishment of much stronger systems of financial supervision and protection of shareholder rights than have ever existed before in developing countries.

In fact, many of the economic 'fundamentals' that had existed during the boom were unchanged at the time of the crash: hard-working populations, high savings, high rates of technological innovation, and high rates of growth. The problem is that such fundamentals do not always explain how markets will perform. While investors' expectations exceeded rationality during the latter phase of the boom, the same occurred in reverse during the crash. In an analysis of the Asian crisis, the SED group wrote:[11]

> We are often asked, 'Why did the Best and the Brightest miss the Asian crisis?' The best short answer is that they *should* have missed it. For the Best and the Brightest are taught that currencies (e.g. the Indonesian rupiah) could never have behaved as they did in Asia. Received economic theories predicted that, given the news about Indonesia's external accounts and other problems, the rupiah should have dropped 12 per cent, and not 80 per cent.

Clearly, new factors are at work. Globalization has created a level of complexity that has outpaced the ability of economic analysis to explain its consequences, and the ability of international organizations to deal with them. The operation of hedge funds is a good example.

Hedge funds are, in effect, the latest global organism to develop in the same evolutionary process that produced transnational companies, world securities markets, and so on. Like other investment funds, hedge funds pool capital from investors and put it into domestic and foreign markets. They have, however, a number of special characteristics. In general, hedge funds cater to big investors – some have minimum entry limits of $10 million. Rather than employing a traditional investment strategy aimed at medium-term profits in one country or market, they play markets around the world, seeking short-term advantage. They look for anomalies between, for example, US bond yields and Russian bond yields. They buy some securities 'long', sell others 'short', and make considerable use of derivatives trading. Most importantly, they are often heavily leveraged, meaning that they borrow money, in some cases several times the value of their assets.

Traditional economics would suggest that hedge funds should serve as a stabilizing force in the market by adding liquidity and ironing out gaps. In fact, the experience of the emerging markets crisis is just the opposite. No one knows the extent, or whether they were the leaders or the followers, but the general view is that a large part of the extremity of the 'meltdown' in Asia and Russia occurred as a result of hedge funds pushing vast sums of money in and out of these markets.

The fact that respected and conservative financial institutions in the US and Europe had invested money in hedge funds completes the global loop: when things go wrong, the effects turn up in unexpected places around the world. The crisis of the late 1990s left the world's leaders and global organizations struggling for answers. In a frank interview on Australian television in March 1999, Mark Malloch Brown, a vice-president of the World Bank, admitted as much. Asked if economists simply did not know what was going on, Malloch Brown hummed and haahed, then agreed that they didn't.

Over the next few years it is likely that major institutions designed to promote stability in international markets, such as the International Monetary Fund and the World Bank, will develop strategies to deal with the new maturity of globalization. In February 1999, the Group of Seven (G7) leading industri-alized nations endorsed a plan to bring together the world's top financial market regulators in a bi-annual forum to deal with such issues. However, there was no indication of any consensus on where this process would lead in policy terms. By 2000 a new threat to growth and markets emerged as a result of a rapid upturn in oil prices and the weakness in the European single currency.

In the meantime, the outlook is one of considerable uncertainty. In the final section of this chapter, we outline some of the key themes we will explore in this book for dealing with these interesting times.

The European investor in the Information Age

The world is entering a period of epochal change from the Industrial Age to the Information Age and, in the transition, investors face an environment that is both difficult and exciting. Britons live in a part of the world where neighbours and major trading partners have experienced enormous growth. The indications are, however, that the sorts of investment approaches that relied on simply cashing in on such expansion are going to be much more difficult to implement successfully than was the case in the past.

The British economy has taken the best part of half a century to find its feet in the new world order which has developed in the second half of the 20th century. Throughout most of the first half of the century the UK economy had been coasting, living on the wealth accumulated during its golden age of industry in the 19th century. This wealth financed a permanent trade deficit in food, raw materials and manufactured goods, while the leadership in industry passed to the United States.

Much of that accumulated surplus was sold to finance the Second World War and most of the nation's infrastructure was run down by the war effort. The UK ended the war virtually bankrupt and its infrastructure was in no position to compete effectively or to refinance its modernization. Although the UK borrowed what at the time was the massive sum of $5 billion from the US and Canada and received a substantial share of Marshall Aid, it was insufficient to make UK companies competitive. The UK in 1946 was nominally still the richest country in Europe after Switzerland and Sweden, but over the next two decades it was steadily overtaken in output per head by its continental rivals – France, Germany, the Netherlands and Belgium, Denmark and Norway, and then by Austria, Italy and Finland.

Economists in recent years have put the blame on the emphasis which post-war Labour governments placed on National Plans, and a policy of attempting to 'pick winners' without a coherent plan for supporting them. Others blamed the state of labour relations which gave trade unions a virtual veto on the introduction of new labour-saving technology.

Some blamed the post-war governments' attempts to maintain Britain's status as a world power and preserve a military and diplomatic presence as far afield as the Indian Ocean and the Far East. Others have emphasized the failure of the UK to join the European Common Market established in 1958. The Common Market gave the founder members – France, Germany, Italy and the Benelux countries – the opportunity to reorganize their industries to take advantage of a common market of nearly 200 million people – four times the size of the UK. There is more general agreement that the UK was simply too small to compete on a global scale with the US and the renascent economies of Japan and the Common Market, and too big to find a specialized niche in the world economy like Sweden, Switzerland and the Netherlands.

Britain eventually joined the Common Market in 1973, but it was not until 1979 that radical attempts were made to restructure the UK economy. Exchange controls were lifted in 1979, allowing the free flow of capital into and out of the UK for the first time in 40 years. Deliberate plans were introduced to break the power of the main trade unions. Efforts were made to eliminate restrictions on the supply of labour, goods and services and to reduce state subsidies, deregulate state industries, sell off state assets and cut public sector spending. Tax rates were cut, leaving interest rates as the main instrument of government economic policy.

The effects were drastic in the extreme. Unemployment rose from well below 1 million in the late 1970s to anywhere between 3–4 million in the mid-1980s, depending on the definitions used. Traditional industries were drastically pruned or destroyed.

There is no doubt that the process would have proved even more painful, and might even have proved impossible, but for the fortuitous discovery of oil and natural gas in the North Sea, and the proceeds of the privatization programme. Also crucial was the successful policy of attracting overseas investment into Britain with the prospects of cheap and docile labour, low taxes, and a minimum of regulations and requirements for spending on support costs.

Following the Thatcher reforms and the recession of 1980, the UK has managed to average real GDP growth of around 2.4 per cent, as shown in Figure 1.3. Labour productivity growth has also slightly exceeded that of the OECD average, as demonstrated in Figure 1.4.

By the end of the century the UK economy had been transformed into a much more modern, compact and specialized structure, based on a small number of major industries including pharmaceuticals and international finance and tourism, supported by a steady flow of oil and gas and a range of niche industries able to compete successfully at home and abroad.

It would be foolish to pretend that the transformation has been complete or so successful that no major problems remain. At the start of the new millennium the UK economy has yet to grasp the nettle of membership of the European single currency. The official position of the Conservative government in the late 1990s was one of wait and see. The incoming Labour administration in 1997 adopted a policy of joining when it would be in Britain's interests to do so, while

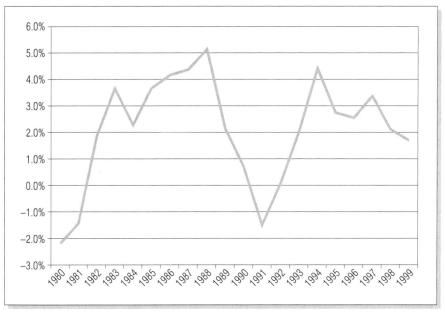

Source: Datastream

FIGURE 1.3 UK real GDP growth rate

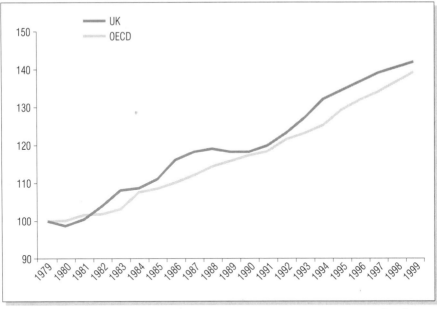

Source: Datastream

FIGURE 1.4   Labour productivity in the UK versus OECD average

the Conservative Party in opposition hardened its attitude and committed itself to staying out of the single currency during the lifetime of the next parliament, which could be as late as 2007.

Although the Labour government's attitude appears to be positive, it has done little or nothing to try to co-ordinate the UK economy with its continental partners or to make a smooth transition to a single currency possible. The government vigorously opposed EU efforts to impose a common withholding tax on all investments held inside the EU borders, on the grounds that such a tax will drive away the vast and highly profitable market in investments held in London by non-resident investors who use it to evade tax either in the UK or at home. If and when a decision to join is taken, the exchange rate at which sterling is integrated and the interest rates current at the time, will be crucially important.

For the time being the UK and the 11 countries in the eurozone have to be seen as distinct entities. The 11 economies that signed up to the single currency in 1999 did so after struggling to bring their individual inflation rates within the 1.5 per cent permitted range, but the single interest rate determined by the European Central Bank did not necessarily fit all their requirements. Initially it was significantly lower than had been the case in both Ireland and Spain, both of which were growing faster than the zonal average, and significantly higher than in Germany, where growth was already below average. It left Ireland in particular facing a real risk of over-heating and rising inflation and Germany facing economic stagnation.

The European Union also continues to pursue social policies such as the reduction in the average working week in France, which could be at odds with the need to reduce labour costs and increase the flexibility of production. At worst it could lead to the eurozone retreating behind a wall of protection and creating a 'Fortress Europe' to protect its lifestyle against external competition.

It is always dangerous to project current trends indefinitely but at the start of the new century North America and East Asia, including China, are expected to be the most competitive global players and the major growth centres of the world in the first quarter of the 21st century. If so, Europe and smaller economies such as the UK could be left with uncomfortable choices to make about their economic allegiances and orientation.

It is clear that British and European investors will, for the foreseeable future, face an investment scene that is at once exciting and full of opportunity but complex and prone to pitfalls. For this reason, they will need a strategy that will cope with, and take advantage of, the new world economic order. In a global marketplace, investors must take a global outlook and determine whether a country, industry or company has a sense of vision, urgency and commitment. Not only is it essential to assess the inclination and ability to adapt and use new technologies, it is also vital to compare how competitive one country or company is against others.

Logically, then, to gain full advantage from the technological revolution, British and European investors alike will have to put at least some of their money offshore. But these investment decisions are likely to be far more difficult than they were ten years ago. Investors who go offshore in an indiscriminate fashion are setting themselves up for disappointment. What often appears to be a strong market is robust only in certain areas. For example, the Dow Jones index of leading US stocks rose 25 per cent in 1999 and the Nasdaq composite index was up more than 80 per cent. But the returns came from a small number of very large companies whose prices leapt while many shares actually fell in value.

Against this background, investors need a framework for a dynamic world: a means of sifting through the mass of data now available to glean information, establish knowledge and – to use an old-fashioned word in a modern sense – to develop wisdom.

The four investment principles developed in *Fortune Strategy* will underpin such a framework: learning how to identify *quality*; learning how to identify *value*; working to achieve *diversity*; and allowing the strategy to work over *time*. More than ever before, it is essential to understand what produces return, what constitutes risk, and how to design a plan that deals with uncertainty.

Coming chapters explore how to maximize the opportunities, and manage the risk, to promote both wealth and survival for the man or woman living on the global village street.

Notes

1 In this book the term 'portfolio theory' is used in a broad sense. It refers not just to what academics may regard as modern portfolio theory but also to the broad array of recent theoretical and empirical research on investment.

2 Markowitz, H.M. (1952) 'Portfolio selection', *Journal of Finance*, vol. 7, no. 1, March, pp. 77–91.

3 Higgins, Benjamin *An Author in Search of Six Characters: a semi-anthropological approach to development*, (to be published).

4 Hale, David (1999) 'Will the world economy recover in the year 2000?', *The Global Economic Observer*, Zurich Research, January 28.

5 *McKinsey Quarterly*, Volume I, 1997.

6 *Strategic Economic Decisions*, November 1997.

7 Bloomberg news service, 9 March 1999.

8 Mantoux, Paul (1961) *The Industrial Revolution in the Eighteenth Century*, Jonathan Cape, London, p. 27.

9 Wriston, Walter (1984) 'The information standard', *Euromoney*, October, p. 92.

10 Hale, David op cit.

11 *Strategic Economic Decisions*, August 1998.

CHAPTER 2

Return: fallacies, facts and formulae

Summary

▦ All investors seek higher return, but they need to know how to measure it and how to compare the return from one investment with another.

▦ Inflation or deflation can radically affect investment strategies, and need to be taken into account.

▦ 'Compounding' of income acts as an antidote to inflation, and provides the correct basis for comparing investments.

▦ Tax can cut into returns, but with varying effects on different investments. The aim of tax strategy, however, is to maximize after-tax returns, not just to minimize tax.

▦ Overseas investment is alluring, but the impact of currency fluctuations must be considered.

Introduction: what you see may not be what you get

At a conference in London some years ago, a young investment adviser had just finished his usual spiel about the importance of correctly calculating returns. He had issued the standard warnings about inflation, tax and the like, and opened the floor to questions. An older gentleman got up in response, and delivered not a question but a riveting ten-minute speech. It went something like this:

> Young fellow, you might be interested to hear a real story about inflation. I retired in 1974, with a lump sum of £50 000. In those days, that was a lot of money – you could buy 60 Morris Minors for that. Like the sensible bloke I was, I put it in the bank at 8 per cent. The interest I received was enough to buy five Morris Minors a year, so I thought I'd be all right for my retirement.
>
> But it didn't turn out that way, because of inflation. Do you know what £50 000 can buy you now? About eight Morris Marinas, and boring cars they are too compared to the old Minor. Now today, I could get 12 per cent interest from the bank. But with that interest on £50 000, I could only afford about one Marina.
>
> The real problem, though, is that I don't even have that £50 000 left. I started living on the interest, but inflation meant that as the years went by it wasn't enough. I had to start eating into some of the £50 000 each year, so it was £45 000 after a couple of years, then £35 000 a couple of years later, then £25 000. Then within a few more years, it was nothing. So now, I'm living on the old age pension.
>
> I did everything the government suggested. I made sure I had lots of money when I retired, I didn't take chances, I put money in the bank. The net result is that I'm scraping by in a little one-bedroom flat. That's what inflation is, my friend.

This anecdote (adapted from an actual case) reinforces what investment is all about: preserving and then increasing wealth in terms of *buying power* over time. It also raises the question of how to assess the true return from an investment.

What matters to investors is the total real return after allowing for the effects of both inflation and taxation. Total return includes any capital gains or losses from increases or decreases in the value of the assets plus any income from interest, rent or dividends. Real return allows for the effect of inflation and net returns allow for the effects of taxation on gains and income.

To compare the value of the vast array of investments on offer, the investor needs a clear idea of the factors that make up return. The straightforward interest rate (or dividend, or increase in capital value) does not on its own determine how much an investment will yield in terms of buying power, as the pensioner in the anecdote discovered. In this case, inflation wiped out the benefits, and the real return after deducting the rate of inflation from the nominal return was negative.

Since the end of the First World War in November 1918 the price of a typical basket of goods has risen almost exactly 20-fold, so that a pound now will buy only the equivalent of what one shilling (5p) would buy back in 1918. The rate of inflation varies continuously, and after an initial leap in 1920, prices fell by almost 40 per cent in the next 15 years. The cost of living measured by the retail price index did not regain the 1918 level until 1948. Inflation gradually accelerated in the 1950s and 1960s, however, and reached a peak of 25 per cent in the mid-1970s. It was in double figures for eight of the nine years from 1973 to 1981 inclusive, and remained a recurring threat through the 1980s, only falling back in the 1990s to an average of around 2.5 per cent.

In other situations, returns can be adversely affected by taxation or, in the case of international investments, by adverse currency movements. In the 1960s the UK government levied an extra rate of income tax on investment income which forced the top rate charged on high earners up to an incredible 98 per cent. Since 1979 investors have been free to invest money in other currencies, but many have been caught by falls in the value of other currencies against sterling which can be either gradual or sudden.

The pensioner was also caught by the difference between *capital growth* and *income*. Capital growth provides an increase in the value of an asset, which is realized only when it is sold or cashed in. Income provides a regular stream of money to live on. The pensioner thought he was well off with an income from interest equivalent to five Morris Minors a year. But while he lived off the interest, the capital value of his investment remained static in sterling terms and then, as inflation started eating into it, declined dramatically.

Finally, the pensioner fell into the trap of regarding fixed-interest investments as inherently safe. He probably saw the stock market as the dangerous domain of speculators. As it happened, his 'safe' investment led him into financial ruin. Had he put perhaps half of his money into a sensibly diversified share portfolio, he would have spent his retirement in comfort and had an enviable estate to pass on to his children.

As we will discuss later, some investments, such as equities, are risky in the short term but have traditionally provided the best way of preserving wealth over time. According to the long-term survey by Barclays Capital, that records data since 1918, share prices beat inflation in 47 out of the next 80 years and dividend income beat inflation in 50 of those years. The combined returns on capital and income also beat inflation in 50 of those years often by a substantial margin. The returns on cash investment, in the form of Treasury bills, beat inflation in 54 of those years, but by relatively small margins. Gilts (fixed interest securities issued by the UK government to finance its longer-term borrowing needs) did even worse, with total returns beating inflation in only 28 years.

Looking at events since 1945 in more detail, a fund invested in equities and reinvesting gross dividends beat inflation in 34 out of 54 years, gilts on the same basis beat inflation in 28 years, and Treasury bills beat inflation in 35 years. But the successful years in equities were appreciably more profitable than the best years in gilts and cash. The equity fund would have turned £100 in 1945 into £85 000 by 1999. A similar fund in gilts would have grown to just £3500 and in Treasury bills to £3800.

The greater reliability of shares as the best long-term defence against inflation is shown when one considers not just individual years but longer time periods. Figure 2.1 shows how over all rolling periods of five years and longer since 1945, shares consistently outperformed cash and gilts, and of particular interest for long-term investment, shares provided a return greater than inflation in every 20-year

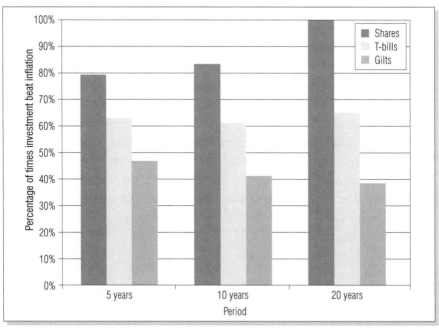

Source: Barclays Global Investors/ipac

FIGURE 2.1 Comparative performance of shares, cash and gilts against inflation over rolling periods, 1945–99

period. By comparison, the return on Treasury bills beat inflation in only about two-thirds of the 20-year periods. Gilts, which generally could be expected to outperform Treasury bills, in fact were defeated by inflation in most of those periods. This reflects the long-term exposure of gilts to inflation on the gilt market during the post-war period.

To make investment worthwhile, the result must be to stay ahead of inflation, taxation, and currency movements where relevant, and transaction fees involved in buying and selling assets.

Different tax regimes apply to different investments. Capital gains on shares may be liable to tax on disposal, dividends are subject to income tax but in the case of interest bearing investments, only the income is liable to tax. The combination of tax and inflation can have a devastating effect, particularly for people in higher tax brackets. For example, even if inflation is within the government's target at 2.4 per cent, an interest rate of 4 per cent will only just maintain buying power for an investor in the top tax bracket paying out two-fifths of his or her income in tax.

Transaction costs are another aspect of the return calculation which are often overlooked. These costs apply to shares and bonds through stockbrokers' commission charges, to property through agents' fees and other costs including stamp duty payable to the government on most deals in stocks and shares and property, and often to interest-bearing accounts in the form of bank charges and penalties for early withdrawals. Transaction costs are of particular importance to investors who try to 'pick the market' through an active trading strategy. Most 'day traders' who buy and sell stocks several times a day actually lose money after paying charges even if their stock-picking selections are quite successful.

The combined effect of transaction costs, tax and inflation can make what at first seems to be a lucrative investment dribble away to nothing. The lesson is clear: any investment strategy must focus on the bottom line, the real return after allowing for inflation, tax and expenses. This chapter looks at the factors that must be taken into account.

Inflation and deflation

A look at economic history shows that inflation, and its out-of-control extension, hyperinflation, are nothing new. Newsreels show German workers in the 1920s using wheelbarrows to collect their daily wages in almost useless currency. In the UK inflation was much less of a threat thanks in part to the deflationary effects of pegging the pound to gold, and for much of the 1920s and 1930s the UK economy suffered from deflation which starved producers of the consumer spending power needed to justify increased production. Even in the post-war period Sir William (later Lord) Beveridge, the architect of the welfare state, considered an inflation rate of 3 per cent as desirable to encourage the owners of capital to put their money to work.

Investors were happy to put the bulk of their savings into bank and building society accounts. These savings, in addition to the proceeds of insurance policies and pension plans, provided the main form of retirement income. During the 1950s and 1960s, this strategy worked satisfactorily for the average saver, thanks to the battery of controls on prices, wages, interest rates and taxes, and on bank lending in the hands of post-war governments. But as controls were relaxed in the 1970s, inflation began to rise.

In the UK the retail price index (RPI) rose by 4.7 per cent in 1969, accelerating to 7.9 per cent in 1970 and 9 per cent the next year (*see* Figure 2.2). In 1973 it topped 10 per cent even before the Middle East oil crisis broke, and quadrupled the cost of oil. In 1974 the RPI soared by 19 per cent, then 25 per cent in 1975, and for five of the next six years it stayed in double figures.

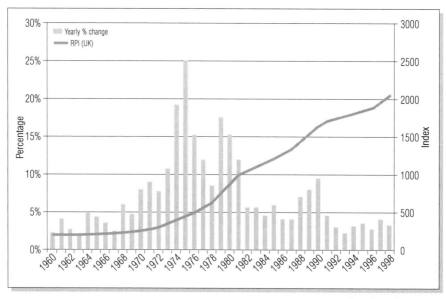

Source: Barclays Global Investors

FIGURE 2.2 UK RPI and yearly changes, 1960–98

Table 2.1 shows that £10 000 in 1970 was worth less than 12 per cent of its real value just 28 years later, with most of the damage being done between 1970 and 1985. People retiring in the early 1970s with typical lump sums of between £40 000 and £50 000 found that they could sustain their lifestyles for only a few years. A pensioner who invested £10 000 in 1970 would have had to see it grow to over £50 000 by 1985 just to maintain its real value. The same £10 000 would have had to have grown to nearly £86 000 by 1998 to break even with inflation.

TABLE 2.1   Effect of inflation on the purchasing power of £10 000, UK, 1970–98

Year	Change in buying power of £10 000 from 1970 (£)	Amount required to equal £10 000 of buying power in 1970 (£)
1970	10 000	10 000
1985	1 995	50 124
1998	1 166	85 759

Source: Barclays Global Investors

Figure 2.3 shows how a difference of just a few percentage points in the inflation rate can have a huge impact on buying power over time. As a rule of thumb, to calculate the rate at which inflation halves the value of money, divide the annual rate of inflation into 70. At 2 per cent a year it will take 35 years to double the cost of living and halve the real value of the currency, but at 7 per cent

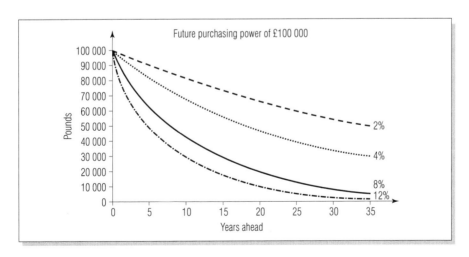

FIGURE 2.3   Impact of different rates of inflation on buying power

it will take only ten years, and at 10 per cent it will take only seven years. This formula works well enough for inflation rates below 10 per cent but it quickly breaks down when rates exceed 10 per cent.

Inflation does not just erode the value of savings, it also reduces the value of wages, triggering annual attempts by trade unions to negotiate pay increases, often to compensate for future as well as past inflation. It also reduces the supply of savings to finance business investment and discourages companies from taking investment decisions because of the uncertainty of future returns on capital, even if interest rates are less than inflation rates and the current real cost of borrowing is negative. Low rates of industrial investment became a serious problem in the UK in the 1970s, further reducing the supply of goods and services and leading to a succession of short spurts in economic growth brought to a premature end by the need to check rising levels of inflation.

One of the most dramatic changes in Western economies over the past decade has been the move from high inflation to a new environment where low inflation is increasingly taken for granted.[1] Figure 2.2 shows the pattern in the UK. After peaking at 25 per cent in the 1970s and averaging about 10 per cent between 1970 and 1990, consumer price inflation had fallen to just 2–3 per cent by the late 1990s. In Japan, inflation was negative for most of the 1990s and in 1998/99 many British and American economists were looking seriously at the possibility of deflation – a sustained period in which asset values and consumer prices decline.

The reasons for this fundamental change include a reorientation in the basic economic strategy of most Western governments, which has made fighting inflation the first priority, following the precedent set by the post-war German government. In many countries the key weapon for doing so, monetary policy, was handed from politicians to central bankers, a policy pioneered by post-war Germany which handed responsibility to the council of the Bundesbank. Handing over control from the Treasury to the Bank of England was one of the first policy initiatives of the new Labour administration in the UK in 1997. The newly established European Central Bank, which took over monetary policy in the member states of the single European currency in 1999, also has complete freedom to set interest rates at the levels necessary to control inflation.

These officials all have less day-to-day fear about job security and housing affordability, and more concern for long-term policy than politicians, for whom the temptation to engineer a pre-election boom has often proved all too strong. Other factors that have been put forward include the impact of deregulating markets to remove restrictions on supply, of technological change and of globalization, which has greatly increased competition.

Improved productivity has lowered unit production costs, which means that companies can often pay higher wages without passing on the costs to consumers. The privatization of state-owned assets has also increased competition and efficiency.

This low-inflation scenario has significant implications for investment strategy, since it alters the equation of return, tax, and real value between the asset classes. These strategic considerations are discussed in more detail in Chapter 9.

Shrewd investors will take low inflation into account in making tactical investment decisions. But they will also remember that sooner or later, in their lifetime, inflation of at least a moderate level is likely to return. In the 200 years since supply and demand replaced climatic fluctuations as the main driver of economic activity, there has never been a low-inflation period that lasted even half a lifetime. And they will consider the broader strategic need to protect their assets from the erosion of buying power over time.

Whether inflation is low or high, it is essential to focus on the *real return* and *real value* of an investment – the return or value *after* taking inflation into account. The critical point is that when measuring investment return – and many economic indicators such as growth in gross domestic product – it is essential to compare it against the inflation rate and calculate the real rate of return after inflation, which is what matters to investors. The corollary is that, if price deflation does become widespread, assets that maintain their value in *nominal* terms – the price at the time – will actually be increasing in *real* terms, as shown in Table 2.2.

TABLE 2.2 Real return at different rates of inflation and deflation

		0%	4%	8%	Nominal return
Inflation/deflation rate	–3%	3%	7%	11%	*Real return*
	0%	0%	4%	8%	
	4%	–4%	0%	4%	
	8%	–8%	–4%	0%	

While simplistic, Table 2.2 shows the big impact that different rates of consumer price change can have on determining whether or not an investment provides an attractive *real* return. For example, if an investment is providing a fixed 4 per cent nominal return a year, and inflation is also running at 4 per cent, the investment is providing zero real return. But if the economy moves into deflation, with consumer prices falling at 3 per cent a year, it suddenly becomes an excellent investment, providing a return that is 7 per cent above the change in consumer prices.

Inflation is just one factor in the investment equation. Another, once nominated by Albert Einstein as mankind's most powerful discovery, is compounding.

Compounding: making time do the work

A tale often told to demonstrate the power of compound returns is that of the inventor of chess and the Emperor of China. The story goes that the Emperor was so impressed with the new game that he asked the inventor what he would like as a reward. The inventor said: 'Highness, I would like a humble gift of rice. Put one grain on the first square of the chessboard, then double it in the next, to two grains. Double it again to four grains in the third square, and so on. My reward will be the rice on the 64th square.'

Depending on who tells the story, the inventor either became the richest man in China, or was sent to an imperial re-education camp. The 64th square would have yielded 9 million trillion grains of rice, equivalent to that produced if the entire surface of the earth were covered in rice fields twice over.

One of the cardinal elements of successful investment is maintaining a medium- to long-term time frame. And one of the best weapons in the investor's armoury is compounding return over time. Understanding the effect of compounding is also essential for comparing returns on a correct basis, as Table 2.3 shows.

TABLE 2.3 Simple and compound return for £10 000 invested at 10 per cent over three years

	Simple (interest consumed) £	Compound (interest accrued) £
Year 1	10 000	10 000
Interest	1 000	1 000
Year 2	10 000	11 000
Interest	1 000	1 100
Year 3	10 000	12 100
Interest	1 000	1 210
Total interest	3 000	3 310

An investor who leaves money in the bank for a year will receive a particular interest rate. On £10 000 at 10 per cent per year, the interest is £1000 gross, i.e. before tax. If the investor spends the £1000 each year, the original investment remains at £10 000, and £1000 interest is paid each subsequent year. This approach, using a *simple* interest rate of 10 per cent, yields £3000 over three years. However, if the investor adds the £1000 interest to the original £10 000 instead of spending it, the investment is now £11 000. In the second year the interest is 10 per cent of £11 000 (£1100), bringing the total investment to £12 100. By the end of three years the investment is worth £13 310 because the interest *compounds*. At the *compound* interest rate of 10 per cent, the investment yields £3310 over three years. Reinvesting dividends from stocks and shares and rental income from property has the same beneficial effect on total returns. Many companies and managed funds encourage shareholders to reinvest dividends in extra shares by making only nominal brokerage charges.

The difference between simple return and compound return is one of the most important concepts for comparing the value of investments. Some investment salespeople will quote the simple rather than the compound interest rate when calculating expected return. For example, a promoter might say that £10 000 invested ten years ago in a particular product is now worth £31 000, and cite this £21 000 profit as a 21 per cent (simple) average annual growth rate of £2100 per year. Such a growth rate would, however, be equivalent to only about 12 per cent in compound terms. While the simple return calculation has some specific uses, the truest way of measuring long-term growth rates is in compound terms.

While the concept of compounding is straightforward, the implications for the investor are immense. A difference of just a couple of percentage points in return can produce radically different results in the value of a portfolio over time. Table 2.4 and Figure 2.4 provide illustrations of this point, and a handy ready-reckoner.

TABLE 2.4 Future value of £10 000 at different interest rates

Period of investment	Compound interest rate				
	5%	*8%*	*10%*	*12%*	*15%*
Now	10 000	10 000	10 000	10 000	10 000
5 years	12 760	14 690	16 110	17 620	20 110
10 years	16 290	21 560	25 940	31 060	40 460
15 years	20 790	31 720	41 770	54 730	81 370
20 years	26 530	46 610	67 280	96 460	163 670
30 years	43 220	100 630	174 490	299 590	662 110

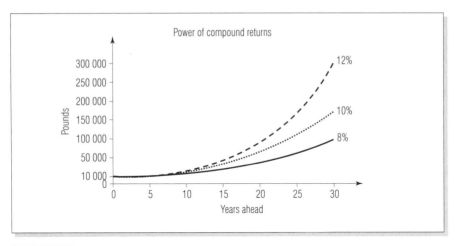

FIGURE 2.4 Power of compound returns

Suppose a pension salesman offers a package in which the investor puts in only £10000 and receives £100000 in 30 years' time. While this may sound great at first, it represents a compound interest rate of only 8 per cent. If the investor could find an investment that would produce a return just two percentage points higher – a 10 per cent compound return – the same £10000 investment would be worth £174490 by the end of the period. A 12 per cent compound rate would produce nearly £300000 – *three times* the return from an 8 per cent compound rate.

Compounding makes it well worth regularly putting money into long-term investments – as long as they stay ahead of inflation. If a 30-year-old starts putting £200 each month into an investment fund today, and the fund averages a return of 10 per cent a year, by the time the investor turns 60 their entitlement will be worth £455832. Even assuming, for example, that inflation averages 5 per cent, the real value of the investment will be £167142 in today's pounds.

Apart from the compounding/inflation equation, an investment's real return also depends on tax. While tax is a bore, the principles are not as difficult as is often made out. In the next three sections, we explore the key aspects of tax and their strategic implications for investors.

Tax: the core principles

Perhaps the most enduring topic in publishing, after sex, is tax. Virtually every budget incorporates some fundamental alteration to the tax system. As a result, comprehensive tax guides are useful for only a short time. With this in mind, *Fortune Strategy* concentrates on general tax principles that affect strategic investment decisions. It illustrates the application of these principles taking into account key features of the UK tax structures as at the time of writing. However, the principles will have general application across most European tax regimes.

The best way to keep up with the changing minutiae of the tax regime is to buy a good tax guide so that you know what to look for, then consult a competent independent financial adviser, tax adviser or accountant. The UK government introduced self-assessment in 1997 promising to calculate the tax liability for individuals who returned their completed returns by the end of September, six months after the end of the relevant tax year. However, for all but the simplest of accounts, the cost of getting an accountant to prepare a tax return (which is itself tax deductible) is perhaps the easiest and most cost-efficient decision an investor can make. It also helps to stay on the right side of the law.

Specific tax considerations for each asset class are outlined in Part Two of *Fortune Strategy*. However, in this chapter, we introduce some concepts that are essential to understanding investment return.

The shrewd investor applies two fundamental, and counterbalancing, principles when looking at the tax implications of an investment strategy. The first principle is that tax can substantially reduce what is left of real return after inflation and transaction costs. Therefore, it is worth ensuring that tax is legally minimized. For example, a number of deductions, rebates and exemptions may be available.

A broader strategic issue for investors is based on the fact that the tax office treats income returns differently from capital gains returns. Capital growth is the profit made between the price an investor pays for something and the price for which it is sold. Income, in tax terms, is a somewhat more amorphous concept. In practice, it means all revenue earned or otherwise received through specific payments, such as salaries, wages and income from self-employment, interest payments, dividends, and so on. Because of the different tax treatment of capital gains and income, it is important to have a mix of investments that produce the desired balance between income (usually through interest and dividends) and capital growth. The right mix depends on each investor's individual circumstances.

This type of consideration is lawful and ethical. Tax laws are designed to achieve the goals of the government of the day, in raising income from certain types of activities, and channelling savings into particular parts of the economy. Tax *planning* is simply good financial practice, and is fundamentally different from tax *evasion*, which is unlawful.

The second principle is: don't go broke by saving tax. Any tax strategy should increase the net after-tax return from investment. If so much income is given up in reducing tax that the tax 'saving' is less than the income forgone, the strategy is counterproductive.

In the next sections we look at how to apply these principles to some of the most important strategic decisions that investors face.

Income tax

Tax rates can change, but the principle is likely to remain. All individuals, including children, can receive a certain amount of income that is not liable to tax. At the time of writing, in the UK this was £4385. This amount is indexed annually at the rate of change in the RPI but can be varied up or down at the Chancellor of the Exchequer's discretion. Older people also get an extra tax-free allowance but this is phased out as their income rises.

The tax bands for individuals as at 6 April 2000 were:

Income			Tax rate %
£0	–	£4385	0 (tax-free threshold)
£4386	–	£5905	10 (lower rate)
£5906	–	£32 785	22 (standard rate)
£32 786+			40 (top rate)

Interest on bank and building society deposits, gilts and bonds is usually paid out net of withholding tax at 20 per cent. Non-taxpayers can reclaim the full 20 per cent, while taxpayers on the 10 per cent rate can reclaim 10 per cent. Standard-rate taxpayers have nothing more to pay, while top-rate taxpayers are liable to pay a further 20 per cent, making 40 per cent in all. In the case of dividends from shares, the tax system provides investors with a credit which at least partially takes into account the fact that companies have already paid tax on their profits. This helps to minimize the extent of double taxation of company profits distributed to investors.

Since April 2000, companies pay tax on their annual profits at a rate starting with 10 per cent for companies whose profit is below £10 000. This rises in various steps to 30 per cent for companies with annual profits in excess of £1.5 million. While the system of tax credits is convoluted, in effect it results in taxpayers on the standard rate and below having to pay no additional tax on dividends received. Top-rate taxpayers pay tax at 25 per cent of the dividend received. In practice this means that in the case of companies earning more than £1.5 million annually, their profits distributed to top-rate taxpayers are effect-ively taxed at 47.5 per cent and for all other taxpayers at 30 per cent.

Capital gains

Capital gains are usually less reliable than income from interest and dividends in the short term, but in the long term they have proved to be both larger and more tax-efficient. Even capital losses can be offset against gains or carried forward to offset future gains.

Seeking capital gain, rather than annual investment income, can be one of the best tax strategies, particularly for investors in higher tax brackets. It is at its most effective when inflation is high, as it defers paying tax while an investment grows in nominal value.

In the UK, capital gains are taxed separately from income, and the annual tax-free allowance for gains of £7200 (also indexed annually) is well above the tax-free allowance on income. Gains are not liable to tax until they are realized by the sale of the assets. Realized gains in excess of the annual allowance are liable to tax at the taxpayer's marginal (i.e. highest) rate. Some assets, including interest-bearing investments such as gilts and bonds, and an individual's home or principal residence, are exempt from capital gains tax (CGT).

The value of taxable assets acquired before April 1998 is indexed to allow for inflation up until that date. Gains on assets acquired subsequent to April 1998 receive no further indexation benefit. But the rate of tax on realized gains is subject to taper relief. The tax rate is reduced in stages from 40 per cent and 20 per cent for top- and standard-rate taxpayers respectively on assets held for less than three years, to a low of 24 per cent and 12 per cent after ten years.

The Budget in 2000 improved the concession on investments in so-called 'business assets' such as unquoted company shares, those listed on the Alternative Investment Market, shares held by employees in their own company, and on investors holding more than 5 per cent of a quoted company. The tax in these cases has effectively been reduced for top-rate taxpayers to just 10 per cent of the gain after four years and 5 per cent for standard rate taxpayers.

Effectively this means that investors, especially high taxpayers, get a significant benefit to the extent that their investment returns are in the form of a capital gain rather than income, and that this benefit is increased to the extent that they are willing to take more risk by investing in emerging, rather than established, company shares. Major shareholders of any company now enjoy a particularly large concession, reflecting the government's desire to encourage enterprise.

To understand how the tax regime works, let us first consider a situation where there is no CGT on individual investments, and compare it with tax on investment income from interest or dividends. The process is shown in

Table 2.5. An investor who is in the 40 per cent marginal tax bracket and earns £5000 of additional income from interest on an investment of £100 000 will pay £2000 in tax. On the other hand, if the investor bought an investment property or a parcel of shares for £100 000 and sold it a year later for £105 000, net of dealing costs, the whole £5000 of profit would be retained because the realized gain is less than the annual tax-free allowance of £7200.

TABLE 2.5 Comparative tax treatments of income and capital gain

	Interest-bearing investment (income) £	Property or shares (capital gain) £
Initial investment	100 000	100 000
First-year return	5 000 interest	5 000 capital gain
Tax liability at 40%	2 000	0
After-tax return	3 000	5 000

Table 2.6 illustrates another example of capital-versus-income investment, using a different set of assumptions. It compares the effect of inflation and tax on a 5 per cent return from income, against a 5 per cent return entirely from capital growth on assets bought today and held for ten years and then sold. It assumes a low inflation rate of 2 per cent, and a high income earner on a marginal tax rate of 40 per cent.

In this case, as Table 2.6 shows, the interest-bearing investment boosts the portfolio after ten years to a compounded value net of tax of £134 392. The net real return after adjusting for inflation as well is £12 493. On the other hand, the growth-oriented investment produces a net real return some 124 per cent higher, of £28 003. This reflects three effects. First, despite being a high-income earner, the investor has benefited by fully taking advantage of the separate tax-free threshold of £7200 for capital gains, indexed for inflation. Second, thanks to tapering, the tax on the realized gain is only 24 per cent. And finally, the investor has also received the compounded benefit of deferring tax over the ten-year period. In practice, the tax liability in the case of the growth investment could be lower still by, for example, utilizing structures such as an ISA, partially investing in the AIM market, and by not realizing all the gains in one year.

This demonstrates, once again, a major theme of investment: two investments that ostensibly yield the same return can in fact produce markedly different results, depending on the tax circumstances of the investor.

| TABLE 2.6 | Comparative tax treatments of 5 per cent return on £100 000* |

	Interest-bearing investment £	Capital growth Investment £
Gross value after ten years	162 889	162 889
Assessable gain adjusting for indexation of tax-free allowance	N/A	54 112
Tax liability	28 497	12 987
Net value	134 392	149 902
Amount needed in ten years equal to £100 000 of today's buying power	121 899	121 899
Net real return	12 493	28 003

* with 2 per cent inflation after ten years. 40 per cent taxpayer using separate tax-free allowance and taper relief for capital gains.

Note: Tax liability on capital gain has been calculated assuming that the annual tax-free allowance of £7200 for gains has been indexed for inflation and that taper relief reduces the tax rate to 24 per cent.

Gearing: getting a lever on investment

Borrowing for investment – called *gearing* or *leveraging* – has acquired a mixed reputation after a series of high-profile corporate crashes over the years. Done incorrectly, it can lead greedy investors to financial ruin even faster than they would get there otherwise. However, there are circumstances where, with good assets and a solid income base, it can pay off. Gearing does this by providing the investor with access to more investment capital. It magnifies the profits or losses of an investment, but the evidence suggests that even after tax the return on stocks and shares and also property has, on average and over time, been greater than the cost of borrowing. The margin is even greater if, as in the case of investing in property, the borrower can charge the cost of interest against tax.

Total return, once again, is comprised of income plus capital growth. If the return is greater than the interest and associated costs, it may be worth gearing. Where investors go wrong is if the income falls short and, instead of rising in value, the asset stagnates or declines. The interest still has to be paid off and, worse still, the interest burden can rise, if set on a variable rate.

Let us take an example, for the moment leaving tax and inflation aside. Suppose an investor has £10 000, but can borrow another £10 000 at 16 per cent interest. The investor has in mind a share parcel that is likely to produce a 6 per cent dividend yield per year. The investor predicts, correctly in this case, that the price of the shares will rise in value by 50 per cent in a year. Table 2.7 shows the results of choosing between borrowing and not borrowing. Even after interest charges, the investor will do far better by borrowing.

TABLE 2.7   Effect of borrowing on return: dividend paid

	No borrowing (£10 000 invested) £	Borrowing £10 000 (£20 000 invested) £
Capital gain at 50%	5 000	10 000
Dividend income	600	1 200
Total gross return	5 600	11 200
Less interest	n/a	1 600
Total net return	5 600	9 600

Suppose now that the economy and share market turn bad and, instead of rising as the investor predicts, the shares lose half their value and no dividends are declared. Table 2.8 shows the different effects of borrowing and not borrowing. If the investor does not borrow, the £10 000 investment will be reduced to £5000. But if the investor does borrow, not only will the whole of the initial investment be lost, but the investor will be a further £1600 in debt. If that person has no funds on hand, they may literally have to sell the car to repay the bank. On a grander scale, this is what happened to many of the 'entrepreneurs' who lost out in various spectacular stock market crashes.

TABLE 2.8   Effect of borrowing on loss: dividend not paid

	No borrowing (£10 000 invested) £	Borrowing £10 000 (£20 000 invested) £
Capital loss at 50%	5 000	10 000
Dividend income	0	0
Total gross loss	5 000	10 000
Less interest	n/a	1 600
Total net loss	5 000	11 600

It should be obvious from this example that a few basic rules apply to gearing. If there is any possibility that the value of the asset, and the income from it, may decline, gearing increases risk greatly. The investor also has to consider whether he or she can afford a rise in interest rates, or whether it would be better to take a fixed rate and possibly pay a premium in interest. On the other hand, for those who are prepared to take the risk with the prospect of substantially higher returns, gearing offers financial leverage.

When tax is taken into account, gearing offers other advantages, particularly for people paying high marginal tax rates. At the time of writing it was possible for UK investors to claim a tax deduction against the rental income on a residential or commercial property for the cost of the interest on borrowing to buy such a property. No such deduction was available for investment in shares. If the interest costs were greater than the rental income from the property – so-called *negative gearing)* – the loss would be carried forward to offset income tax liability from future rent (but not future capital gains) from the property. The loss could not be used to claim a rebate against other tax liabilities. Of course, if the property's rental stream failed to increase materially in the future, this loss might never be claimable.

This discussion returns to the second fundamental point about tax: the objective is not to minimize tax but to maximize net return. Negative gearing and other 'tax losses' involve losing income in the expectation of making more money through tax-advantaged capital gain. Plenty of 'tax-effective' schemes fail on exactly this criterion.

Considerations for international investment: currency

Investors who confine their choice of investments to their home economies juggle with the relative returns in income and capital after allowing for the cost of borrowing and the effects of inflation and tax. People who invest offshore accept an additional element of risk, arising from possible fluctuations in the currency in which the asset is purchased.

Currency risk adds a whole new dimension to investment. Like gearing it can magnify gains or losses. It can save a poor investment from costing money, or it can destroy the benefits of a good investment. The value of any overseas investment to a UK investor is what it is worth in pounds sterling, and to an investor inside the single European currency zone, its worth in euros.

Suppose an investor buys £10 000 worth of shares in a Thai commercial property development company, Siamese Twin Towers. The Thai currency, the baht, is trading at 50 to the pound, and Siamese is trading at 1000 baht per share. If £1 buys 50 baht, £10 000 will buy 500 000 baht. This in turn will buy 500 shares in Siamese.

Initial investment	£10 000
Conversion to baht at £1 = 50 baht	500 000 baht
Number of shares at 1000 baht per share	500 shares

Suppose Siamese rises to 1250 baht per share on the Bangkok exchange – a gain of 25 per cent in Thai currency. However, at the same time, the baht falls 33 per cent in value against the pound so that it takes 67 baht rather than 50 baht to buy a pound. The value of the share parcel, in Thai currency, has risen from 500 000 to 625 000 baht. But what is this worth in pounds to the UK investor? The local value of the investment, 625 000 baht, is divided by the current number of baht to the pound, now 67, to give £9328 – a significant net loss.

Initial investment	500 shares
Conversion to baht at 1250 baht per share	625 000 baht
Pound value of shares at £1 = 67 baht	£9328

Predicting currency movements in a free market is very prone to error. According to traditional economic models, currency should reflect relative changes in 'fundamentals' among nations, such as inflation, trade balances, investment flows and interest rates. In fact, emotional issues such as political confidence are often more important in determining market movements. The experts were near unanimous that the newly formed European single currency, the euro, which began life in 1999 would quickly rise in value against the US dollar partly because of demand from other central banks anxious to add it to their reserves and partly because the US economy was set for a recession. In fact, the euro fell almost 16 per cent in its first year.

The above examples show that currency risk on individual overseas investments can be substantial, and investors should have no illusions about it. It is possible, however, to reduce or eliminate currency risk by taking out a *currency hedge*. This is a derivative financial instrument that guarantees that an investor can change foreign money for a certain rate in the future. The problem is that such a hedge can be expensive and difficult to manage for the private investor. There are, however, quite a few complexities of international currency that can reduce overall risk. In the next chapter, we explore in detail 'natural' hedges and discuss how applied portfolio theory can help to manage currency risk.

As with any other market, currency is subject to supply and demand. The day-to-day demand and supply of dollars, yen, euros, sterling and especially the currencies of smaller trading nations such as the Thai baht, or the Mexican peso leads to short-term fluctuations in the price of one currency against another. If more foreign traders than usual suddenly want to pay for Japanese contracts or buy goods, they need to buy yen, and the value of the yen is likely to go up. Speculation by currency traders can also push a currency up or down and lead to a great deal of short-term volatility.

Long-term trends in currencies are more open to fundamental analysis, that is, to looking at the underlying economic factors. A key factor is the level of interest rates. If interest rates are high, it attracts overseas investors, who have to buy the currency in order to purchase bonds or other interest-bearing financial instruments. Interest rates are determined largely by government monetary policy, discussed in Chapter 4. Another fundamental determinant is the overall state of a country's economy and, more specifically, its trade balance.

These fundamental factors do not always dominate. Intangibles such as political confidence, or speculation, often prove more important, as we discovered with the Asian crisis discussed in Chapter 1. However, as a broad rule of thumb, over the long term the direction of a currency will reflect the performance of a national economy. Economic performance, in turn, should be reflected in the prices of assets, such as shares and property. And this means that investors who pick the country correctly are likely to win both ways in the long term: in value of assets and in value of currency.

It is easy to become deceived by the concept of return, and the astute investor starts with the question: what is the return being *compared* with, and is it relevant? Unfortunately, many investors fall into the trap of comparing the returns that they receive with those of their neighbours, with other investments, and so on. Return is, after all, only a way of generating money, and money is only a means to achieve personal goals, not an end in itself.

The most important benchmark is how well a particular return provides for the investor's needs and aspirations, after taking into account the tax profile and level of risk that the investor is prepared to take.

The trade-off between risk, return and time is the central equation in investment. To achieve higher rates of return, investors may have to accept more risk, but there are various strategies available to get the best from this trade-off. We look at these strategies in Chapter 3.

Note

1 Economists tend to distinguish between different types of price inflation, such as asset price inflation and retail price inflation. Unless otherwise specified, this book uses the term 'inflation' in the way it has come to be most commonly identified: retail price inflation.

Risk, return and diversification

Summary

▪ While people usually look first at the *return* of a potential investment, the likelihood of getting that return depends on the *risk* associated with the investment.

▪ No investment strategy can succeed without a framework for comparing the risks of different investments, including against the return they provide.

▪ An investor's overall portfolio is what counts, and investments that are quite risky on their own may actually combine to reduce the volatility of a portfolio.

▪ Effective diversification can help get the best out of the trade-off between risk and return, but the investor has to understand why different investments perform in different ways.

▪ While investors often concentrate on picking individual investments, what will principally govern the long-term performance of a portfolio is the diversification among the major asset classes.

▪ Investors cannot just look to the past when assessing risk and return; they need to make a judgement on what the *future* holds for investments, and to do so they need to assess the fundamentals which lie behind investment markets.

Introduction: a retrospective on 'greed is good'

The late 1980s introduced a generation of Britons who had grown up with memories of low wages, high taxes, rationing and controls to a new world of unlimited opportunities for getting rich. The mood was captured by Gordon Gecko, the hero of the film *Wall Street*. 'Loadsamoney' and 'Greed is Good' became the watchwords for a new generation of yuppie. The stock market became the new casino, where everybody won and the luckiest won more than most.

Terry Bond was a typical young professional who was intrigued by the fortunes that were being made. Recently married, he was visiting his wife's family in early October 1987. His father-in-law enthused over the virtues of investing in penny shares, which seemed to offer an unbeatable formula. Buy a share for 5p and the worst it can do is fall 5p, but the upside is unlimited. Buy tens of thousands of shares for thousands of pounds and the sky is the limit. Terry surreptitiously stole his father-in-law's Penny Share Guide, invested his entire savings in ten different penny shares and sat back to wait for the cash to roll in. In fact, of course, the stock market crashed and the main share index fell 30 per cent in a matter of days. Everyone rushed to sell their penny shares as well, but there were no buyers for these speculative issues, prices collapsed and Terry lost nearly 90 per cent of his investment within a week.

There is a happy ending in this case. Terry learned his lesson, set about mastering the fundamentals of the stock market, taught himself the basic rules of investment analysis, and with the help of a few trusty reference books set about rebuilding his portfolio on sound lines. Now, in addition to a core, diversified portfolio, he has an active portfolio of about a dozen shares, trades once or twice a week, and writes a column on private investment each week in the *Independent* newspaper.

But his story raises a number of topics that will be brought out in this chapter, including risk, return, and diversification. He sought high return. He thought that he could reduce risk through diversification, but his strategy was ineffective because it breached some basic principles. His portfolio concentrated on one asset class, shares; one small sector of the share market, penny shares, for which there is a limited market; and one country, the UK. Most importantly, he failed to 'look behind the price' at what really underpinned these companies. And, as a result, he failed to realize that the boom was unsustainable.

What drove the boom of the late 1980s was the immediate flush of financial deregulation. This created a surplus of capital and a surplus of banks eager to find homes for that capital through lending. As conservative lending rules were thrown aside, entrepreneurs borrowed large amounts of capital for often ill-judged, poorly defined, high-risk investment projects which relied on cheap borrowings and on the largely psychological engine of the boom itself.

As discussed in Chapter 1, many of the recent problems in Asia and the emerging markets reflect a similar boom-bust pattern, as does the volatility of technology stocks. The US and UK stock markets in particular were being driven by a mania for high technology and dot com issues, many of which had yet to turn a profit, and some of which were exposed in the shake-out of April 2000. Rising markets were also supported by a rash of mergers, especially in the finance and media industries, using borrowed funds and highly valued share offers in the hope of recouping part of their investments by selling off redundant assets.

Never has there been a greater need to understand risk and how to manage it. Most investors incur far more financial risk, usually without knowing it, and get far less return than they should. As a result, few have benefited fully from the opportunities that deregulation has made available.

Chapter 3 is the most challenging of the book. It is also the most important for readers who wish to learn not just the mechanics of individual *markets* but of investment *strategy* itself.

To understand superior strategy, readers will have to challenge some of their natural assumptions. It seems reasonable, for example, that more risky invest-ments should provide the potential for higher returns. But it is not that simple. Some investments may be high risk on their own, but because they have different characteristics from most others, they may actually help to reduce the total risk of a portfolio. Investors may be prepared to accept less return from such higher-risk investments because of this *diversification* benefit. Or, put another way, much of the additional risk can be 'diversified away'.

The relationship between risk, return and diversification requires a depth of understanding to get the best out of it. But careful study of these concepts will provide the investor – whether adventurous or conservative – with a strong foundation for designing rewarding investment strategies.

Horses for courses

The expression 'modern portfolio theory' is probably not the greatest conver-sation-starter at an Ascot Gold Cup gathering, for example. But many racegoers know more about it than they realize. In its more sophisticated form it can involve considerable mathematics. However, it is not necessary to be a mathematician to understand, and use, portfolio theory. In fact, anyone who has punted on a horse should be able to understand the basic principles. Risk, return and diversification operate in much the same way on the track as they do in investment markets.

The key to modern portfolio theory is the relationship between the risk of an investment and the return it provides. This trade-off is a key factor governing the value and price of an investment. It is the principle used to compare one investment with another and to determine superior mixes of investments to make up a portfolio. At its simplest level, the concept follows common sense. Investments that carry low risk can offer a low return and still attract buyers. Investments that involve medium risk must offer a better return. And investments that entail high risk have to lure investors with the prospect of high returns.

The betting industry operates on the same trade-off. Some horses attract better odds than others because they have a good chance of winning and others hardly stand a chance. The odds are based on past performance, current form and expectations of what this trend implies for the future – specifically, the next race. Some horses perform fairly consistently, while others seem to be erratic. What is it, though, that enables a bookie to work out whether a horse should pay 10–1, 5–2 or 1–2?

Bookies sell bets to the public. For the favourite, call it Victor, a bookie has to offer only very short odds because the horse is fairly assured of a first, second or third place. The bookie may offer odds of 1–2 for a place – for every £2 bet, the punter gets £3 back less tax (including the original £2). Before tax the punter makes a profit of £1, or a 50 per cent return, on a successful bet. Because the risk of losing the £2 stake is not so great, the punter is prepared to make the bet, even though the prospective return is not spectacular compared with other horses.

Suppose now that another horse, Dud, has never won a race and has won a place only once in ten starts. The only way the bookie can attract bets on the lesser horse is to offer the prospect of a fabulous return. So the bookie offers 10–1 odds on Dud; that is, for every £1 the punter puts up, the bookie will pay £11 back (including the original £1 stake) if the horse wins a place. These odds offer a prospective return of 1000 per cent, which compensates for the high risk.

Similarly, only the prospect of higher return will attract investors to a higher-risk investment. The principle applies, in different ways, to all types of investments. The *junk bond* is a fixed-interest financial instrument in which investors lend money to companies that have a less than first-class credit rating. They are higher risk because the companies have a greater chance of going broke and not paying back bondholders. Junk bonds offer a higher rate of interest than bonds for companies that have a better credit rating, to compensate for this extra risk.

The risk/return factor for all securities is worked out through the market. For assets such as property and shares, the pricing mechanism itself matches risk and return. Assets that involve more risk trade for a relatively lower price, providing a higher prospective return. This introduces the concept of investment *yield* – the return of an investment relative to its price.

To examine the relationship between risk, return and price, let us take a property example. Two blocks of flats are on the market. One, Downtown Mansions, is already established, providing £100 000 a year in rent with good prospects of rental growth. The other, Suburban Villas, is a new development in a less fashionable part of town. The developers also expect it to earn £100 000 a year in rent, but the prospects are less certain. Suppose both blocks come up for auction, and Downtown Mansions sells for £1 million. This represents an initial rental yield of 10 per cent on the purchase price. But the same investor will not pay the same amount for Suburban because it represents a higher risk. He might offer just £800 000 for the property in order to secure a rental yield of 12.5 per cent. Table 3.1 shows the calculation.

TABLE 3.1   Return on two properties compared

	Downtown Mansions	Suburban Villas
Annual rent (A)	£100 000	£100 000
Auction price (B)	£1 000 000	£800 000
Rental yield (A/B x 100)	10%	12.5%

The stock market is a little more complicated, but the same basic principle applies. Established companies with good profit records can command a higher relative price for their shares than companies that are just starting out. The higher prospective return is what entices some investors to make a longer-term investment.

The discussion has so far dealt with the intuitive concept of risk as it relates to individual investments, or horses. However, sensible investors – and punters – do not invest or bet on one-offs. Rather, they assess a range of options and their risk/return characteristics, and spread their money over options and also over time. This approach opens up more dimensions of risk and return, including diversification, diversifiable risk and correlation. In particular, it raises the complication of how some higher-risk options can, because of their diversification value, sometimes offer a lower prospective return and still get takers.

Diversifying risk: the racecourse

Returning to the racecourse, suppose that a few days before the race a punter has put a fair bit of money on the favourite, Victor. However, after analyzing past performance, the punter discovers that Victor does best on dry tracks and the forecast is for rain. So the punter wants a way to cover the bet should the track become very wet.

After looking at Dud and finding that it too is a dry-weather horse, the punter comes to Raindrop on the form guide. In dry weather, Raindrop has done even worse than Dud. However, the few times it has won a place have all been in the wet. The punter may put some money on Raindrop, on the basis that if the track proves wet, Victor may lose, but Raindrop may win a place and cover the main bet. The punter may accept odds of about 5–1, half those on Dud, even though Raindrop has, historically over all her races, less chance of winning.

In effect, the punter has tried to *diversify away risk* by looking for a horse with characteristics opposite to those of the main bet. To use a term explained more fully in coming sections, the *correlation* between the performances of the two horses is low. Because of its diversification benefit, Raindrop is an attractive bet, despite its high risk. The betting industry will probably know this, and the odds on Raindrop will offer far less return than its win/loss record suggests. Seen from another angle, a large part of the risk of Raindrop is *diversifiable* risk: while the horse never wins in dry weather, it is easy to diversify this element of risk by putting money on a dry-weather horse.

Applying this to investment, certain types of assets also tend to move in opposite ways to others. Stock markets do not behave as a unit, and at any one time there will be big variations in performance between different markets, between different sectors in the same market, and above all between shares in different companies. Some sectors are known to be more influenced by spurts and slowdowns in the economy, others are much more consistent. Some respond early in the economic cycle, others react relatively late in the cycle. Some shares are carried along by the cycle but many will be affected by specific influences and will move against the trends.

Take 1999 for example. Over the year as a whole the FTSE 100 share index rose 21 per cent, but the information technology sector more than trebled, the electronics and mining sectors more than doubled, while 14 out of 39 separate sectors including retail trade, food retailing, pharmaceuticals, water, electricity and insurance all ended lower than they had started. Variations between companies were even greater, with ARM, the best performing share in the FTSE 100 index, multiplying 13-fold in the year and many top companies rising more than 50 per cent. But famous names such as Marks and Spencer, Sainsbury, Boots, Lloyds TSB, SmithKline Beecham, and the Prudential actually fell over the year.

With hindsight these changes were explicable, even predictable. But if it were that easy to anticipate the course of share prices in relation to the performance of the economy, investors would simply follow an established pattern and make fortunes all the time. In fact, like history, economics never repeats itself exactly. No one economic cycle is exactly like any previous cycle because some new factors intervene to alter the pattern. The performance of individual companies is even more unpredictable because they are prone to individual factors – such as an enlightened management or a technological breakthrough, or to a takeover bid – which completely alter their valuations.

Sophisticated investors look for a mix of assets with opposing characteristics to reduce the risk of an overall portfolio. The scope for profit then relies not on one asset doing well or badly on any one day or week, but on the whole portfolio doing well over time. The time factor is essential: in the short term, the investor may experience fluctuating fortunes, but a disciplined strategy will work in the medium to long run.

A further point from our racing analogy relates to information. Bookies do not generally accept a bet outside their overall book, unless they believe that they have 'inside' knowledge. The bookie knows that all the information about a horse and race, including form, track conditions, jockey, rumours and so on, is already incorporated in the odds. The only reason to accept a special bet would be if the bookie believed that he or she knew something beyond all this which the market did not.

This principle is critical to investment strategy, where it is known as the *efficient markets hypothesis*. Markets work in such a way that most of the information about a particular investment is already reflected in its price. Unless the investor has special information that is not yet 'priced in', the most efficient diversification is across the market as a whole – in racing terms, the whole book.

This section has sketched the whole picture. The main point is that risk, return, diversification and time are all part of the same equation. We now turn to the individual components of the equation in greater detail.

Risk: the search for a measure

Everyone has an intuitive concept of risk, and some sorts of investments appear to be more or less secure than others. However, to apply logical analysis to choosing from *all possible* investments, it is essential to have a consistent basis for comparing risk.

In sports such as cricket, averages are worked out to compare the performance of players. A 'batting average' to compare investments would also have obvious advantages. Return is comparatively easy to measure and, as discussed in the previous chapter, the measures of total return and compound return are the norm. Measuring risk, however, has presented more of a challenge for the investment industry.

It might at first appear that a measure of 'downside' risk would be sufficient. After all, most investors associate risk with the chance that they may lose some or all of their money. However, any measure of risk should take into account potential 'upside' as well. Volatility works both ways, up and down. Time is also important. Ultimately, the investor wants to know the potential range of gains and losses, how likely they are to occur, and over what period.

The financial community has come up with a generally accepted measure that draws all of these factors into a single figure: *standard deviation*. This measures volatility in the return of an investment. An investment with a high standard deviation is a high-risk investment in terms of volatility. One with a low standard deviation is low-risk when it comes to volatility. But standard deviation is not, on its own, the definitive guide to risk. It also requires fundamental analysis and good judgement – techniques that are developed in *Fortune Strategy*. However, like a batting average, it provides a rough basis for initial comparison.

Standard deviation indicates the range of returns that an investment provides with a reasonable level of confidence. It is worked out through a mathematical formula that measures volatility in the return of an investment – that is, the ups and downs of its return compared with its average over time. The band that covers the greater part of the returns around the average is then assessed. And the result is a measure of the range of returns that can be expected around two-thirds of the time.

Put technically, standard deviation expresses the range from the average return within which 68.3 per cent of observed returns fall. Fortunately, the result can be easily understood without knowing the details of the mathematics.

Simple risk measures

Suppose an investment's average return, based on past performance, is 15 per cent with a standard deviation of 8 per cent. This means that, based on past performance, in about 68 years out of every 100 the investment will probably provide a return within 8 points either side of the average return, that is, between 7 per cent and 23 per cent. In the other 32 years out of every 100, the return will probably fall outside this range because of unusual events, which may range from stock market crashes or booms to foreign wars.

The percentage used for standard deviation, 68.3 per cent, is close to 66.6 per cent, or two-thirds. And the two-thirds guideline makes the whole idea easier to comprehend. For instance, a stockbroker might say of a stock with a 10 per cent average return and a standard deviation of 2 per cent: 'This stock is pretty reliable; it has shown a 10 per cent average return over the past ten years. It is a fairly stable performer, and most of the time – that is, in two years out of three – you are likely to get a return of between 8 and 12 per cent.' The stockbroker might look at a stock with a 15 per cent average return and a 15 per cent standard deviation and conclude: 'This stock has shown good average return, about 15 per cent, but it's more risky. In two out of three years it will probably provide a return in a pretty wide range, from 0 per cent to 30 per cent.'

Comparing risk and return: a two-company example

The standard deviation, and the average return, are two useful measures of an investment. They can provide a quick comparison of two or more assets in terms of the risk/return trade-off. The following example compares the performance of two imaginary companies: the first high-risk and high-return, the second low-risk and low-return.

Farflung Airlines, a transport company, has recorded the following returns over the past 12 years:

Year:	1	2	3	4	5	6	7	8	9	10	11	12
Return:	10%	40%	20%	30%	0%	10%	60%	20%	30%	10%	20%	–10%

Average return: 20%
Standard deviation: 18%

Figure 3.1 shows the performance of Farflung Airlines, and the notional range of standard deviation. This sort of analysis can provide a good overview

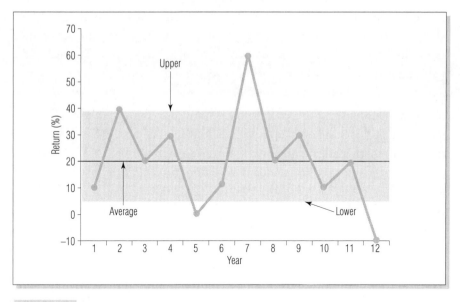

FIGURE 3.1   Returns of Farflung Airlines over 12 years, with upper and lower range of standard deviation

of an investment. Farflung's average return is 20 per cent, but the range of returns is wide: from 60 per cent to –10 per cent. The standard deviation tells us that, if this pattern continues, the investor will have a roughly two-in-three chance of getting a return within a range 18 per cent higher, or 18 per cent lower, than the target 20 per cent. If an investor were relying on this stock alone for regular income, it would present problems. However, an investor who could hold it for a long time could expect a generous 20 per cent return from the average of the ups and downs.

In contrast, Universal Utilities produced the following returns over the same 12 years:

Year:	1	2	3	4	5	6	7	8	9	10	11	12
Return:	10%	7%	12%	13%	8%	11%	7%	6%	10%	12%	13%	11%

Average return: 10%
Standard deviation: 2.5%

Figure 3.2 shows this stock's performance. The average return for Universal Utilities is 10 per cent per year, but the range of returns is nowhere near as wide as for Farflung Airlines. The company's return ranged from 6 per cent to 13 per cent over the period. This would be a far superior stock to produce assured return in any one year. The standard deviation of 2.5 per cent tells us that, if the pattern continues, in two out of three years the return will be within a range of about 7.5 to 12.5 per cent. This stability would suit an investor who needed a regular return, or who planned to invest for only one or two years and could not take the risk of losing money. However, the overall return is far lower than for Farflung Airlines.

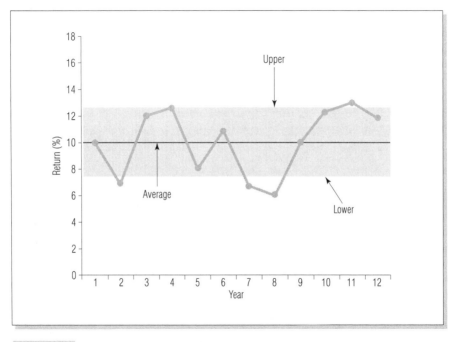

FIGURE 3.2   Returns of Universal Utilities over 12 years, with upper and lower range of standard deviation

Each investment has its own historical risk and return profile, which can be illustrated for easy comparison on a risk/return graph. Figure 3.3 shows what Farflung Airlines and Universal Utilities look like. Low-risk, low-return investments are placed in the lower left-hand corner, and higher-risk, higher-return investments towards the upper right. Most companies should lie along that line from lower left to upper right of the graph. If companies lie significantly below or above this line, special factors may be at work.

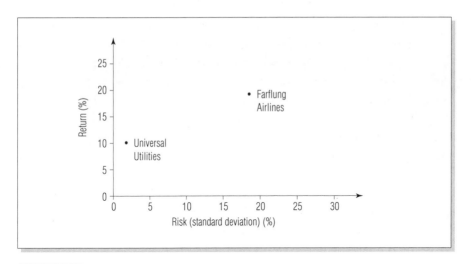

FIGURE 3.3   Risk/return graph of Farflung Airlines and Universal Utilities

This discussion introduces some broader strategic implications of the trade-off between risk and return. For the rational investor there are two basic approaches. First, an investor can aim for a certain level of return. In this case, the objective is to find investments that will provide this return, but with the lowest possible level of risk. Alternatively, an investor may be able to tolerate only a certain level of risk. The strategy then is to identify investments that provide no more risk than this level, but with the highest possible return.

The risk/return trade-off is the starting point in working out the overall investment equation. However, other factors have to be taken into account. One of these is that, as soon as more than one investment is involved, what counts is the *combination* of investments. The risk/return characteristics of individual assets become less important than the performance of the portfolio as a whole. And this is where the question of diversification – getting the best out of a combination of assets – comes into play.

Diversification: managing up return, managing down risk

In constructing a portfolio, it may seem logical that an investor who can accept only a low level of risk should invest in assets that have a low standard deviation. But in fact, the best way to reduce the risk of a portfolio may be to buy certain investments that have a *high* standard deviation – a high risk. This paradox is the essence of modern portfolio theory.

As soon as an investor has more than one investment, what counts are the risk/return characteristics of all the investments together. Each investment's individual risk is not so important for itself as for what it will do to the risk of the portfolio. Each investment performs in a certain way in relation to every other investment. Some tend to go up when others go down, some move in roughly the same pattern, and some seem to move in totally unrelated fashions. This relationship is known as *correlation*, and investors who apply it effectively can do better from the risk/return trade-off.

Suppose an investor has a single risky investment, such as Farflung Airlines. The investor wants to hold onto it because in the medium term it yields good returns, but also wants to reduce the risk of the total portfolio. The intuitive move would be to sell half the shares in Farflung and use that money to buy into a safer asset, such as Universal Utilities.

Table 3.2 and Figure 3.4 show what happens to a portfolio of the two companies over the next five years, assuming the two stocks record a similar pattern of returns as in the past. The average return over the five years falls to 15 per cent instead of 20 per cent if all the money were held in Farflung. The diversification slightly reduces the risk of volatile returns in any one year, but not by all that much. The return for the portfolio still ranges wildly from 23.5 per cent down to 4 per cent. So, for all the loss of return, the portfolio still does not perform consistently.

TABLE 3.2 Portfolio return: Farflung Airlines and Universal Utilities

Year	1	2	3	4	5	Average
Farflung Airlines	10%	40%	20%	30%	0%	20%
Universal Utilities	10%	7%	12%	13%	8%	10%
Total portfolio	10%	23.5%	16%	21.5%	4%	15%

Now, suppose there is another imaginary stock on the market, a petroleum company called Slick Oil. Like Farflung, its return is a solid 20 per cent. It is, however, just as risky, with the same standard deviation of about 20 per cent. What would happen if the investor sold half the Farflung shares and put them into Slick Oil? Intuitively, one would say the risk would increase or be the same.

Research shows, however, that while Slick Oil has a similar long-term return and volatility, it tends to do well when Farflung does badly, and vice versa. This is because, when oil prices are high, the oil company makes a profit but the

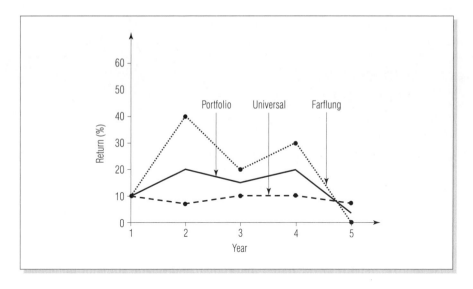

FIGURE 3.4 Returns over five years of Farflung Airlines and Universal Utilities with portfolio of both stocks

airline company suffers high operating costs because of the rise in fuel prices. When oil prices are low, the oil company does poorly but the airline company does well. When oil prices are steady, both companies have an average year. A portfolio of the two stocks could reflect the benefits of this inverse relationship.

Table 3.3 and Figure 3.5 show the movement of the two stocks over the next five years, and the performance of the portfolio made up of them. The return is constant every year – 20 per cent – and the standard deviation of the portfolio is zero.

TABLE 3.3 Portfolio return: Farflung Airlines and Slick Oil

Year	1	2	3	4	5	Average
Farflung Airlines	10%	40%	20%	30%	0%	20%
Slick Oil	30%	0%	20%	10%	40%	20%
Total portfolio	20%	20%	20%	20%	20%	20%

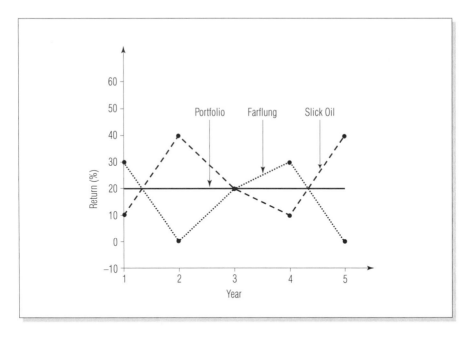

FIGURE 3.5   Returns over five years of Farflung Airlines and Slick Oil with portfolio of
both stocks

Compared with diversification into the safer Universal Utilities, which would significantly reduce return but only slightly reduce risk, diversification into the riskier Slick Oil maintains a high return while turning the overall portfolio into a risk-free investment.

What explains this paradox? The answer forms part of the *Markowitz model*. Two investments that display *negative correlation*, that is, move in opposite directions, cancel out each other's risk. Two investments that display *positive correlation*, that is, move in the same direction, do little to reduce the overall risk of the portfolio.

Comparing performance patterns: correlation

As with risk, the financial planning industry has a shorthand way to measure correlation that is fairly easy to grasp. Correlation is measured on a scale of –1 to 1. Two investments that move in perfect positive correlation – they go up or down together – have a correlation of 1. Those that move in perfectly opposite directions, such as Farflung and Slick Oil, have a perfect negative correlation, expressed as –1.

Most investments lie somewhere in between, with correlations expressed as positive or negative fractions. A pair of investments with a correlation of 0.8 would be described as having a high correlation, while a pair with a correlation of 0.3 would have a fairly low correlation. (Note that the word 'positive' is frequently omitted.) A pair with a correlation of –0.3 would be described as having a low negative correlation.

To produce a low or negative correlation consistently, there must be an underlying fundamental factor. Farflung and Universal Utilities display no steady pattern in their movement. But there is a fundamental factor that makes the returns of Farflung and Slick Oil move in opposite directions – oil prices.

Of course, in the real world it is not easy to pick investments that demonstrate consistently low or negative correlations. And if the investor does find a pair, the chances are that the market will have already factored in the diversification benefit. The return will then have been adjusted downwards, as in the case of Raindrop in our horse-racing analogy.

There are 'active' strategies undertaken by investment professionals, with varying degrees of success, to add value to a portfolio by trying to search out individual diversification opportunities. Yet even for the investor who does not want to engage in detailed applications, there is still a major advantage in understanding what makes diversification effective.

The most powerful lesson of diversification is that whatever an investor's target rate of return, a properly diversified portfolio will achieve it at lower risk than an undiversified or poorly diversified portfolio. Some diversification strategies reduce risk, while others do not. And the concept of correlation is useful in distinguishing good diversification from bad.

Diversification: more than 'spreading money around'

Many people, even some investment promoters, think that diversification is simply 'spreading money around'. However, such a strategy may not be effective. It depends on whether the portfolio covers a range of assets that are likely to have consistently low or negative correlations, for underlying fundamental reasons. Put another way, *random* diversification may average only returns and risk down, while *effective* diversification can manage down risk and manage up returns.

As with standard deviation, correlation is really only a tool in looking at the fundamentals. The real value of correlation for the private investor lies not in the numbers but in the concept: that assets react in different and sometimes opposite ways to the same *investment theme*.

One of the most important rules of investment is to look *behind* the price of an asset, to see what supports it. What is keeping its price high or low? And what will change its price? An investment theme is something that fundamentally underpins the performance of an industry or individual investment, although it may not be obvious at all times. In fact, it may not manifest itself until a major event makes it apparent.

Oil prices are a good example. For more than two decades after the Second World War, the world enjoyed cheap oil. This theme underpinned a substantial part of the whole Western way of life. In the United States, petrol stayed between 25 cents and 33 cents a gallon. Transport companies, airlines and other industries that relied on petroleum products prospered. This investment theme underpinned what has been termed by some as the Long Boom.[1] The oil shocks of the 1970s brought a traumatic end to this theme and reversed it. Industries reliant on oil suffered, and higher oil prices worked their way through the economy, pushing up inflation. Investors exposed solely to adversely affected companies lost money.

The oil shocks also showed how investments and markets could be affected by a theme, in less obvious and often intriguing ways. In the UK property market, for example, the value of inner city houses rose while more distant towns in the commuter belt did poorly. The reason was that commuters became worried about the future availability and price of oil and whether they would be able to travel to work for an affordable price, if at all.

Understanding investment themes is largely common sense. However, it is often handy to see how well common sense fits with historical data. A useful tool for this purpose is a *correlation table*, which shows the correlations of investments or sectors over a period. Table 3.4 lists the correlations of some of the main sectors on the London Stock Exchange between 1985 and 2000.

TABLE 3.4 Correlations of selected UK stock exchange indices December 1985–January 2000

	Mining	Telecoms	Construction	Household goods	Banks
Mining	1				
Telecoms	0.69	1			
Construction	0.86	0.75	1		
Household goods	0.32	−0.26	0.15	1	
Banks	0.77	0.89	0.85	−0.14	1

Source: Barclays Global Investors/ipac

This table can be used to explore some real-life themes. An important investment theme is that of international stability and confidence, which is critical for the construction and building materials industry. When people are confident about the economy and the world in general, they are more likely to construct houses or commercial buildings. When things look uncertain, they do not want to risk commitment to new expenditure and are less likely to build. The banking industry is also affected by confidence since the demand for loans and banking transactions generally is higher when money is cheap and the default rate is lower. The correlation between the construction and banking sectors is a high 0.85. So for an investor looking to diversify a portfolio dominated by construction stocks, there would not be much diversification benefit in the banking sector.

The telecommunications service sector has a high correlation with the banking and construction sectors, indicating that it too is significantly influenced by the overall level of economic activity and interest rates. But it is inversely correlated with the household goods and textiles sector. This may suggest that in part the purchase of new telephony services such as mobile phones, the internet and so on is coming at the expense of traditional household goods providers.

The household goods sector, on the other hand, which includes textiles and basic appliances, has a relatively low correlation of 0.15 with construction and a negative correlation of –0.14 with banking. It indicates that people's spending patterns on such goods is relatively stable, notwithstanding fluctuations in the global and domestic economy.

There is another sector that is affected by the theme of international stability and confidence, but in the opposite way: gold. The price of gold tends to go up during heightened international tensions, as investors divert funds from financial and equity investments to 'hard' investments that they believe will survive any crisis.

Gold shares are included in the mining sector and comprise mostly offshore-based companies with a UK listing. The mining sector, which is dominated by companies such as Rio Tinto, is generally highly correlated with the theme of international confidence and stability and hence with the banking and construction industries. After all, many of the outputs of the mining industry end up as inputs into the construction industry.

However, during the early part of the 1990–91 Gulf crisis, gold prices surged, even though other mining companies and construction stocks did poorly. From October onwards, when it appeared likely that Iraq would leave or be forced out of Kuwait, the two sectors changed tack, with gold falling and the building sector rising.

Gold shares are among the most volatile. However, they offer considerable diversification benefit against investments that rely on the international confidence theme. Despite a relatively low return in recent years, this benefit might make it worthwhile for investors who require protection against adverse international events, or a catastrophic political or financial crisis.

In a similar vein, the construction index has a relatively low correlation with the food and drug retailers index, at 0.28. However, as can be seen in Figure 3.6, from about mid-1988 following the stock market crash of October 1987, both indices briefly had a high correlation for about a year before they moved in opposite directions, the construction index being severely affected by rising interest rates, which was exacerbated in 1990 by the Gulf crisis and prolonged by the weakness of the banking sector in the early 1990s. The food retailers index, however, performed well during this period, reflecting in part a flight of investors to safety.

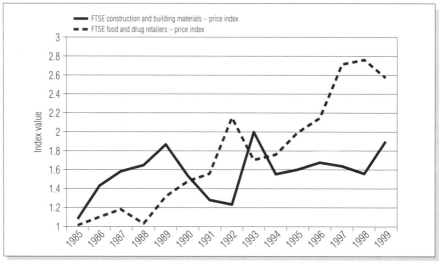

Source: Barclays Global Investors/ipac

FIGURE 3.6 Diversification in practice: construction and building materials and food and drug retailers indices, UK stock exchange, December 1985–December 1999

On the other hand, the food index declined from mid-1987 to mid-1988 while the construction index rose. This reflected the fact that action by the Bank of England to lower interest rates in the aftermath of the 1987 crash boosted interest rate-sensitive stocks, such as those in the construction index, while having little benefit for basic industries such as food retailing.

These examples show how the three-way equation of risk, return and correlation can work itself out, often in apparently paradoxical ways.

Diversification in practice: climbing the risk ladder

So far, this chapter has covered what constitutes risk, how diversification works, and how these factors relate to return. Now we look at how these concepts can be applied to investment strategy.

The key to successful investment is the efficient management of risk. To achieve this, the investor must analyze the risk of individual assets, then work out ways to reduce that risk through diversification.

The riskiness of each investment hinges on a multitude of factors. These range from the state of the international economy to whether a company's managing director suffers a heart attack, or whether the company reads the market trends correctly. To fully understand an investment's risk, it is important to identify the different risk components. The following *risk ladder* provides a useful classification, dividing risk into five levels:

1 **Investment (company) risk:** factors that may affect the returns of a specific investment entity. For a company, these may include the loss of key personnel, a strike, a discovery, natural disaster, and so on. For property, the risk may relate to the location, local planning considerations, and occupancy factors. For 'junk' bonds issued by companies with a limited track record, it may be the confidence of the capital markets in the success of a particular project.

2 **Industry (asset class subsector) risk:** factors that may affect some groups of investment entities, but not all. For companies, this will be defined as risk factors that affect the returns of all the companies in an industry, but not companies in any other industry. These may include changes in the regulatory environment, new safety standards, new technology, changes in the pattern of consumer demand for tourism and airline travel, for example. For property, the risk may refer to factors that affect commercial rather than residential property.

3 **Asset class (market) risk:** factors that affect all stocks, or all bonds, or all cash investments, or all property markets. These may include the introduction of a tax or regulations affecting a particular asset class.

4 **Country (economy) risk:** factors that affect all asset classes in an economy, such as the level of economic confidence and consumer demand, or political stability, interest rate policy and exchange rate trends.

5 **International risk:** factors that affect investment entities globally, such as world recession or financial system collapse.

So, how does the investor deal with these components of risk? Returning to the racecourse, there are choices to make. Like the punter putting money on individual horses, the investor can take a bet on one-off investments and hope for the best. This approach may provide a win here and there, but not a consistent means of managing risk and providing assured income. Alternatively, investors can take an approach similar to that of bookies, and spread the risk on the basis that over time the odds of such an approach will be in their favour. Bookies diversify their books over different horses, different tracks, different races, and over time.

The shrewd investor will try to diversify away risk at each rung of the ladder. Country risk can be diversified away by investing in overseas markets. Asset class risk is diversified away by spreading the range of asset classes in the portfolio. Industry risk is diversified away by buying into several industries. Investment risk is diversified away by selecting a number of investments within each industry. Figure 3.7 shows the process.

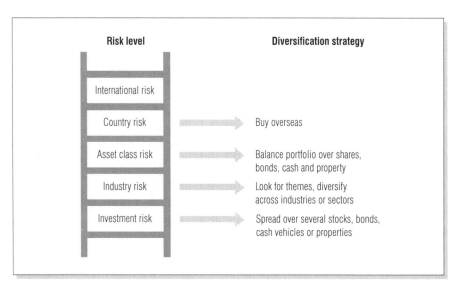

FIGURE 3.7 Climbing the risk ladder

The question now is: how does the investor choose from the wide range of assets to produce a diversified portfolio? Some professionals adopt an 'active' approach to asset selection in a bid to find sets of assets that, they believe, will produce particularly good returns in relation to their diversification benefit. This approach is more difficult than it might sound because the market tends continuously to factor in the diversification benefit of each asset, and price the asset accordingly.

This is one place where the efficient markets hypothesis comes in. It is based on the view that financial markets are generally well informed. Hundreds of punters, institutional investment analysts and brokers are looking for, and acting on, market information. As a result, unless the investor has information that is not already incorporated into prices, it is very difficult to 'beat the market' because, paradoxically, everyone is always trying to beat the market.

This fact may come as a disappointment to investors who are looking for a magic wand. The flip side, however, is that *most of the time* the market provides a fair assessment of the risk, return and diversification benefit of an asset, and the price reflects this assessment. If the investor chooses a portfolio that represents the market as a whole, it should be an efficient portfolio in terms of the risk/return trade-off. The investor can expect, over time, to achieve the historical return normally associated with that market. As we will discuss in Chapter 7, the development of the managed fund industry makes this sort of broad-based strategy easily accessible to the private investor. Even without investing in managed funds, however, the private investor's ability to diversify away risk is easier than it sounds.

Studies have shown that, in a particular asset class, the investor reduces both the industry risk and the firm-specific risk with a relatively small spread of randomly picked investments. In the stock market, for example, about 20 stocks can eliminate most of the diversifiable risk. One US study found that an investor who held 20 US stocks selected randomly would reduce risk by only another 3 per cent by adding another 50 stocks.[2]

To understand why this may be so, consider an investor who is thinking about putting money into the gold sector. The various gold companies are unlikely to suffer the same firm-specific risk at the same time. They will probably not strike new ore bodies at the same time, nor are their managing directors likely to suffer simultaneous heart attacks. On this basis, even a random selection of companies or investments would substantially reduce the firm-specific risk. Remember, investors are not rewarded for taking pointless risk; that is, they gain no benefit for taking risk that can be diversified away.

By investing in a single gold company of average expected return for that sector, an investor would face greater risk than by investing in a collection of gold companies. There would, however, be no corresponding benefit in expected return. A one-company portfolio would face all of the risks associated with the gold industry, but would also face substantial company-specific risk. Such company-specific risk could be largely diversified away without lowering the expected return.

At the next level up the risk ladder – the spread of a portfolio over industries – the investor might think about an 'intuitively improved' approach to diversification. It is clear that concentrating on a narrow range of industries that could be subject to the same sort of risk factors, such as the retail and building sectors, would subject the investor to more risk than a more diversified portfolio. So, bearing in mind the concept of the investment theme, it would not take much knowledge to work out a portfolio that would diversify away much of the industry risk by selecting half a dozen or so industries. Such an approach would come close to 'buying the market' at the asset class level; that is, investing in a set of industries that would broadly represent the market as a whole.

This leaves the question of how to diversify among the asset classes. While many investors spend most of their efforts selecting individual assets or industries, it is in fact the mix of *asset classes* that is most likely to determine their ultimate fortune.

Asset classes, time and the efficient frontier

The four *asset classes*, or principal investment markets, are cash (the short-term money market), bonds (the long-term money market), property, and equities (the stock market). It seems natural to continue the diversification process and spread the risk among these asset classes. The question, of course, is how much to put into each.

This is the most important decision the investor will take. In the past, some analysts have suggested that the decision accounts for 75–90 per cent of the risk and return of a portfolio. While the basis for this assertion has been challenged, it is generally accepted that asset allocation is the focal point of investment strategy.[3]

In Chapter 8, we look in detail at how to use asset allocation to devise a rational strategy that caters to the investor's particular goals and aspirations. The tax considerations of the various asset classes are also taken into account. In this section, we look at some basic principles of asset class diversification.

Part of the reason why it is worth devoting so much attention to the asset classes is that, more than on any other rung of the risk ladder, the risk, return and correlation of the asset classes are fairly consistent over time. In the short- to medium-term, say one to five years, the performance of each class, and their relativities to each other, may stray from the norm. Over the long term, however, the investor can know with a fair degree of confidence which asset classes will provide the highest and lowest risk and return. Just as importantly, the investor can have a fair idea of the correlations of the asset classes or, put in practical terms, of what sort of combinations will provide what diversification benefit.

In the next three chapters, we look at the characteristics of the asset classes in detail. Here we provide a brief overview.

Cash is the safest asset class and provides over time the lowest return. It covers such investments as instant-access and savings accounts subject to one year's notice or less in banks and building societies, cash unit trusts, and similar short-term, interest-bearing investments such as Treasury bills, bank and commercial bills, and certificates of deposit that will be repaid in one year or less. Cash generates income but no capital gains. It provides no protection against the effects of inflation on the value of the capital invested, but interest rates do usually rise with inflation and offer some compensation. At the same time the risks of loss as a result of fraud or defaults are low. Because in normal conditions cash is the safest investment market, it is used as a benchmark against other investments. When deposit rates are low, other investments become more attractive and tend to rise in price. Cash therefore tends to have a low correlation with all other asset classes.

Bonds are also interest-bearing investments, but involve a longer period of maturity, from one up to as long as 30 years. Some bonds, including the War Loan originally issued to help finance the First World War, are undated, which means there is no set date for redemption. Most bonds pay a fixed rate of interest. While this locked-in interest rate may seem safer, it actually exposes the investor to more risk: if inflation or short-term interest rates go up during the period to maturity, the market value of fixed-rate bonds falls and the investor loses out. Index-linked bonds reduce this risk, often at the expense of lower returns. Bonds in general are low-to-medium risk investments, and provide low-to-medium returns over time.

Property covers both residential property, including established homes and newly built or converted blocks of flats, and commercial property, which includes everything from working farms and country estates to office blocks, retail parks, shopping malls and industrial estates down to individual shops and restaurants on single sites. It is a medium-to-high risk asset class, with returns proportionate to this risk. Rents and prices usually rise with inflation but often after considerable time-lags. Because the property market is generally adversely affected by rises in interest rates, it tends to have a low correlation with interest-bearing investments, especially cash.

Equities are the highest-risk, highest-return category of investment. Investors take a direct share in the profits or losses of companies, and hence in the economy itself. They offer the best protection against inflation because over time they are best able to pass on higher costs and benefit directly from economic growth.

As discussed in Chapter 2, an important principle in examining the asset classes is the time horizon and inflation. Although in the short term cash and fixed-interest bonds are somewhat safer, in the longer term they provide limited protection against inflation. This means that for long-term investment, they are actually riskier in terms of maintaining real buying power, while property and equities are safer. Tax considerations generally accentuate these factors.

Analysis of long-term investment returns on cash, bonds and equities by Barclays Capital dating back to 1918 and returns from commercial property dating back to 1963 prepared by International Property Data suggests that, over time, the four asset classes are likely to produce the following *real* (after inflation) returns in the long run:

Cash: 0–2%
Bonds: 1–3%
Property: 5–8%
Equities: 7–10%

Since 1918 the total real return on equities, including gross income and capital growth, has averaged 8 per cent a year, while bonds have averaged 2.4 per cent and cash 1.5 per cent. The calculations assume that gross income is reinvested each year. Even if allowance is made for tax and transaction costs, the return on equities is significantly higher than property and gilts.

This does not mean that the typical investor should put all their funds into shares. Such a move would subject the investor to significant short-term risk. There is no absolute right or wrong class of investment. The investor's time frame and objectives are both important in the choice of asset class.

Shrewd investors will juggle time, return and risk to get the best mix of asset classes to suit their particular needs and objectives. The aim, however, is to get an *efficient* mix of assets with different risk/return characteristics. This is where modern portfolio theory comes in. The correct combination of assets can often maintain much of the high-return advantages of riskier investments but reduce the overall risk towards levels associated with safer investments. Conversely, good diversification can maintain the low-risk levels of safer asset classes but provide at least a measure of the higher returns associated with riskier investments.

This efficiency comes from the same principles of correlation and diversification benefit described above. Because cash and shares, for example, tend to have a low correlation, adding some shares to a cash-based portfolio has the potential to raise return significantly without substantially raising risk. Similarly, adding some cash to a share-based portfolio can significantly reduce risk without significantly reducing return.

This does not mean that there is one 'best' portfolio. There are, in fact, any number of efficient portfolios, at different points in the trade-off curve. This concept is known as the *efficient frontier*. Figure 3.8 provides an example. The graph shows a conceptual trade-off between risk and return. Points C and D represent individual investments. The curved line represents where the most efficient portfolios, or combinations of investments, lie. Portfolio A is a lower-risk, lower-return portfolio. It represents the best return for that level of risk, and the lowest level of risk possible for that level of expected return. Portfolio B is also an optimal portfolio, but at a higher level of risk with a higher level of expected return. The individual investments C and D are less attractive than the portfolios. Investment C produces the same level of expected return as portfolio A, but for a higher level of risk. Investment D involves the same level of risk as portfolio B, but for a much lower return.

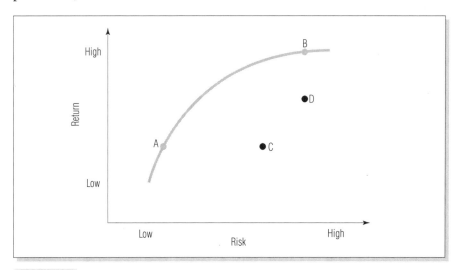

FIGURE 3.8 Conceptual risk/return graph with efficient frontier

The objective of investment strategy is to get as close as possible to the efficient frontier at the point of the trade-off between risk and return that best suits the investor. Portfolios towards the bottom left of the curve (portfolio A) tend to be dominated by cash and bonds, and those towards the top right (portfolio B) by property and shares. The point is that a balance among the asset classes will produce a more efficient investment vehicle than any individual investment.

Figure 3.9 shows the performance of the key asset classes, both domestic and foreign, some individual assets, and an 'evenly spread around' portfolio over the period 1991 to 1999. As expected, domestic cash was at the low end of the risk/return spectrum, with a return of just over 7 per cent and a low standard deviation. UK and international shares over this period displayed equally high levels of risk, with a standard deviation of around 10 per cent, while returning just over 18 per cent. Gilts over this period, which was a very strong one for equities, had a slightly lower risk, of 9.6 per cent, but a much lower return, at 11.4 per cent, than shares.

The graph illustrates the effect of diversification. Investors who concentrated their money on some well-known individual companies, such as Marks and

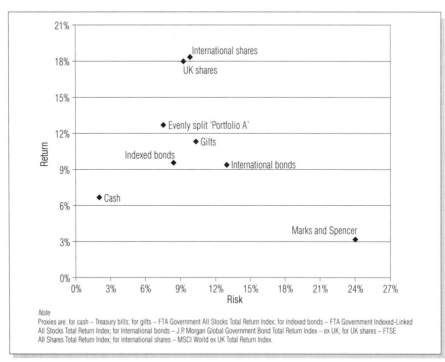

Note
Proxies are: for cash – Treasury bills; for gilts – FTA Government All Stocks Total Return Index; for indexed bonds – FTA Government Indexed-Linked All Stocks Total Return Index; for International bonds – J.P. Morgan Global Government Bond Total Return Index – ex UK; for UK shares – FTSE All Shares Total Return Index; for international shares – MSCI World ex UK Total Return Index.

Source: Barclays Global Investors/ipac

FIGURE 3.9 UK and international markets, December 1991–December 1999

Spencer, would have done worse than those who invested in any of the other options. Marks and Spencer produced a return that was one-sixth that of the stock market as a whole, with more than twice the volatility; it did not even keep pace with cash.

In contrast, a portfolio composed of simply 'spreading around' funds among all the asset classes in question would have performed quite creditably. The 'evenly split' Portfolio A shows what would have happened if an investor had divided available funds evenly among UK shares, UK indexed bonds and gilts, international shares, international fixed interest and cash – the investor would have put 16.67 per cent into each category in 1991 and held this portfolio through to 1999. Such a portfolio would have produced a return of 12.4 per cent with a volatility of 7.3 per cent.

An investor could, however, have done better. Table 3.5 and Figure 3.10 illustrate this point. Suppose the investor with the evenly spread portfolio, Portfolio A, had wanted to get the same return but for reduced risk. By adjusting the allocations to the different asset classes, the investor could have achieved this goal through Portfolio B. This portfolio puts more money into domestic and foreign equities, which produce good return, but offsets the volatility of shares by putting half the portfolio into cash. Similarly, an investor who wanted to increase return, but for the same level of risk, could have done so through Portfolio D. That portfolio is concentrated in shares, but again a quarter of the portfolio is in cash to maintain diversification and hence reduce volatility to maintain the same risk level. An investor who wanted to slightly improve both risk and return could opt for Portfolio C, which is an interpolation between the minimum-risk and maximum-return portfolios.

TABLE 3.5 Comparison of portfolios, arbitrary and optimized, for 1991–99, UK

	A Evenly split portfolio	B Minimum-risk portfolio	C Medium-risk and return portfolio	D Maximum- return portfolio
UK shares	16.7%	26.7%	33.7%	40.6%
International shares	16.7%	21.6%	28.0%	34.3%
Gilts	16.7%	0.0%	0.0%	0.0%
Indexed bonds	16.7%	0.0%	0.0%	0.0%
International bonds	16.7%	0.0%	0.0%	0.0%
Cash	16.7%	51.7%	38.3%	25.1%
Annualized 13-year return	12.4%	12.4%	13.9%	15.3%
Risk	7.3%	4.9%	6.1%	7.3%

Source: ipac

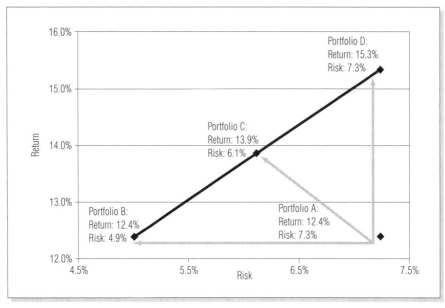

Source: ipac

FIGURE 3.10 Moving to the efficient frontier

The exercise of choosing these improved portfolios was conducted, of course, with the benefit of hindsight. But it illustrates that the *potential* exists to improve portfolio performance by superior diversification among the asset classes. While practice is much more difficult than theory, what's important here is the *objective*: to get as close as possible to the efficient frontier.

To sum up, good diversification involves moving up the risk ladder and diversifying away risk at each level. Spreading funds around a range of individual investments and industries within an asset class to reflect the market provides the investor with the risk and return of that asset class. Diversifying judiciously among the asset classes provides an opportunity to fine-tune the performance of a portfolio, and get as close as possible to the point on the risk/return curve that the investor seeks.

Many investors try to select individual stocks or other investments in a bid to get a portfolio of superior assets. Later chapters provide skills to assist in this process, but achieving consistent success this way is difficult. The strategy outlined in this section shows that the investor does not have to rely on such micro-selection to achieve overall investment goals.

However, even after all the levels of diversification discussed so far, the investor is still left with an element of undiversifiable risk: the national economy.

The way to reduce this risk is to move another step on the risk ladder: across national boundaries.

International dimensions: making the world your oyster

If civilizations with investment markets are ever found elsewhere in the universe, it will presumably be possible to reduce planet risk through intergalactic diversification. Until that happens, the next best strategy is to make use of differences between the countries on Earth.

International diversification reduces risk for exactly the same reasons as domestic diversification among companies and industries. Since national economies are never the same, they tend to move in different patterns. Each country has a distinctive mix of natural and human resources, industries, political direction, and economic priorities and aspirations.

There are fundamental reasons why some economies do well when others do poorly, based in part on the fact that what is produced in one country is often consumed in another. Some economies perform well, others perform poorly over both the short and longer term. Over the decade from 1990 to 2000, US stock market values quadrupled while the Japanese market halved. Some markets perform relatively consistently. Others, including Russia and Hong Kong, are notoriously volatile. By investing internationally, it is often possible to get in on both sides of the transaction and reduce the price risk.

Suppose, for example, an investor wants to diversify the risk of investments in UK transport stocks. The return from such investments, beyond the company-specific risk, depends almost entirely on the demand for transport and that is heavily influenced by the international price of oil. So by buying into international oil companies, the investor would have an excellent investment theme working both ways. When the price of oil goes up, the transport companies do poorly, but the profitability of the oil companies should improve in proportion. When the price of oil is low, the reverse applies.

The principle extends to national economies. Investment can be diversified among what economists describe as the *comparative advantage* of nations. For example, Australia's commodity-based economy tends to do well when commodity prices are high. In contrast, the Japanese economy is more devoted to adding value to raw materials and is more likely to do well when commodity prices are low.

Of course, as described in Chapter 1, world investment markets often move in unison in response to certain stimuli. The US and UK stock markets in recent years have tended to move quite closely in parallel, while the Japanese market has shown a very low correlation. This is the top of the risk ladder: international risk. It appears that many markets, particularly in Europe – are coming closer together, probably as a result of formal and informal international economic integration.

However, the correlations between UK markets and many international markets are surprisingly low. Table 3.6 shows the correlations among six countries for the major share and bond indices in local currency.

TABLE 3.6 Correlations of international shares and bonds in local currency

	UK	Ger	Jap	NZ	Aus	US
Shares*						
UK	1.00					
Ger	0.59	1.00				
Jap	0.35	0.36	1.00			
NZ	0.49	0.35	0.30	1.00		
Aus	0.60	0.52	0.39	0.70	1.00	
US	0.68	0.56	0.41	0.47	0.61	1.00
Bonds**						
UK	1.00					
Ger	0.58	1.00				
Jap	0.11	0.22	1.00			
NZ	0.13	0.10	0.10	1.00		
Aus	0.33	0.29	0.19	0.25	1.00	
US	0.41	0.45	0.22	0.13	0.43	1.00

* 1988–99. Share indices: Australia – All Ordinaries Accumulation; Germany – DAX;
   Japan – Nikkei; NZ – NZ40; UK – FTSE; US – Dow Jones Industrials.
** 1982–99. Based on ten-year bond yields of those countries.

Source: Barclays Global Investors/ipac

A number of studies, including one by the authors, have identified the potential that international diversification has for reducing portfolio risk. Adding foreign stocks and bonds to a portfolio can considerably improve the potential efficient frontier. The increasing growth of emerging markets in Eastern Europe, Asia, Latin America and Southern Africa is also adding to this potential.

Buying international assets involves two separate investments: in a foreign market and in a foreign currency. So what happens to currency risk in an internationally diversified portfolio? As previously discussed, currency risk can be substantial; studies have shown it to be more volatile than most investment markets. However, there are a number of approaches to managing this risk.

At least conceptually, currency has no value of its own; its value exists only in relation to other currencies. As a result, extending exposure from one foreign currency to a basket of several currencies can smooth currency risk over time. Downward movements in some currencies tend to cancel out upward movements in others.

One example of how diversification can reduce currency risk is shown in Table 3.7. In this case, we are putting ourselves in the shoes of five investors from different countries who have put money into a basket of currencies: sterling, the US dollar, the Deutschmark, the Japanese yen and the Australian dollar. The experiment looks at how a portfolio, worth 100 000 units of their domestic currency and divided equally among the foreign currencies, would have performed over different periods ending in February 1999. Investors with a strong domestic currency will tend to lose money on share portfolios invested in weak currency markets while investors with a weak domestic currency will tend to do better from investing overseas in shares in a strong currency.

TABLE 3.7 Changes in the value of a five-currency portfolio worth 100 000 units of investor's currency over different periods to February 1999

Investor's currency	Start	1 year	3 years	5 years
British (sterling)	100 000	105 516	84 591	89 028
Australian (A$)	100 000	108 187	112 545	108 852
German (mark)	100 000	96 976	106 901	101 541
Japanese (yen)	100 000	90 269	98 752	111 093
US (US$)	100 000	101 778	89 846	94 554

Source: ipac

Ignoring the actual performance of the portfolio we see that over just one year, the greatest currency loss was for the Japanese investor, whose portfolio declined by nearly 10 per cent from 100 000 yen to 90 269 yen in the year to February 1999. Over a three-year period, the British investor would have lost the most money, with a portfolio declining by more than 15 per cent from £100 000 to £84 591. Over five years, the British investor again suffered the greatest loss, of about 11 per cent. This is of course because the pound was strong and most of the other currencies in the UK investor's portfolio were weak.

What is interesting is that in this case, the longer the time frame, the lower the relative currency risk. The currency loss to the British investor over five years, at 11 per cent, represents only about 2 per cent per annum. The strategic issue here is whether currency risk is outweighed by the benefits of investing in overseas assets, which involve a diversification benefit and in some cases a benefit from better performing assets. It is well worth remembering that there have been many periods when sterling has been weak over the past 30 years. We explore this point in greater detail when we look at interest rates and foreign currency hedges in Chapter 4.

Of course, if an investor's own currency weakens, the currency risk of overseas investment can also work to advantage. The Australian investor, for example, would have done extremely well out of a diversified foreign holding. In one year, the investor's overseas portfolio would have improved by 8 per cent, by 12.5 per cent over the three-year period, and by 9 per cent over the five years to February 1999. However, in all cases the risks of a diversified portfolio will be less than investing in a single foreign currency.

What this exercise shows is that, although diversification reduces currency risk, some risk remains, both on the upside and downside. The downside risk in a diversified portfolio is that one's own currency will rise in value against a basket of everyone else's. But there are, in fact, ways of reducing this remaining currency risk. One approach is the *natural hedge* – rather than take out a formal hedge contract, investors offset their exposure to currency fluctuations by a countervailing financial transaction or exposure. Major companies limit their foreign currency risk by borrowing money in a currency to which they have exposure through exports or investments in hard assets.

A UK company that exports, say, $1 million worth of widgets to the United States in a dollar-denominated contract may do some of its borrowing in the United States so that its interest payments come to $1 million per year. If the value of the greenback goes down, the UK company will receive fewer pounds for its exports, but its interest payments will cost less in pounds by a commensurate amount.

Some of the same principles can be applied to private investment. William F. Sharpe, a Nobel prize winner mentioned in Chapter 1, made an intriguing suggestion on this topic: 'Other things being equal, it may make sense to invest more in countries whose products and scenery one admires, for the effective exchange risk is likely to be smaller there than elsewhere.'[4]

A British citizen may plan to visit the US in a year's time, estimating that the trip will cost £3000 based on the current exchange rate. Investing £3000 in a dollar-based deposit for a year will eliminate the exchange risk. If the value of the dollar goes up, the cost of the holiday will go up in sterling terms, but so will the sterling value of the dollars invested.

The other point raised by Sharpe, relating to foreign products, is far more relevant to the average Briton or European than they may realize. This is that every working and living day, Britons and Europeans are exposed to currency risk. Every time they consider buying a foreign-made electronic good, an imported book or jar of jam, they face an exchange risk. If the currency value of the country in which these products are made goes up against one's own currency, the goods are likely to become more expensive.

Just about everything a person consumes has some element of foreign input, directly or indirectly. Even in the case of a basic meal such as a Cornish pasty, a significant part of the value added, from fertilizer, farm machinery, transport equipment and food preparation equipment, may be sourced from overseas. Just as there is no reward for investing in a single stock, industry or asset class, there is no reward for investing in a single currency, including one's own, when diversification can reduce that risk.

So how much currency diversification makes sense? Research conducted by ipac securities limited shows that there are two countervailing issues to consider. First, a basket of currencies adds to diversification for a total portfolio, i.e. it helps to reduce total portfolio risk. Second, exchange rates tend to be highly volatile. Up to about 20 per cent of a portfolio, there is a net diversification benefit from holding unhedged international assets; much beyond this point, however, and the increased currency exposure *adds* to total portfolio risk. This is simply another way of saying that you can have too much of a good thing!

Derivatives: investment management to infinity and beyond

A whole new dimension of hedging and risk reduction has been introduced with the broader use of investment instruments known as derivatives. Over the past decade or so, the business of managing portfolios has been revolutionized by their use. These much-misunderstood instruments have done more than anything else to create highly cost-effective ways for investors to manage down risk and manage up return. At the same time, because derivative contracts can usually be bought for relatively small margins, they create considerable potential for leverage, speculation, and the loss of fortunes very quickly.

The well publicized abuse of derivatives for speculative purposes by rogue traders such as Nick Leeson – who caused the £800 million collapse of Barings Bank in 1995 – has given the public a lopsided view of derivatives. The potential for abuse, however, should not blind astute investors to the wide range of possibilities that derivatives open up to improve returns and reduce risk.

The first thing to understand about derivatives is that they are not an asset class. Rather, they are contracts in which two or more parties agree to future arrangements in relation to a real asset or a set of assets. That is, they are *derived* from a real market, called the physical market. In general, they are used in one of three ways: for hedging, speculation, or arbitrage.

The term derivatives came into vogue in the 1990s, when their range and usage expanded rapidly. They are not, however, a new thing. Options and futures in the tulip market were traded on European exchanges in the 17th century. But, in fact, the principle of the futures contract goes back hundreds and possibly thousands of years to the time when traders would agree in advance on the price at which a commodity would be bought and sold at a date in the future. Alternatively, traders sold each other options to purchase or sell. Whereas a futures contract is a firm commitment, an option is exactly what it says, a payment which gives the right but not an obligation to deal at a fixed price in the future. They are exercised only if it is profitable to do so.

The modern derivatives market grew out of these same concepts. Until relatively recently the great majority of futures and options deals were based on commodities such as copper, wool or rubber. The Chicago Futures Market also traded in foodstuffs, including pork bellies and orange juice. More recently these staple products have been overtaken by contracts trading in interest rates, shares, share indices, and currencies.

On top of these, there is an unlimited range of *over-the-counter* arrangements between individual parties, usually organized by merchant banks and other financial intermediaries, for example, swapping long- and short-term interest rate contracts in different currencies, which can get exceedingly complex.

Many applications of derivatives are high risk, but probably the majority of derivative contracts are aimed at risk reduction. Derivatives can be used to hedge an investment on the physical market by counteracting the effect of any unfavourable future market movement. The very low transactions costs typically associated with derivatives, together with the information revolution, has meant that trading, be it for the purposes of hedging or speculation, is now done very much on an international basis.

The principles of derivatives are essentially the same whether one is dealing with financial instruments or commodities. For an easily digestible example, we will consider the futures market, and a well-known commodity: wool. Let us put ourselves in the shoes of an Australian grazier, although the example could apply equally to a wool grower anywhere.

Hedging with futures: the grazier and the wool broker

Suppose it is April and a grazier is planning to shear his flock in October. At the same time, a wool broker is pondering how to acquire wool. The wool broker has committed to provide a certain amount of wool for a fixed price to an Italian clothing manufacturer around October. The price quoted for the October wool contract is A$5 a kilo, and both parties believe that they can make a profit at this price. Without ever meeting each other, the grazier and the wool broker could match their requirements by taking out opposite positions on the Sydney Futures Exchange. The grazier would take out a standard contract to sell 2500 kilos of wool in October, roughly equivalent to the expected wool clip. The wool broker would take out a matching contract to buy 2500 kilos. Whatever happened to the physical price of wool between the signing of the contract in April and the delivery date in October, both parties would have locked in the price at which their contract would be transacted. The grazier has hedged against a decline in the price, and the wool broker has hedged against a rise.

For a speculator, derivatives offer a way of taking bets that a physical market will move either up or down, but with a highly leveraged position. Still using wool, let us take an example of speculation by *going long*, i.e. betting that the physical market will rise. This is shown in Figure 3.11.

Suppose it is April and a speculator decides that the physical market is likely to rise substantially in six months, from A$5 to at least A$6 a kilo. The speculator could buy wool now and sell it in six months, but this would involve storage costs and tying up money which could be doing other things. Instead, the speculator could take out a futures contract to buy 2500 kilos of wool in October at A$5 a kilo. Entering the contract would require a comparatively small deposit. When the contract fell due in six months, the speculator would pay the pre-agreed price of A$5 a kilo and take delivery of the wool. Let us say the speculator was correct in his gamble, and the physical price of wool rose to A$6.50 a kilo by October. The speculator would then sell the wool on the physical market for this price and make a profit of A$1.50 a kilo, taking home A$3750.

Conversely, a speculator who thought that the wool price was going to fall would take out a futures contract to sell. Figure 3.12 follows such an example of *going short*. Again, it is April, the current price is A$5, but the speculator takes

April

Physical
market
Wool $5 per
kilogram

Futures
market

Futures contract
Speculator agrees to
buy 2500 kilograms
of wool at $5 per
kilogram in October

October

Physical
market
Wool $6.50
per kilogram

Futures
market

Speculator resells
2500 kilograms of
wool on physical
market at $6.50
per kilogram,
totalling $16 250

Futures contract
Speculator takes
delivery of 2500
kilograms of wool at $5
per kilogram, totalling
$12 500

FIGURE 3.11 Futures speculation – going long

April

Physical market
Wool $5 per kilogram

Futures market

Futures contract
Speculator agrees to sell 2500 kilograms of wool at $5 per kilogram in October

October

Physical market
Wool $4 per kilogram

Futures market

Speculator buys 2500 kilograms of wool on physical market at $4 per kilogram, totalling $10 000

Futures contract
Speculator delivers 2500 kilograms of wool at $5 per kilogram, totalling $12 500

FIGURE 3.12 Futures speculation – going short

out an October contract to *sell* 2500 kilos of wool. In October, when the contract fell due, the speculator would buy wool on the physical market where, to her delight, the price had declined to A\$4 a kilo. She would then deliver this wool to fulfil the futures contract, which commands the higher pre-agreed price of A\$5 a kilo. The speculator would earn a profit of A\$1 per kilo or A\$2500. Of course, if speculators get the bet wrong on a futures contract, they can be up for a considerable loss since they must deal on unfavourable terms in the physical market to fulfil the futures contract.

The point about speculating on futures, and many other derivatives, is that one does not have to put up much initial capital to take a very large speculative position. In futures, brokers require a deposit, and then make 'margin calls' to cover adverse movements over the course of a contract between the physical and futures price. Speculators who simply deal without having a supply or a use for the product can get caught if the price goes against them and they have to put up cash to settle their deals. But if the bet goes the right way, a speculator can make a lot of money for a small outlay.

Arbitrage involves trying to profit from a temporary price anomaly, such as between the physical and futures market. For example, a trader might observe that the futures market price for wool in the contract month about to fall due is higher than the physical market. In this case, depending on the carrying costs, a trader might see a profit in the difference. The trader would take out a 'sell' contract on the futures market and simultaneously purchase wool at the lower price on the physical market to fulfil the futures contract.

In practice, most futures traders 'close out' their positions before the delivery date. They do this by taking a position in the futures market that is opposite to the one originally taken, so that the contracts cancel each other out leaving a profit or loss on the price difference. Many contracts do not require having to deliver the physical commodity – contracts still open at the delivery date are 'cashed out' by calculating the difference between the futures price and the physical price as measured by an index. However, the mechanism of hedging or speculation works anyway; the closing out or cash settlement provides a profit or loss equivalent to going through with the physical trade.

The world of derivatives has expanded enormously from the comparatively simple days of futures and options, with high-flying investment analysts or 'rocket scientists' designing ever-more-complex deals. It is now a colourful and complex world with an array of exotic-sounding instruments and applications. These include alligator spreads, bells and whistles, contango markets, curve locks, down-and-in options, interest-rate condoms, legs in the air, long positions, naked warrants, negative straddles, reverse floaters, roller-coaster swaps, strip hedges, triple witching hours, vanilla products, and zero-cost collars. For investors who want to learn about the gamut of derivatives, a number of good books are available including *Risk Management with Futures and Options* (Pearson Education, 1998) by Keith Redhead. For the purposes of overall investment strategy, it is worth at least gaining a general idea as to what derivatives are, and how they can be employed.

In the next three chapters we outline the main derivatives that apply to each asset class. The main point to remember about derivatives is that, correctly employed, they have the potential to engineer the risk/return equation in investment to either better manage risk, or increase leverage for speculation. As they become better known and demystified, they are likely to become an integral part of the mainstream investment industry.

Developing a successful portfolio for the future: looking for high-quality risk

Readers should by now have a grasp of the key concepts of investment: the basics of risk, return and diversification, and how the main asset classes reflect these characteristics. From here, we will focus on applying this knowledge.

Overall, *Fortune Strategy* aims to provide the reader with the most essential tool of the investment trade: wisdom. The wise investor bases decisions on information. But in the era of the internet there is no shortage of information and of itself it is of limited value. Wisdom therefore includes the ability to gain insight from analyzing information, to make judgements, and to exercise common sense.

Why are these things so important? Investors who understand risk, return and correlation have powerful conceptual tools at their disposal. But to develop a successful portfolio, it is critical to be able to determine reasonable estimates for each of these factors *in the future*. Most published information on investments relates purely to the past. Yet if history were a sure predictor of the future, investment would be easy. The dynamic nature of investment markets, which, unlike the laws of physics, directly reflect changes in society, means that the past is a lousy guide to the future. It is the future that will determine how well the investor does. Strategy cannot tell you what to pick, only how to pick it.

In periods of epochal change, such as that the world is going through at the beginning of the new millennium, the risks of the unknown can be particularly pronounced. Finally, while investment markets overall are remarkably efficient in terms of pricing assets, they can periodically be distorted by manias of greed or fear, or by investors acting on incorrect beliefs. The events that led up to the Great Crash of 1929 are an obvious example. Recent research by academics such as Mordecai Kurz of Stanford University has shown how individually rational investors can still make 'correlated' mistakes that push prices to excessive highs or lows.

For these reasons, investors need to look beyond the historical results of investments to find out what lies behind them and what can affect them in the future. This is where wisdom and judgement come in, and it is the most challenging and interesting part of the investment process. There are no simple laws to provide clear-cut answers. However, a powerful approach is one based on the systematic pursuit of *high-quality risk*. This approach is particularly recommended by those investment professionals concerned with achieving *reliable* long-term investment performance.

The concept involves the rigorous and systematic evaluation of investments, taking into account the probability of the *expected return* being achieved and the probability of loss. The higher the expected return in relation to the expected standard deviation, the higher the quality of the risk or investment.

Given the limitations of historical measures of risk and return, a more powerful framework for analysis is necessary. And this is where applying the principles of *quality, value, diversity* and *time*, introduced in Chapter 1, comes in. Constructing a successful portfolio involves applying all four of these elements, not just one or two.

Quality means focusing on assets that have sound fundamentals – for example, in the case of shares, companies that have sound management, strong core businesses and solid prospective earnings.

Value means buying those assets at the right price. A quality asset that you have paid too much for is a bad investment. Indeed, some of the most dangerous words in investment are: 'You can't go wrong buying ...'. Some of the greatest investment disasters have come from people who have paid too much for what have essentially been good-quality assets.

Diversity is essential because, in a dynamic world, even the best analysts sometimes get their assessments of quality and value wrong. Investors need a diverse range of assets to spread the risk, but that spread has to be effective.

Time, as distinct from timing, is the final vital ingredient, provided that the previous three elements of a successful portfolio are in place. But this involves more than simply adopting a 'buy and hold' policy. It is a matter of knowing how certain investments will react over different time periods, how to make use of this, and regularly monitoring the portfolio to determine the impact of change on quality and value.

To assess quality and value, achieve diversity, and make time work effectively, the investor has to gain a clear understanding of what makes a company, industry, or asset class really work. In the next three chapters we do just that, looking at the main features of each asset class, how the market operates, the main types of products, risk and return characteristics, trading strategy, and what lies behind the price.

Notes

1   M.T. Daly and M.I. Logan explored the Long Boom concept in *The Brittle Rim*, Penguin, Victoria, 1989.

2   Solnik, B.H. (1974) 'Why not diversify internationally rather than domestically?', *Financial Analysts Journal*, July–August, p. 49.

3   Jahnke, William (1997) 'The asset allocation hoax', *Journal of Financial Planning*, February.

4   Sharpe, William F. (1985) *Investments*, third ed., Prentice-Hall International, New Jersey, p. 714.

PART TWO

The asset classes

CHAPTER 4

Interest-bearing investments: riding high on the yield curve

Summary

- While cash and bonds might seem less intriguing than other investments, they actually offer great potential for analysis and strategy, and can produce substantial profits or big losses.

- Deregulation has opened up a wealth of investment options in interest-bearing products, but many investors still put their money into traditional bank and building society accounts.

- The money market operates much like any other market, except that the Treasury and the central bank participate directly and their policies have an important influence.

- The money market divides naturally into a market in cash sums which mature in 12 months or less, and the bond market where parcels of money maturing in more than 12 months are traded. Cash and bonds have quite distinct characteristics in terms of risk and return.

- Bonds are normally tradable – they can be bought and sold before they are due to be repaid.

- Long-term fixed-interest rates are a more risky investment than a short-term variable rate.

- For people in the top tax bracket, interest-bearing investments will generally not maintain their buying power after inflation and tax in the long term. But when interest rates are falling, tradable fixed-interest stocks could produce very good returns over the short term.

- In the UK, capital gains on fixed-interest securities are not liable to capital gains tax.

Introduction: why the banks are bastards

Traditionally, Britons have invested in banks and building societies as the safest option. The figures show they still do – even though interest rates in recent years have often been abysmal and many higher-paying alternatives are effectively just as safe.

While many investors have worked out the opportunities in the share market, news about the revolution in interest-bearing investments has been slower to filter through. This is ironic, since deregulation probably brought the biggest immediate changes to this asset class. Until 1971, bank deposit rates were set by the Committee of London Clearing Banks. The Building Societies Association continued to recommend savings rates until 1983 and only a very limited range of interest-bearing accounts were available to the public. Virtually all were current or short-term deposit accounts which gave the banks and building societies the right to change the rate of interest paid at little or no notice.

Deregulation removed most of these restrictions, and encouraged individual banks and building societies to offer competitive rates for deposits, including different rates for larger and smaller sums and longer or shorter periods of time.

Conventional banks and building societies now face increasing competition from banks set up by insurance companies such as the Prudential, Standard Life, and Legal & General; by stores such as Marks and Spencer, Sainsbury, and Tesco; and specialist companies such as Virgin Direct, the banking arm of Sir Richard Branson's private business empire. Internet banks like the Prudential's Egg and the Co-op Bank's Smile have added yet another tier of competition to the banking sector. It seems, however, that it is the commercial dealer and the financially literate private investor, rather than the average consumer who have reaped the benefits. Why is this?

Interest rates paid by banks and building societies are linked loosely to the base rate set by the Bank of England for interest rates in general because banks can accept deposits equally from personal customers and from the London money markets, where rates are closely related to base rate. But private customers almost always receive lower rates of interest than large commercial customers because of the higher administration costs needed to handle smaller sums of money. These costs are often expressed as a spread between the average interest rates banks and building societies earn on lending money and the rates they pay to small savers.

Although banks and building societies have been desperately cutting costs, closing branches, sacking staff and streamlining services, operating costs remain in excess of 2 per cent. When interest rates were con-sistently in double figures, as they were through most of the 1970s and 1980s, banks and building societies could afford to pay high nominal rates of interest and still remain profitable. But as inflation and interest rates declined to reach their lowest level in 30 years during 1999, so the nominal rates paid to savers have been disproportionately squeezed in order to cover costs and maintain profits.

Deregulation has, however, opened up a whole new range of alternatives for private investors to get more value out of interest-bearing investments, including money market accounts, money market unit trusts, and bond funds. These avenues enable individuals to get almost as competitive returns from their money as large commercial investors.

Market overview and concepts

Money is a fascinating commodity, but it is still a commodity. Borrowing and lending money is, in effect, the process by which one party gives up the oppor-tunity to obtain goods and services now and passes this opportunity to someone else. The lender expects a reward for this opportunity cost. In financial markets, the reward is interest payments. Interest rates change because the needs of borrowers for funds, and the willingness and ability of lenders to provide funds, vary from time to time. The use of money is like any other market: it is subject to the laws of supply and demand, and the price changes accordingly.

In recent years, the term 'money market' has tended to be used to describe the business of trading large parcels of credit and fixed-interest securities among companies and financial intermediaries, including banks and specialized traders, as well as commercial investors such as insurance companies, investment fund managers and pension funds. The *money market* is exactly what the name implies: a market in which parcels of credit are exchanged. Banks borrow and lend each other huge sums of money in order to balance their books. Most of these loans are 'overnight', although longer dates are taken from seven days up to a year or more.

One factor makes the market for money different from other asset classes: the government and central bank play a major role in determining supply and demand, and hence price. Not only do governments borrow money to buy goods and services, through central banks they also attempt to influence the market to achieve economic objectives. The Bank of England administers the rules that limit the amount of credit individual banks can create. It manages the financing of government debt and in 1997 it also assumed the role of setting the base rate, on which all other rates are based. Hence, any examination of what lies 'behind the price' requires analysis of these operations, known as *monetary policy*.

The Bank of England can regulate the total amount of money in the market, injecting cash by making money available at attractive rates of interest, or by acting as a lender of last resort and lending at penalty rates of interest. It can take money out of the market, which is usually done by selling investments to the banks that participate in the London market.

The Bank of England is also responsible for raising the cash the government needs to pay its day-to-day debts and whenever necessary top up the money it receives from taxation. Every week the Bank of England auctions Treasury bills, which are IOUs redeemable in three months' time. It also sells gilt-edged securities, which are bonds repayable at a set time in the future, usually between five and 30 years from now.

For every borrower there has to be a lender or investor, and to paraphrase Shakespeare, individuals, banks, companies and even the government in their time play the part of lender. The price the borrower pays the lender for the privilege of being able to enjoy the right to spend the borrowed money is the rate of interest. At any one time, rates of interest will vary with the balance of supply and demand and with the size of the sums of money involved.

Time is another key factor in borrowing and lending. Like individuals, governments and companies sometimes need to borrow funds for long-term development, but they may also have short-term money requirements depending on cash flow and commitments. Interest rates on short-term and long-term instruments can and do vary considerably according to expectations of what interest rates will do in the future. At any one time fixed rates for longer periods of time of a year or more are usually higher than those paid on short-term deposits, which can be withdrawn more quickly without penalty.

Interest-bearing investment is often regarded as boring, low-return and safe. But these descriptions are not necessarily correct. Interest-rate market strategy can involve some of the most complex and intriguing analysis of domestic and international economic and political trends. Done well, it can provide large returns; getting it wrong can result in substantial losses.

In this chapter, we look at two distinct asset classes: cash and bonds. Both are interest-bearing, however cash is usually defined as an asset that matures or comes up for renewal in 12 months or less. It is usually a deposit negotiated solely between the borrower and the lender and cannot normally be transferred to a third party. Bonds are investments that have a life in excess of 12 months and can be bought or sold readily at the current market price, allowing the lender to unwind the transaction, at a price.

Cash only earns interest, and because most cash assets cannot be bought and sold before maturity there is no possibility of making capital gains or losses. But bond prices can go up when interest rates fall or down when interest rates rise. Investors can therefore make capital gains or losses (which are also tax-exempt). This distinction makes the risk/return trade-off between cash and bonds fundamentally different. Each has a different correlation with other assets and hence different diversification benefits.

The best way to approach the different instruments and markets is to start with some fundamental concepts.

- All interest-bearing investments involve three elements: an interest rate, a maturity, and a principal amount, often termed the face value. The *interest rate*, which can be fixed or variable, is the return on the investment expressed as a percentage. The *maturity* is the time span between the date of issue of the security or deposit and the day that it 'matures', when the borrower is required to pay the money back. The *face value* is the amount to be paid back at maturity, excluding any interest payment. The interaction between these factors determines the nature of the investment, and its price.

- Interest-bearing investments can be split into two basic categories: short-term investments where the interest rate is variable or the maturity for less than a year (usually defined as 'cash' in terms of investment strategy), and long-term investments where the maturity is longer than a year and the interest rate is usually fixed (usually defined as 'bonds').

- A second division is between non-tradable investments and tradable or 'securitized' investments. Most (but not all) tradable investments have a maturity of a year or more.

- In the case of non-tradable investments, the borrower usually a bank or building society sets the terms of the deal, including the rate of interest and the conditions under which the investor can withdraw money without penalty. But in most cases the borrower will offer a range of options to appeal to a variety of investors. Most non-tradable investments have a maturity of one year or less, they do not involve third parties, and the investments cannot be bought or sold. Bank and building society current and deposit accounts are the best examples.

- Securitized or tradable investments are also parcels of money, but crucially they are invested in return for a receipt, a certificate of deposit, or a bond. This is a piece of paper which can be bought and sold and transferred to third parties, allowing the original investor to get his or her money back and make a profit or loss in the process. Once again the terms and conditions vary in order to attract investors, and the City of London has shown astonishing ingenuity in dreaming up new kinds of instruments with different features, irreverently known as bells and whistles, to match every conceivable need.

- All interest-bearing investments carry some risk that the borrower will default, and the quality of the borrower is usually reflected in the rate of interest needed to make the investment attractive to lenders and investors. The investor therefore has to understand who is ultimately required to pay back the money, what credit risk is associated with this person or entity, and the nature of any guarantees or security arrangements.

- Blue-chip borrowers pay the lowest rates; smaller, riskier or less established borrowers have to offer premium rates. If the rate of interest rises and falls with market rates there is little or no risk of either gain or loss through being out of line with market trends. But if interest rates are fixed there is a risk that the return will look unattractive if current market rates rise, and vice versa. Borrowers usually impose penalties if lenders want their money back early and the risks and penalties increase with the length of the fixed term. With tradable securities, of course, investors can get their money back at any time by selling the investment and the risks are reflected in the price.

- There are two markets for tradable securities: the primary market, in which the security is sold by the issuer to the intermediary or the investor for the first time, and the secondary market, in which the security is traded from one endholder to another.

- Most interest-bearing securities fit into one of two categories: discount securities or coupon securities. Treasury bills are discount securities. As such they earn no interest. With *discount* securities, the lender buys a security for less than its face value. For example lenders may bid £98.75 for each £100 worth of Treasury bills on offer. This 'discount' is the equivalent of £1.25 worth of interest on an investment of £98.75 when the face value is paid back on maturity three months later.

- *Coupon* securities pay a certain interest rate on a regular basis, be it monthly, quarterly, half-yearly or yearly. In practice, tradable bonds often provide the investor with a combination of both capital gains (or losses) and coupon interest.

- The concept of *price* can apply to tradable investments, just like it does to hard assets. A parcel of credit has a value which can move up or down, presenting the potential for a capital gain or loss. As with other types of investments, the price is inversely related to the *yield*, which in this case is represented by the interest rate.

An important factor in assessing the desirability of various fixed-interest investments (as with all investments) is how easily they can be traded or sold. This depends in part on the volume of securities on issue, and the *depth* of the market, which refers to turnover of trade on the secondary market. One advantage of government securities and bank bills is that the market is deep: they are traded in huge quantities all the time. As Table 4.1 shows, the amount outstanding in the commercial fixed-interest market in gilts, corporate bonds and the short-term money market exceeded £1 trillion at the end of 1999, putting them in the same league as the equity market. Turnover was far greater still. In the first three quarters of 1999, daily turnover in the gilt-edged market averaged £5.3 billion, and turnover in the overnight inter-bank market ran at more than £8 billion a day.

TABLE 4.1 Amounts outstanding in sterling markets (November 1999)

	£
Gilts	296 billion
Corporate bonds	249 billion
Short-term money market	473 billion
Interest rate swaps	2732 billion
Equities	1664 billion
Total	5414 billion

Source: Bank of England Quarterly Bulletin, March 2000

We now look at the main investments available in these asset classes.

Types of investment

Non-securitized investments

Interest-bearing deposit accounts: savings accounts or interest-bearing cheque accounts pay interest on whatever the balance of the account happens to be. They may have a variety of names, such as high income accounts, or notice accounts, usually with a set notice period such as 60 days or 90 days to define the amount of notice required to make withdrawals without penalty. The interest rate is usually variable, and credited once a year.

Fixed-interest deposits: these are usually fixed at the time of making the deposit. During the term to maturity, the investor is either unable to withdraw the funds or incurs a penalty charge or lower interest rate for doing so. Banks and building societies offer fixed-rate deposits for up to five years, and a number of insurance companies offer guaranteed income bonds which are fixed-rate investments usually for one, three or five years.

Money market accounts: one particularly useful avenue for private investors has been the opportunity to invest money in accounts linked directly to the rates payable in the London money markets. A number of banks now offer a range of notice accounts from as little as one week, two weeks, a month, three, six or 12 months, which pay fixed rates of interest agreed at the outset for set amounts and periods of time. Most require minimum investments of £50 000 for one- and two-week deposits, but most will open money market accounts for the longer periods for as little as £10 000.

Cash in a money market account can be rolled over each time the notice expires, and the interest earned can be reinvested. Interest on cash which is rolled over starts earning more interest immediately so that the actual interest earned in a year, known as the annual equivalent rate, will be higher than the amount earned on a conventional bank or building society account where interest is usually credited only once a year.

For example, if £10 000 is put into a one-month notice account at 5 per cent and interest is rolled up 11 times in a year, it will earn £512. A three-month notice account will roll up three times and earn £509, a six-month account will roll up once and earn £506, while a 12-month account will earn only the final interest payment of £500. When rates are moving, shrewd investors can bet on the trends by choosing an appropriate rollover period. For example, in 1999 when rates bottomed out in the middle of the year and started rising again in the final quarter, a three-month roll-over would have outperformed the one, six and 12 month roll-overs.

Money market accounts are also allowed to pay interest gross on deposits of £50 000 or more. This can be a significant advantage even to UK resident investors who will eventually be liable to income tax on the interest but can legally defer it until they have made their tax returns and tax payments are due.

Investors can also invest money in offshore accounts in places such as Jersey, Guernsey and the Isle of Man, where most banks and a number of building societies now have branches. Most of these accounts are denominated in sterling, but accounts can be opened in all the leading currencies, including dollars, euros, yen and Swiss francs. All offshore accounts can earn interest paid gross, that is, before deduction of tax, but once again UK residents are legally bound to declare the untaxed income on their tax returns.

Securitized investments

The general public until recently never thought of venturing away from non-securitized investments. There is no reason why private investors should not move into the more exciting and potentially rewarding world of securities investments. But it is a different ball game and the risks as well as the rewards are also different.

Investors have thousands of tradable interest-bearing investment options to choose from. But the best way for the private investor to get a grip on this market is to concentrate on one basic distinction: securities with a maturity of less than 12 months (short-term); and those with a maturity of more than a year (long-term). Long-term securities fall into the 'bonds' asset class for the purposes of investment strategy, while short-term securities fall into the 'cash' asset class.

Short-term securities

Short-term government instruments: securities issued by the government for periods of less than a year, usually as a means of fine-tuning monetary policy. In the UK the main instrument in this category is the Treasury bill issued each week by tender, usually for terms of 13 weeks.

Bills of exchange/promissory notes: securities issued by companies usually to finance exports. Bills of exchange are drawn up by the exporter and signed by the importer. Promissory notes are drawn up by the importer and used as a means of payment. Both securities promise to pay a fixed amount after a fixed period, and can then be sold at a discount (which depends on the creditworthiness of the borrower) to raise immediate cash. Maturity is usually 90–180 days, and the face value is usually in six digits.

Bank bills: discount securities accepted or endorsed by banks on behalf of companies for terms normally between 30 and 270 days. These bills are rapidly traded in the commercial money market, and are the principal investments for money market unit trusts. *Endorsement* or *acceptance* by a bank means that the bank itself assesses the creditworthiness of the borrowing company, and effectively guarantees the debt. A closely related instrument is the *negotiable certificate of deposit*, issued by banks on their own behalf.

Commercial bills: discount securities issued by companies or individuals under similar terms to that of bank bills but, like promissory notes, without bank endorsement or acceptance. Most of these short-term securities are issued in very large denominations, and are traded almost exclusively between banks and other players in the London money markets. Interest rates are generally higher than those available to individuals.

However, small investors can gain access to them by investing in money market funds that private investors can buy and sell. These are managed funds, which pool the funds of many investors into lumps big enough for commercial trading. About a dozen different funds accept lump sums as small as £500, although £1000 is more usual, and most accept regular monthly contributions, some as small as £25. The interest can be paid out at regular intervals, annually, quarterly, and in a few cases monthly if the investment is large enough. Most of these funds have the added advantage that investors can cash in their investment at short notice.

Long-term securities

Government bonds: these are long-term IOUs issued by governments. A bond is a piece of paper that promises to pay the bearer a certain amount of money on a certain date in the future. The maturity of bonds varies widely. UK government bonds, known as gilt-edged stocks or gilts, are the main instruments by which the Treasury raises money. Gilts with up to five years to their repayment date are 'shorts', five to 15 years 'mediums' and over 15 years are 'longs'. Stocks such as War Loan that have no set repayment date are 'undated'. They have proved very poor long-term investments and no new undated stocks have been issued for many years.

Each year a number of stocks reach their maturity date and may be replaced by fresh issues or further tranches of existing stocks if the government needs cash. But on those relatively rare occasions when the Treasury is running a surplus thanks to a combination of a buoyant economy and a growing tax base and a lower level of public spending, the redemptions may exceed new issues, creating a relative shortage of stock for investors to buy.

Because interest rates on most bonds are fixed, prices will rise when interest rates fall, and vice versa. Yields rise as prices fall, yields fall as prices rise, but fixed interest gilts are always repaid at par when they mature, i.e. £100 for each £100 of nominal value.

In order to raise money more cheaply while giving investors protection against inflation, the government began issuing index-linked stocks in the 1970s. Both the capital value and the interest are increased in line with the retail price index, although the interest is all taxable. The coupons on some index-linked bonds have been as high as 4.125 per cent but others offer as little as 2 per cent plus inflation, which in an environment of low inflation represents a considerable saving to the government on its interest payments.

Unlike fixed-rate stocks, index-linked stocks will be repaid at their accumulated value, which makes them attractive to pension funds which have long-term commitments. The capital value of index-linked stocks increases over time, and some of the early issues are now relatively expensive. The current market price will, however, reflect the accumulated value as well as the guarantee of future indexation.

In 1997 the Bank of England allowed the six-monthly interest payments and the capital repayment on certain gilt-edged stocks to be bought and sold separately as gilt 'strips'. All gains or losses at the end of each tax year are treated as income for tax purposes, but strips held as part of an individual savings account are tax-exempt.

Corporate bonds: commercial companies have also issued bonds over the years in order to raise capital for fixed periods of time at fixed rates of interest. They are riskier than government bonds, but offer significantly higher coupons and yields. Until the 1990s the cost of raising long-term capital in this way was more than most companies were willing to pay and they preferred to rely on short-term bank finance and long-term capital raised by issuing new shares on the stock exchange. Then in 1994 the government allowed private investors to hold corporate bonds issued by UK and European companies in a personal equity plan, where they were exempt from income tax as well as capital gains tax. With long-term interest rates generally falling in anticipation of a permanent low level of inflation, issuing corporate bonds became an attractive option.

Corporate bonds are unsecured, which means they are not backed by the company's assets, and initially only companies with a long track record could hope to raise finance this way. But as confidence grew, even companies with a relatively erratic financial track record found it possible to issue bonds paying interest which was high enough to be attractive to investors starved of high returns in conventional assets but still low enough to be attractive to the issuers.

Debentures: corporate interest-bearing securities backed by a charge over the assets of the company. Debenture holders rank ahead of other creditors and shareholders (but not before employees and the tax office) in the repayment of principal and interest should the company be wound up. Because of the extra security, yields on debentures are significantly lower than on corporate bonds.

Convertible bonds: corporate bonds that involve an option to convert debt into equity, i.e. at some point in the future the holder of the security has the option to exchange the note for shares in the company at a price fixed at the time the notes are issued. The more tempting the conversion price, the lower the coupon on the convertible and the cheaper the cost of finance to the company.

Permanent interest-bearing shares (PIBs): these are special securities issued by a number of banks and building societies. They pay high fixed rates of interest, but have no guaranteed redemption date. Investors can get their money back only by selling the PIBs to other investors at prices which vary inversely with current interest rates.

Mortgage-backed securities: an extension of the mortgage: interest-bearing securities backed by mortgages over real estate. A growing number of companies have raised money by issuing securities backed directly by anticipated future rental incomes, secured by long-term leases. In 1999, for example, NHP, the nursing homes operator, raised £194 million before fees by offering securities backed by the rental income on 81 nursing homes on terms that represented an approximate yield of 6.95 per cent to the institutions that bought the issue. King's College Hospital and Keele University have also raised capital by issuing long-term bonds paying interest secured on rent from student housing.

Although most interest-bearing securities are traded predominantly by the commercial money market, there are some opportunities for the private investor. Small investors can buy gilts in multiples as small as £100 of nominal value. They can be bought and sold through stockbrokers, including special low-cost dealing firms, which will charge a small commission, or through the Bank of England. New issues can be bought direct from the Debt Management Office, which will not charge a commission. Investors can buy and sell corporate bonds, debentures, preference shares and convertibles through a bank or stockbroker.

Most private investors looking for a spread of fixed-interest securities buy corporate bond funds, which are effectively unit trusts that reinvest small investors' cash in a variety of corporate bonds, usually at least 50 different companies in order to spread the risk and average out the income. Corporate bond funds expect to earn mainly income, but they also hold out the possibility of earning tax-free capital gains if interest rates generally decline and the fixed coupon bonds go to a premium over their face value. Investors can buy corporate bond funds in amounts as small as £100. There is no upper limit, although most investors choose to invest initially through an ISA which allows them to invest a limited amount each year free of both income and capital gains tax.

Zero-coupon shares issued by split-capital investment trusts have also become popular. Zero-coupon shares which sell initially at a heavy discount to their face value, but investors know that they will be redeemed at par on the set date, so they in fact behave like long-dated, fixed-interest bonds on which the interest accumulates to maturity. They often appeal to investors with set require-ments at future dates, such as annual school fee payments to meet or a mortgage to repay. Split capital trusts are examined in more detail in Chapter 7.

Investors who buy into the bond market through bond funds and gilt funds are in fact delegating the management of their money to professionals. Investors who deal direct are backing their own judgement. But all private investors need to know when medium- to long-term economic trends are likely to make bonds more attractive than cash, and vice versa.

Risk and return

More so than for other asset classes, the way risk and return work for interest-bearing securities is counter-intuitive: everything seems to be upside down. This section looks at how:

- when short-term interest rates go up, the value of long-term, fixed-interest investments goes down, and vice versa;

- the more 'secure' the investment, in the sense of paying a fixed interest rate for a long period of time, the greater the 'maturity risk'. Investors can find their money locked into a fixed return that is considerably below, or above, what it could be earning from the market rates of the day;

- the question of maturity risk is amplified by inflation: the danger emerges that a long-term investment will pay substantially less, or substantially more, than inflation over the period in question.

When looking at interest-bearing investments, it is important to bear in mind the effects of compounding. The investor must calculate return in compound terms, whether interest is paid via fixed rates at maturity, periodic interest (coupon) or discount (zero coupon). This approach provides a common basis for comparison, and helps in understanding another crucial point: the *time value of money*. All else being equal, an investment that pays a certain amount of interest sooner is more valuable than one that pays the same amount later.

To illustrate this point, here is a simple example. Suppose there are two alternative investments. One is a corporate zero-coupon bond purchased for £10000, which will mature with a face value of £15000 in five years; it pays no periodic interest. The other is a £10 000 debenture purchased at face value, which pays a 10 per cent coupon annually and matures in five years; that is, in five years it will have paid five £1000-coupon instalments. Table 4.2 compares the two investments.

TABLE 4.2 Values of zero-coupon bond and coupon-bearing debenture

	Zero-coupon bond/£	Debenture/£
Investment	10 000	10 000
Interest (reinvested at 10%)		
Year 1	0	1 000
Year 2	0	1 100
Year 3	0	1 210
Year 4	0	1 330
Year 5	5 000	1 460
Total interest	5 000	6 100

The direct profit from each investment is £5000 over five years – a simple return of 10 per cent per year. In the case of the debenture, however, the investor has the benefit of receiving the return progressively rather than at maturity and hence benefiting from compounding reinvestment income. By the time the debenture matured, the additional interest would be more than £1000. The debenture is therefore worth substantially more than the discount bond.

As discussed, *yield* is the critical issue for interest-bearing securities. The key mechanism is that the price falls as the yield goes up, and the price rises as the yield goes down. The important corollary is that when interest-bearing securities are traded, the price reflects the yield available on other interest-bearing investments at the time. If prevailing interest rates go up, for example, the price of an existing interest-bearing security goes down because new securities will carry a higher coupon.

To illustrate the process, let us follow the travels of a £15 000 face value discount bond that matures in five years and is purchased for £10 000. This represents an initial (simple) yield of 10 per cent, since it will provide a £5000 profit over five years, or £1000 per year on an initial investment of £10 000. We can follow the example in Figure 4.1.

Jane buys the bond for £10 000 from XYZ plc in 2005 which will pay £15 000 in 2010, providing an expected return equivalent to the prevailing 10 per cent rate. After two years, however, Jane is forced to sell the bond to meet unforeseen commitments, but the prevailing interest rates for investments of similar maturities have gone up to 15 per cent. If Jane tried to get her original 10 per cent yield, she would try to sell the bond for £12 000. This would provide her with a £1000 per year profit for two years. But no one would buy the bond at that price because they would get less than they could from the prevailing interest rate. This is because any would-be purchaser would be thinking about the yield over the three years between purchasing the bond and its maturity. At a purchase price of £12 000, the profit would be £3000 over the three years to maturity – a simple yield of only about 8 per cent, or about half the prevailing rate of 15 per cent. (This calculation is called the *yield to maturity*.)

The only way Jane can sell the bond is to lower the price so that the yield equals prevailing interest rates. If she offered the bond for £10 400, the buyer would earn a profit of £4600 over the three years to maturity – a simple yield of about 15 per cent. At this price, Jane has made a profit of only £400 over two years – a return of just 2 per cent instead of the 10 per cent she had in mind when she purchased the bond. In this case, Jane lost out by locking in to a long-term security.

However, this can work both ways. Suppose Jane sells the bond to Jack for £10 400 and Jack keeps the bond until maturity. By that time, interest rates have fallen to 5 per cent. But XYZ plc is still obliged to honour its original commitment, so Jack receives the £15 000, providing him with his 15 per cent return. In this case, Jack has won against falling interest rates by locking in a high return.

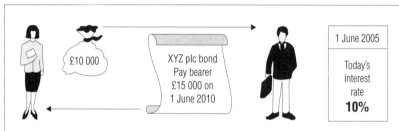

1. June 2005 Jane goes to XYZ plc and pays £10 000 for an XYZ bond, which will mature with a face value of £15 000 in June 2010. Her initial yield, equal to the prevailing interest rate, is 10 per cent per annum.

2. June 2007 Jane sells the bond to Jack for £10 400. She earns only £400 profit for her two-year investment, or only a 2 per cent annual yield. But the price reflects a 15 per cent yield-to-maturity for Jack, which is equivalent to the prevailing interest rate.

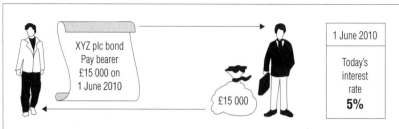

3. June 2010 Jack receives £15 000 from XYZ plc when the bond matures, providing a £4600 profit for his three-year investment equivalent to his expected 15 per cent annual return, despite the fall in interest rates.

FIGURE 4.1   Jane, Jack and the bond

In practice, the trading of bonds and other interest-bearing securities is more complex than this. It combines all of the elements that we have dealt with and a few others: coupon payments, the term to maturity, the compounding effect, projections of future interest rates, and so on. The fact that income is taxable but any capital gains are not is also a factor. However, the principle is what's important: bond prices go down when prevailing interest rates rise, and bond prices go up when prevailing interest rates fall.

The longer the term to maturity, the higher the potential return but the higher the risk as well. If an investor is locked into an interest rate for several years, there is a much greater chance of doing substantially better or worse than by sticking with the prevailing cash rate. Thus, bonds are riskier but tend to pay a higher return than cash, which is always the safest alternative investment.

The 'credit risk' or 'issuer risk' is another crucial element in assessing interesting-bearing investments. At issue is whether the body ultimately responsible for paying the debt is likely to be able to do so. In terms of issuer risk, gilts and Treasury bills are regarded as the safest. A government is unlikely to go bankrupt and, if worst comes to worst, it can print money or raise taxes to pay back lenders. From there, bank bills rank well among private sector securities. Debentures, which carry a charge over assets, are safer than unsecured corporate paper such as promissory notes.

So, with interest-bearing investments, risk is a product of two main factors: maturity risk and credit (issuer) risk. These two factors operate independently, and often in opposite directions. For example, a long-term gilt is extremely secure in terms of issuer risk, but riskiest in terms of maturity risk. Figure 4.2 depicts this situation.

The market is finely tuned to credit risk. The greater risk of corporate bonds results in investors generally demanding a significant, albeit fluctuating, premium in interest over gilt rates, as shown in Figure 4.3.

But the most serious risk to fixed-interest investments is inflation. Index-linked gilts offer protection against inflation, but the price of index-linked stocks has risen and yields though safe are very low. Fixed-interest bonds provide no protection against inflation. If they are issued at £100 they will be redeemed at £100, but the interest and the capital will be eroded by inflation.

A study by ipac securities limited found that bonds were a poor defence against the rising tide of inflation, especially during the 1970s. The total return on a portfolio of gilts went negative in 1968 and remained negative in ten of the next 14 years, by which time its total value in real terms had fallen by almost 50 per cent.

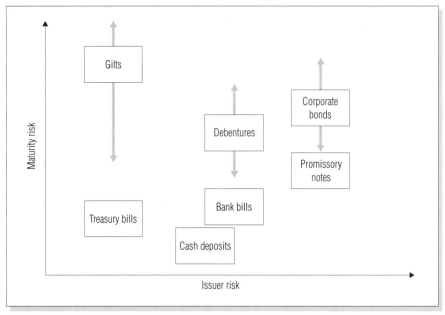

Source: ipac

FIGURE 4.2 Risk in the interest rate market

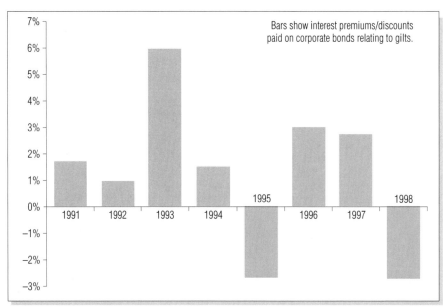

Source: Barclays Capital Equity-Gilt Study, 1999

FIGURE 4.3 Corporate bonds versus gilts: relative total returns

During the 1980s and 1990s, however, when inflation declined, bonds proved a better investment. The study sought to determine how successful a strategy of investing purely in bonds, and holding those bonds for the ten years to maturity, would have been. It calculated the return per £100 invested in bonds, and compared it with the return that would have been required to keep pace with inflation over the ten years. The results are shown in Table 4.3.

TABLE 4.3   Ten-year returns versus inflation for gilts, UK, 1960–98

Years	Bond return (£100 invested)	Value required to maintain purchasing power of £100	Bond or inflation greater?
1960–70	132	152	Inflation
1961–71	181	159	Bond
1962–72	141	166	Inflation
1963–73	123	181	Inflation
1964–74	107	205	Inflation
1965–75	140	245	Inflation
1966–76	153	272	Inflation
1967–77	217	298	Inflation
1968–78	218	305	Inflation
1969–79	225	342	Inflation
1970–80	263	365	Inflation
1971–81	211	375	Inflation
1972–82	330	367	Inflation
1973–83	422	349	Bond
1974–84	533	307	Bond
1975–85	429	260	Bond
1976–86	421	234	Bond
1977–87	336	216	Bond
1978–88	376	213	Bond
1979–89	382	196	Bond
1980–90	333	186	Bond
1981–91	390	173	Bond
1982–92	305	169	Bond
1983–93	339	163	Bond
1984–94	281	161	Bond
1985–95	302	157	Bond
1986–96	293	155	Bond
1987–97	301	155	Bond
1988–98	344	149	Bond

Source: ipac/Barclays Global Investors

This shows again how essential it is to look at the fundamental factors that underpin an investment. We will now explore the elements that take the investor 'behind the price' of interest-bearing securities.

Behind the price

The factors that motivate the money market comprise a seething cauldron of hard-nosed economics, politics, international influences and what is often called 'market sentiment', which more often translates as market paranoia. This makes the interest rate equation both complex and intriguing.

The key is to keep an eye on the big picture, and distinguish between short-term influences and long-term trends. This should help the astute investor to get the best out of the economic cycle, by achieving a balance of cash and bonds in a portfolio.

Short-term interest rates in the UK are dominated by one factor: monetary policy. The government, through its own borrowing, has a major influence on interest rates, but since May 1997 the ten members of the Central Monetary Committee of the Bank of England have set the base rate, to which all other interest rates are indirectly linked. The committee consists of five 'insiders' who are directors of the Bank of England, and five independent outside advisers appointed by the Chancellor of the Exchequer, with the Governor of the Bank of England exercising the casting vote in the event of a deadlock. The government retains the ability to regulate the economy by raising or lowering taxes and public sector spending.

A good way to approach the issue of economic and monetary policy is to ask: what do people and companies borrow money *for*? The answer generally falls into one of two categories, consumption or expansion, both of which raise the general level of economic activity. When funds are cheaper, i.e. when interest rates are low, people are more inclined to build houses and buy goods produced both domestically and overseas. Companies will buy new plant and equipment. The supply of money, controlled by the government and the Central Bank, thus acts on the economy in the same way as the throttle controls the amount of fuel entering the engine of a car.

The primary responsibility of the Bank of England is to regulate demand in order to keep inflation under control. Other economic problems, including the level of unemployment, the exchange rate and the balance of payments, are only of secondary importance. This hard-line approach has yet to be fully tested in all circumstances. It remains to be seen whether the Bank of England can maintain an unyielding hard line in the face of rising unemployment, a recession or social unrest. But it is a quantum leap from the bad old days when governments were tempted to ease monetary policy to 'pump-prime' the economy whenever dole queues lengthened or when mortgage rates were causing hardship for borrowers and an election was approaching.

But monetary policy does not operate in a vacuum. The influence of any government and any central bank on monetary policy should be kept in perspective. Their power is not absolute. They operate within national economies that are primarily private sector, and are locked into the world economy.

This point leads to the second tier of factors that affect interest rates: long-term, fundamental, economic factors. While central banks can influence interest rates in the short to medium term, long-term trends get back to fundamentals. The factors are numerous, but the following are some of the most important.

First, while the Bank of England fiddles with the timing of government borrowings to carry out monetary policy, the extent of borrowing itself depends on the government's ability to balance its budget. If the signs are that in the medium to long term budget deficits will come down or move into surplus, this trend will exert downward pressure on interest rates. This is because government borrowing requirements will be reduced. Conversely, prospects of increased spending act as an upward pressure on interest rates. Balancing the budget, in turn, depends on the government's ability and intention to raise taxes on the one hand, and spend them on the other.

Second, interest rates tend to have a high correlation with inflation rates, although the dynamics are complex. Sustained high interest rates tend to dampen an economy and inflation. If interest rates are much higher than the rate of inflation, i.e. *real* interest rates are too high, the demand for funds will be reduced because the real cost of borrowing will be prohibitive. But the supply of funds tends to expand as investors (often from overseas) seek to cash in on high real interest rates by lending money. This trend tends to reduce interest rates. While high real interest rates can occur in the short term, in the longer term the difference tends to come down to only a few percentage points. The expected future rate of inflation is thus a major influence on long-term interest rates.

Third, the rate of inflation depends on the level of economic or business activity. When business is booming, more people are employed, personal and business consumption is higher, and corporate profits are good. These trends tend to exert upward pressure on inflation as the economy becomes 'overheated'. There is, however, an offsetting factor: boom times should improve the government's tax base, since more people are employed and companies are generating bigger profits.

In total, therefore, interest rates are influenced by a variety of factors, both domestic and foreign. Predicting the peaks and troughs and turning points of the interest rate cycle, and the relative levels of short- and long-term interest rates is a skilled and profitable activity. We turn to such issues next.

Investment strategy

High up in the glass towers of major cities, a peculiar breed, the money market dealers, ride the yield curve. Their eyes are glued to computer screens, which display a Star Wars-like array of interest rate data, with esoteric calculations on how each rate and maturity relates to another. Backed by this real-time microchip analysis and their own educated guesses of where interest rates are heading, the dealers look for the tiniest niche to invest money, with a view to making a profit by lending at one rate for a certain period of time while borrowing at a lower rate for another period.

This type of active trading strategy is not for the private investor. But the small investor needs to know the factors that influence interest rates, prices and yields in order to decide how much of his or her assets to allocate to fixed-interest assets.

The relationship between short-, medium- and long-term interest rates is central to trading strategy. And the money market has come up with a handy way of displaying this relationship: the *yield curve*. The yield curve, shown in Figure 4.4, depicts interest rate yields on one axis and time to maturity on the other. Its shape reflects how the money market believes interest rates will move in the future, but against a background of the traditional risk/return trade-off.

The *normal* yield curve – the one that should happen in theory – slopes upwards, as in the left-hand example of Figure 4.4. Cash, which is safer, offers the base return, and bonds, which carry a higher maturity risk, offer a progressively higher return as their maturity increases.

From time to time, however, the yield curve turns *inverse* – it slopes downwards – as in the right-hand example. This can occur when two factors combine. First, the authorities impose tight monetary policies, making short-term interest rates very high. Second, the market believes that this is a short-term trend and that, over time, lower inflation and easier monetary policy will bring yields down.

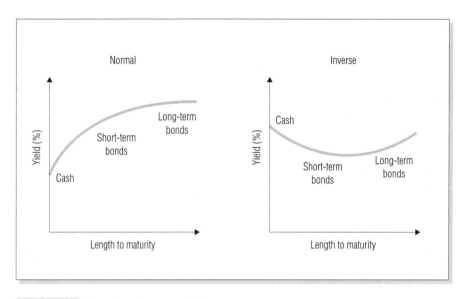

FIGURE 4.4 Normal and inverse yield curves

During periods when short-term interest rates are clearly on the rise but bond yields are still relatively low (that is, the normal yield curve is starting to flatten out or slope downwards), cash is more attractive than bonds. It makes more sense to take the relatively high short-term interest rates if the return on bonds does not compensate for the higher maturity risk. Conversely, when cash interest rates are falling but bond yields are still relatively high (that is, the yield curve is becoming more upward sloping), bonds become more attractive. Buying bonds in such circumstances can lock in higher interest rates for longer periods.

The trick, of course, is to know when interest rates are on a sustained upward or downward trend, and to pick the peak and trough. There is no foolproof way to do this. However, fundamental economic analysis can provide a guide. A lot has to do with picking the current status of the economic or business cycle.

Cash, bonds and the economic cycle

Bond prices tend to do well when inflation and short-term interest rates are falling because, as discussed, prices are inversely related to yield and the yield reflects prevailing interest rates. It follows, then, that bonds show their highest potential to produce prospective profits at the top of the business cycle, when bond prices are low but short-term interest rates and inflation have peaked. As the economy enters the slowdown phase, or recession, interest rates and inflation are likely to drop. By buying when yields are high and prices low and locking in a high return in bonds, the investor is likely to make a substantial capital gain and/or regular coupon return.

The worst outlook for bonds, and the best outlook for cash, occurs when the economic cycle has reached its bottom and is likely to pick up. In that case, inflation and short-term interest rates are likely to rise, which will reduce the capital value and real return of bonds.

An important implication is that an interest-bearing portfolio (which may be part of a wider portfolio) divided between cash and bonds will provide substantial diversification benefit. While investors may adjust the weightings of cash and bonds according to their predictions of the economic cycle, an interest-bearing portfolio diversified over different maturities will help to protect the investor against the vagaries of these cycles. In times of rising short-term interest rates and inflation, the investor's bond investments will fare poorly but the cash investments will provide a handsome return. In times of recession, on the other hand, the bonds in the portfolio will perform well.

International dimensions

As discussed in Chapter 3, investing overseas involves taking on currency risk. If the investor is prepared to accept this risk, or is able to hedge it, there are definite attractions in overseas interest-bearing investments.

Investment in long-term financial instruments in foreign markets is a useful way of further diversifying away national economic risk. Although we speak of 'world inflation', the inflation rates of Western countries vary substantially. Inflation rates in the UK during the 1990s were less than half the average rates of the previous decade, but the UK still appears to be paying the price for past misdeeds and also for the heavy dependence on interest rates rather than taxation for regulating demand, and for its determination to paddle its own canoe and maintain its own currency. As a result, real interest rates in the UK at the start of the new millennium were half as high again as in core countries of the eurozone such as Germany.

A number of studies have shown that the inclusion of international bonds can both reduce risk and enhance return in the typical portfolio. One study described international bonds as 'the most effective means of diversifying exposures to domestic monetary, budgetary, and other financial uncertainties'.[1]

Assessing risks in the bond markets is a specialized activity. Not even managers from major funds try to work this out on their own. Rather, they turn to specialists in the field: credit-rating agencies such as Moody's, and Standard and Poor.

These agencies have a system of grading issuer risk, such as the well-known double A, triple A, and so on. These ratings are crucially important both for borrowers and investors. In mid-2000, for example, a sharp rise in its debt levels to £28 billion raised the possibility of British Telecom losing its A grade status, threatening its borrowing costs, its profits and the price of its shares. In general, most professional investment managers steer clear of all foreign bonds and debentures except those classified as *investment grade*, which rate as triple B or better. These are government-backed securities in countries that are not classified as banana republics, and corporate securities from prime-rated companies. Investments in less solid securities, such as junk bonds, may offer attractive returns. Their place in a portfolio is, however, in the 'money you can afford to lose' category.

Derivative instruments

Derivatives can be used by borrowers and lenders to hedge against adverse interest rate or currency movements in the same way that producers and consumers hedge against adverse future changes in the prices of commodities such as oil, sugar or wool. They also allow investors to speculate on rises and falls in bond prices, currency rates and interest rates as well as shares. The main instruments are options and futures. These allow investors to take a view on future price changes without putting up the full price of the contract and can therefore be used to gear up a bet on future price movements.

In London, options and futures are traded on the London International Financial Futures Exchange or Liffe, which merged with the London Traded Options Market in 1992.

Options: to buy an option requires an investor to pay a non-refundable premium now for the right to buy or sell bonds (or shares or currencies) on set dates in the future. Options to buy are known as *call options*, options to sell are known as *put options*. The price paid for the option is known as the *premium* and the price at which the option can be exercised is the *strike price*. If the contract is profitable, the profit depends on the difference between the option price and the cash price when the contract matures. If it is not profitable to exercise the option, the buyer simply allows it to lapse and loses the premium.

For the *writer*, the premium is the income received for taking the risk that the actual price of the bonds, currencies or interest rates will move in an unfavourable direction and the option will be exercised.

UK investors can also buy options on interest rates in the London inter-bank market (Libor) or the European inter-bank market (Euribor) that can be exercised at set dates from one up to three, six or 12 months ahead. The contract is based on a target interest rate, which is subtracted from 100 to establish the strike price. If, for example, the contract assumes an interest rate of 5 per cent, the contract price is set at 100 – 5 or 95. If interest rates rise to 6 per cent, the contract will fall to 100 – 6 or 94. If rates fall to 4 per cent, the contract price will rise to 96. An option buyer who hopes to gain from lower interest rates buys a call option, if he hopes to gain from a rise he buys a put option.

Options are a popular way of limiting risk exposure of interest-bearing investments. A company that has a loan from a bank, which is reviewed every three months, may fear the next review will raise that rate and decide to hedge the risk. The company treasurer buys put options which will allow him to exercise his option if interest rates rise and make a profit to offset the increased cost of his loan. If interest rates actually fall, his option is useless, but his loan will be cheaper. In effect, the option acts as an insurance policy. The worst-case scenario is if rates are unchanged, in which case the premium has been wasted and nothing gained. Investors who do not have future expectations on which to base their option trading are more exposed, but their loss is limited to the size of the initial premium.

Futures: unlike an option, a futures contract is a firm commitment to take up the contract when it matures, or to close it by taking out an equal and opposite contract in the meantime. There are two main sets of players. Hedgers expect either to deliver or to accept the actual asset in order to match a futures contract when it matures, and simply want to limit their exposure in the meantime. A profit on the futures contract should help offset a loss on the asset and vice versa. Speculators have no such 'real world' needs on the physical market and trade for hope of profit and risk of loss.

Futures contracts in gilt-edged stocks and foreign government bonds, especially German Bundesbank bonds, have been traded in large volumes on Liffe for years. Bonds denominated in euros are also now available. Contracts are in multiples of 100 000 dollars, sterling or euros and changes are measured in percentage points of the price of the underlying securities. Investors can also trade in three-month interest rates in sterling and other leading currencies including the euro.

For big corporate players, these futures offer a readily accessible hedging mechanism. Suppose a company is due to receive a large sum of money in a few months' time and intends to invest it in the short-term money market. The company may, however, be nervous that interest rates will fall between now and then. The company could take out a 'buy' contract for the same sum in bonds on the futures market for the month when the money is due to come in. The price for the bonds, and hence the interest rate yield, would be set in the contract. The company could thus lock in an interest rate several months in advance.

For speculators, futures offer a way of betting on the movement of interest rates. In particular, it is possible to speculate on a rise in interest rates in a way that is not possible on the physical market. Suppose a speculator took the view that interest rates on bonds were going to rise within a few months, more than was reflected on the futures market. The speculator could take out a futures contract to sell bonds. If the bet is right and physical interest rates do rise, bond prices will fall. The speculator can then buy bonds on the physical market at the lower price and use them to fulfil the futures contract at the higher pre-agreed price, pocketing the difference as profit.

The interest rate futures market is, in general, for major players. A single contract for interest rate futures on Liffe is for $1 million or £500 000, so it is not a market for the unprepared or the impecunious.

Currency instruments: as discussed in previous chapters, currency risk is a major disincentive for private investors who wish to put money into overseas markets. The same applies to companies which do business overseas but do not have a natural hedge. This situation creates a market for derivative instruments to reduce currency risk, and opportunities for speculators to get on the 'other side' of such contracts. The main derivatives covering foreign currency include futures, options and swaps.

Foreign currency futures involve tradable contracts in which parties agree to buy or sell standardized amounts of foreign exchange at pre-set prices at specified dates in the future. Investors or companies expect to receive income or make payment in an overseas market over a set time period can hedge by taking out contracts to buy or sell foreign currency in accordance with the amount and timing of their commitments or expectations. The main market is the Chicago Mercantile Exchange which offers futures contracts in multiples of 125 000 euros, 12.5 million yen and £62 500.

Foreign currency options involve one party purchasing the option to buy or sell a certain amount of currency at a pre-agreed rate over an agreed time frame. For hedgers, options offer an attractive and flexible insurance policy against adverse currency movements, although the premium may be high. For the writer of the option, the risk can be substantial. However, financial intermediaries usually offset the risk through natural hedges or other derivative instruments, often running, in effect, a book of various currencies.

Swaps involve two parties agreeing to exchange an agreed amount of currency at a certain date in the future. In this sense they are similar to a futures contract, but they usually involve a tailor-made over-the-counter arrangement struck through an intermediary. They often include an interest rate and a currency swap component, and can become complex.

Tax considerations

Interest-bearing securities provide return in the form of interest, which with the exception of some forms of National Savings is taxable as income in the UK. From April 2000 investment income qualifies for tax at the special low rate of 10 per cent on the first slice of taxable income. The standard rate of tax is 20 per cent. But investment income is aggregated with earned income for tax purposes, and anything in excess of the standard rate band is liable for tax at 40 per cent.

Some forms of National Savings pay interest gross, i.e. without deducting tax, and leave the investors to declare the income on his or her self-assessment form and pay tax in the following year. But the great majority of interest-bearing assets, including interest on bank and building society accounts, and dividends on bonds and equities, are paid net of tax at the standard rate. Standard-rate taxpayers are required to declare the income on their self-assessment forms but are not liable for further tax. Top-rate taxpayers, however, are liable to pay an additional tax charge of 20 per cent on all income above the starting point for top-rate tax. Any additional tax due on dividends is payable in the year following the year in which it was received.

Interest on overseas fixed-interest bonds held by UK residents is payable gross from April 2001, although it must be declared for tax purposes, and paying agents may report payments to the Inland Revenue. Interest on money invested in cash-based individual savings accounts is, however, exempt from tax. Dividends on investments in shares, unit trusts and corporate bond funds invested in equity ISAs are also exempt from tax, and in both cases the exemptions apply equally to lower-rate, standard-rate and top-rate taxpayers. All ISAs are also exempt from capital gains tax.

Interest on money market accounts qualifies for tax even if allowed to accumulate, but increased value on discount securities, including zero-coupon bonds, is treated as capital gains, on which all investors qualify for an annual allowance.

Interest and dividends on offshore investments is usually paid gross and in spite of the best efforts of the UK government to track down tax evasion by UK residents with income received on money invested in the Channel Islands and the Isle of Man, these territories have full control of their tax regimes. They are also not members of the European Union – a fact which will give them continued exemption from any EU-wide withholding taxes on income from savings and investments.

Interest on gilts is taxable but is normally paid gross. Interest on other fixed-interest securities is taxable and normally paid net, but capital gains or losses on fixed-interest securities are exempt from capital gains tax.

Note

1   Cholerton, K., Pieraerts, P. and Solnik, B. (1986) 'Why invest in foreign currency bonds', *Journal of Portfolio Management*, Summer, p. 4.

CHAPTER 5

Equities: taking the dogs for a random walk

Summary

- The stock market offers a fantastic avenue for individuals to take a direct stake in the economy and increase their wealth. However, too many investors treat it as a casino, adopting highly risky tactics that usually fail.

- A broadly based portfolio of 20–30 shares per major market should give the investor most of the overall market's gain in the long term.

- It may be possible to make additional gains by 'tilting' the portfolio to exploit a theme the investor believes has not been recognized or correctly priced by the market.

- Overseas stock markets offer exciting ways of taking an interest in the global economy. Done wisely, overseas equity investment can achieve a better diversified portfolio.

- Tax incentives to invest in venture capital projects and the treatment of capital gains make shares a very tax-effective investment, especially for high-income earners.

- Historically, shares have offered the best return of any asset class, although they are vulnerable to short-term market emotion and volatility. People who wish to preserve and increase their buying power over the long term will require a significant exposure to shares, and a strategy for managing stock market risk.

Introduction: a piece of the action

Lending money to companies can produce a comfortable return, but to get more out of wealth creation you have to own the company. This is where the stock market comes in: buying shares makes the investor a part-owner. And, through the stock market, the investor can secure a piece of every sector in the world economy.

A common perception about equities is that success comes from 'playing the market', using an active trading strategy to pick winners, track down 'inside information', work out price trends through complex charts, and get the timing right. This puts the stock market in the same category as the great British sport of gambling.

There is nothing inherently wrong with speculation, but it is not *investing*. The benefits from equity investment stem from watching the big picture while taking a long-term view. The private investor can use this approach since it relies mainly on common sense and knowledge.

Since it came into being, the stock market has yielded good returns over the long term. This is not to say that for individual stocks, and for the entire market over periods, an investor cannot lose money. What it means is that overall, the odds are in the investor's favour. Gambling, on the other hand, is weighted against the gambler.

Mathematician Hans Eisler studied forms of gambling and ranked them according to how much, on average, a person could expect to get back.[1] Based on this study, blackjack would return about 99 pence in the pound, horse racing 85 pence, and lotteries 61 pence. Using return data since the First World War the corresponding figure for UK shares would be £1.12 a year, i.e. the average nominal return has been just over 12 per cent per year.

The game is weighted in the investor's favour, and there is no need to be a professional analyst to play. Various studies have shown that a portfolio selected by throwing about 30 darts at a newspaper stock market list will perform about as well as one selected by professionals. It is very difficult to 'beat the market', and few managers of investment funds do so consistently.

The reason for this has to do with the efficient markets hypothesis, introduced in Chapter 3. In essence, it suggests that new information is absorbed so quickly and effectively into stock prices that it is difficult for anyone to get a consistent advantage. It also shows that share prices, rather than conforming to historical patterns tend to take a 'random walk' as new information comes in. Past performance provides no reliable indicator of whether a stock is likely to go up or down at any moment.

Many investors regard the process of picking and trading stocks as a key attraction of the stock market. For those who wish to do so, this chapter provides a guide to doing it with structure, knowledge and discipline. However, such an approach is not necessary to get results. The investor can select companies according to a wider strategy, determining which combination of stocks will form the best portfolio according to how much risk the investor wishes to take.

To do this successfully, it is necessary to understand the factors that make up risk and return from equities, the mechanics of the market, and how a stock is valued. And as Gordon Gecko, the evil but attractive villain of the movie *Wall Street*, would say, it is worth being able to distinguish genuinely undervalued companies from dogs, and from those which are still dogs though they may have different fleas.

There are dozens of books about basic stock market investing. Rather than replicate their content, *Fortune Strategy* looks at market characteristics rather than the detail, with a view to developing sound strategy.

Market overview and concepts

An entrepreneur who wishes to finance a venture has two main options: borrow money, or give investors a share of the business. Suppose an investor's friend needs to raise £50 000 to develop a brilliant new idea to create some computer software for a service that does not yet exist, and the bank is unduly sceptical. The friend puts up two propositions. The investor can lend the friend £25 000, to be repaid plus 15 per cent interest, whether or not the software can be developed. This option represents an interest-bearing investment. Alternatively, the investor can put up £25 000 for a half-share in the venture. If the friend sells his idea on for £300 000, the investor gets £150 000; but if the friend has no luck, the investor gets nothing. That represents equity.

Borrowing the money means that the friend is obliged to pay back the principal and interest at a certain date in the future. But selling a half-share leaves no debt hanging over the friend's head. Until the venture makes money, there is no obligation to make any payments; and if the whole venture collapses, the friend has a partner to share the loss.

This shows the attraction of sharing equity for both the entrepreneur and for the investor. Multiply it over thousands of ventures and hundreds of thousands of investors, and we have the stock market.

While the stock market world is full of jargon, the concept behind it is simple: stock market investment involves owning a direct interest in a business venture, the value of which depends on its ability to make a profit.

As with interest-bearing securities, there is a primary and secondary market. When a company first decides to raise capital in an initial public offering or IPO, it issues and sells shares that can then be traded from one person to another. For many years before the stock exchange as we know it developed, shares in various ventures were traded in informal venues, such as London coffee houses. Today's exchange is merely a formal version of the coffee house. A company may seek a *listing*, which means, literally, that it appears on the list of stocks traded at the exchange.

The incorporated business venture – the public limited company – is the basic currency of equity markets. Therefore, investors focus on ways of measuring a company's performance and the interaction among these measures. These are some of the key concepts:

Share: a unit of ownership of the company. If a company, XYZ plc, has 1 million shares on issue and one person owns 100000 of them, that person owns 10 per cent of XYZ plc.

Issued (or *subscribed*) *capital:* the total value of all the company's shares issued to shareholders. If XYZ plc has issued 1 million shares with a value of 100 pence each, it has £1 million of issued capital.

Share price: the price at which a share is trading in the market – what investors are prepared to pay for a share. Newspapers quote a 'mid-price'. The actual buying price is usually a touch higher, the selling price a shade lower. The difference or spread is usually 1–2 per cent but on 'penny' shares can be 5 per cent or more.

Market capitalization: the total market value of a company based on its share price. If XYZ plc shares are trading at £2.30, the market capitalization (or market cap) of XYZ plc is £2.3 million (2.3 times 1 million shares).

Earnings: the profits of a company over a particular period, such as a quarter or year. There are several levels in the corporate profit and loss statement at which earnings are determined – gross, before tax, after tax, and so on. The benchmark most commonly quoted, unless otherwise stated, is net profit after tax and interest payments – the *bottom line*.

Dividend: a sharing out of profits to shareholders. This is usually expressed as a dividend per share. If XYZ plc declares a dividend of 5 pence per share and an investor owns 1000 shares, that investor should receive a cheque for £50.

Assets: in the general sense, everything a company owns or is entitled to claim. In stock market lexicon, the *net tangible assets* or *net asset backing* of a company is most often referred to. This represents, in effect, what would be left in real terms should a company be wound up.

Types of investment

A share is a unit of ownership in a company, but there are many ways in which ownership can be structured. Returning to our computer software friend, the half-share deal could take several forms.

The friend might insist on taking the first £20 000 of any profit, for doing the work, so that he gets *preference* in dividends. The friend may agree that the investor should put up the £25 000 in two parts: £10 000 now, and the rest as required. The friend might give the investor a say in deciding how to market or what equipment to buy; so the investor would have *voting rights*. The different types of shares and companies reflect these sorts of considerations, and we look at them next.

Types of share

Ordinary shares: this is the most basic and common form of share, entitling an investor to a share in the profits, a share of the assets in the event of liquidation (after liabilities have been met), and a share in control of the company. This includes the right to vote at general meetings for company directors, among other things. An ordinary share is usually *fully paid*, i.e. the investor has met all the capital requirements to own the share, with no payments deferred or outstanding.

Preference shares: there are several variations but generally, as the name implies, preference shares offer the holder preference in one or more respects over holders of ordinary shares. Usually, preference shareholders have a right to receive a dividend before ordinary shareholders, and rank ahead of ordinary shareholders in the event of a wind-up. Preference shares are safer than ordinary shares, although depending on the specific case they may provide less potential for return and restricted voting rights.

Convertibles: these are corporate bonds paying fixed interest rates initially, with the right to convert into ordinary shares at set prices in the future.

Risk and return

Return from equity investment is made up of the dividends received from a company, plus capital gains (or losses). Bonus issues and share splits complicate things, and those interested in these complexities should buy a good stock market book and liaise with their adviser. Basically, however, the return from dividends is self-evident, and the capital gain is simply the difference between the amount paid for the shares and the amount received when the shares are sold.

Both elements of return hinge on the same factor: a company's ability to make a profit. A company that has no net earnings cannot pay a dividend unless it has built up reserves into which it can dip. Investors will rush for shares in a loss-making company if they are convinced it will make substantial profits in the near future, but a company that fails to make that profit in the future will quickly become unattractive to investors. Its share price is likely to fall, killing off the investor's opportunity to make a capital gain. The key issue, then, when analyzing the risk of a company, is how the various factors affect the quality and degree of certainty of its future earnings.

An important factor that affects *all* companies is where they are placed in the corporate lifecycle. Companies just starting out involve higher risk than those that are long established with regular earnings.

Business ventures start with an idea – whether it is to build the first successful orbital engine, or to discover gold. The next phase is to see whether the idea will work. If so, that idea has to be commercialized – used to make something that people want to buy. This phase is often overlooked, and many brilliant advances in technology fail to find a market. The Coca-Cola company ran into this problem in its abortive campaign to introduce 'new formula Coke'. It might have been technologically better, but consumers preferred the old 'Coke'.

Once a company has produced a saleable product, it must gear up for production on a large scale. At this stage, the company has reached adulthood, but this is not the end of the story. Companies may seek to expand at any stage to enter new fields or geographic markets.

What makes the corporate lifecycle important for investors is that at every stage the company needs new capital, and this may provide an investment opportunity.

The principals of new companies usually finance the early phases out of their savings or borrowings, then seek public funds to commercialize the concept. This is known as venture capital. Certain public and private investment groups, including 3i, Candover Investments and Cinven, the former Coal Board pension scheme, specialize in this area.

The practice is high-risk. A common belief in the industry is that out of ten venture capital starts, you usually get one star, two failures, and seven walking dead. The profits from the one star have to make up for all the others. Most venture capitalists will not consider a project unless it offers a prospective return of at least 50 per cent per annum. The price per share in relation to prospective earnings is very low at this stage. Venture capitalists usually plan to make their profit by selling their shares for a much higher price once the earnings materialize.

One way for investors to spread the risks of investing in individual projects is to invest in a venture capital trust (VCT) run by one or other of half a dozen specialist managers. Investors in VCTs qualify for a number of tax breaks to help offset the inherently higher risks involved. These are discussed in Chapter 7.

The concept of the corporate lifecycle is shown in Figure 5.1. Most companies seek a public listing at the adolescent, or expansion capital, phase. They may join OFEX, the market only in matched bargains, AIM, the 'junior' stock exchange, or go for a full listing on the London Stock Exchange. Here the prospective returns may be less spectacular than earlier on, but are still substantial because earnings potential has not been proven on a large scale. As

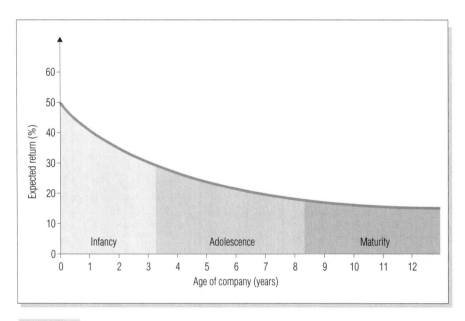

FIGURE 5.1 Investing in the corporate lifecycle

the company matures and income becomes more regular, investors do not require such a high return because the risk is reduced.

Even the most established companies occasionally seek new capital, often through a *rights issue*. In this case, existing shareholders are offered the opportunity to purchase new shares at a favourable price. Investors can take up the offer or not, or sell the right to purchase the new shares (usually offered in a ratio to shares already held). Rights issues enlarge the size of the capital pie so, for practical purposes, shareholders are offered the option to maintain the relative size of their slice in the hope of rising future profits.

The lifecycle factor, however, is only the starting point of risk assessment. Mature companies still have the potential for substantial risk, again dependent on the quality of their earnings. Recall the risk ladder from Chapter 3. A company may depend on a single customer, for example, which may place it in a risky position. One example was the textile manufacturer William Baird which sold more than 25 per cent of its output to Marks and Spencer, which in 1999 summarily cancelled its contracts in an attempt to cut costs.

The investor also has to look at the company's ability consistently to supply that product – no product, no earnings. Some companies may be more vulnerable to industrial action than others. Management quality is also crucial. Even companies with excellent assets producing a good income flow can be destroyed by ill-conceived corporate adventures.

Going up the risk ladder, other factors are industry-specific. Some industries are relatively 'recession proof', the classics being food and alcohol. Others are cyclical, such as commodity-based industries, construction, and capital goods.

Table 5.1 shows the return, and relative risk, of some of the major industry sectors of the UK stock market. One would generally expect those industries that involve higher risk to provide higher returns. However, the timescale and the question of diversifiable versus non-diversifiable risk are important. The index numbers for individual market sectors compiled by the FTSE actuaries show that the returns on different sectors vary greatly. In recent years construction and building materials, conglomerates, engineering, household goods and textiles, personal care and household products, retailing and real estate have performed poorly compared with banks, electronics and electrical engineering, pharmaceuticals, telecommunications, media and technology stocks. Sectors with the lowest returns can also be among the most volatile, along with primary industries such as mining, steel and forest products.

However, these staple industries can provide very useful protection at times of crisis or recession, compared with the more glamorous sectors. As the

TABLE 5.1 Risk and return characteristics of UK stock market indices, January 1986–December 1999

Index	Anual return	Annual standard deviation
Mining	18.0%	28.8%
Oil and Gas	19.3%	21.0%
Chemicals	11.0%	21.8%
Construction and Building Materials	8.9%	24.8%
Forestry and Paper	13.7%	33.0%
Steel and Other Metals	16.6%	33.0%
Aerospace and Defence	10.5%	24.6%
Diversified Industrials	7.7%	21.9%
Electronic and Electrical Equipment	17.7%	23.8%
Engineering and Machinery	12.4%	23.3%
Automobiles	17.1%	27.0%
Household Goods and Textiles	1.1%	24.0%
Beverages	12.1%	20.9%
Food Producers and Processors	11.8%	17.2%
Health	10.4%	18.8%
Packaging	11.0%	24.2%
Personal Care and Household Products	8.8%	23.9%
Pharmaceuticals	21.2%	22.6%
Tobacco	17.3%	25.8%
Distributors	11.5%	22.4%
General Retailers	8.7%	19.7%
Leisure Entertainment and Hotels	13.7%	22.5%
Media and Photography	18.0%	23.0%
Restaurants, Pubs and Breweries	13.3%	18.4%
Support Services	15.0%	20.0%
Transport	13.2%	19.7%
Food and Drug Retailers	10.6%	19.4%
Telecommunication Services	21.7%	21.5%
Electricity*	22.7%	20.6%
Gas Distribution**	17.1%	22.7%
Water***	15.2%	19.8%
Banks	23.3%	24.4%
Insurance	11.0%	22.8%
Life Assurance	21.6%	21.5%
Investment Companies	15.5%	18.4%
Real Estate	8.5%	21.2%
Speciality and Other Financials	17.4%	23.8%
IT Hardware	28.6%	44.8%
Software and CPU Services	23.8%	25.8%
All Share	16.4%	16.7%

Notes
* Calculation since January 1991
** Calculation since January 1987
*** Calculation since January 1990

Source: Barclays Global Investors/ipac

'crashette' of April 2000 demonstrated, glamour stocks are often the ones to suffer most when the market as a whole gets the jitters. This highlights the point that there is no simple relationship between risk and return: the potential contribution of each sector and stock to the risk and return of the total portfolio is what needs to be taken into account.

The stockbroking fraternity has adopted a useful way of measuring the riskiness of an individual stock compared with that of the overall market: the Beta factor. The Beta provides an indication of how prone or resilient a stock is to good or bad news that affects the market generally. Beta labels the riskiness of the overall stock market at 1, and measures individual company riskiness against it. A stock with a Beta of 0.5 is significantly less volatile than the market average, while a stock with a Beta of 1.5 is more volatile. If the overall market rises by 10 per cent, a stock with a Beta of 0.5 can be expected to rise by 5 per cent. But a stock with a Beta of 1.5 could be expected to rise by 15 per cent, and so on.

Beta is an indicator rather than a truly predictive measure, but it can be useful for assessing a portfolio. In general, a portfolio with a concentration of high-Beta stocks is likely to do better in good times but worse in bad times than one dominated by low-Beta stocks.

The riskiness of a company must be reflected in its price. And an assessment of this riskiness must also take into account the diversification benefit of the share: is the company's share price highly or lowly correlated with other share prices? The next section explores the link between risk, return and share price, and ways of analyzing it.

Behind the price

Ultimately, what makes the price of a stock go up or down is the market's perception of changes in its future earnings capability. So it is worth a closer look at what we mean by 'the market'.

As suggested in our discussion of the efficient markets hypothesis, the market is the collection of individual views on what assets are worth. Market perception of future earnings capacity is based on the interpretation of new information and rumour. If a mining company discovers a major deposit, its price will rise as the market perceives that it has a higher future earnings capacity. A company may undergo a major restructuring, such as that undertaken by GEC, an electrical engineering group. It relaunched in 1999 as Marconi, an IT hardware stock, and more than doubled the share value in the process. The same applies for industries and economies. Commodity prices may move on a long trend, or national productivity may develop over time.

Information drives the market. But the problem facing the investor is whether to act on individual bits of information and, if so, which ones. This problem can be largely avoided if the investor chooses a long-term strategy involving buying a diversified portfolio that broadly represents the various wealth-creating sectors of the economy. However, it is still worth understanding the strategies involved in more active approaches.

The best stock market analysts consider each piece of information within a broader framework. To assess quality and value, they look 'behind the price' of a company and the market as a whole to find its underlying strength or weakness. New information can then be scrutinized against these 'fundamentals'. This approach, known as fundamental analysis, is usually divided into two levels: bottom-up analysis, which focuses on the individual company, and top-down analysis, which starts with overall economic trends. We now turn to the main themes in each approach.

Bottom-up analysis

Corporate affairs legislation and stock exchange rules require listed public companies to reveal considerable information about their activities, including financial details. A lot of market information, such as share prices and dividends, is on public record. Analysts scrutinize all of this closely, paying particular attention to ratios – how one statistic relates to another.

Company analysis has two aims. The first is to work out how a company is performing in its own right. Ratio analysis can provide clues to how well a company is managing its debt, using its capital to generate profits, and so on. The second purpose is to work out whether a company's share price accurately reflects its fundamental value. Is it undervalued, overvalued, or valued about right in the market? And how does its value compare with that of another company, or the market as a whole?

Ratio analysis is no substitute for common sense and *knowing* the company, its management and industry. It does, however, provide pointers to what practical questions to ask. Ratios commonly quoted include the following.

Earnings per share (EPS): the EPS provides an indication of corporate profitability by looking at the amount of profit attributable to each ordinary share. It is calculated by taking the company's net operating profit after paying interest and tax, subtracting preference dividends, and dividing it by the number of ordinary shares on issue, and expressing the result in pence. If XYZ plc has 1 million shares, and its earnings were £900 000 last financial year, its EPS is 90p.

Price earnings (P/E) ratio: this is one of the most useful ratios. It shows how much the market will pay for each share in a company in relation to the reported profit attributable to that share. The equation is the current selling price for an ordinary share divided by the earnings per share or EPS.

The figure for EPS is usually based on the last financial year. So, if XYZ plc was trading at 900p when its EPS was 90 pence in the last financial year, its 'historic' P/E ratio would be 10 (900 divided by 90). Most analysts also calculate an EPS based on their forecasts of the economy in the current and future years. The P/E ratio is a key tool used in 'bargain hunting'. All else being equal, a stock with a low P/E ratio would be a bargain, while one with a very high P/E ratio would be overpriced. But because all else is not equal in investment markets, a low P/E company may just be a dog and one with a high P/E an unsustainably rising star destined to fall.

The P/E ratio is most meaningfully used as a pointer to what questions to ask about a company, and for comparison. When the aggregate of P/Es in the stock market is taken into account, it also provides a rough indication of whether the market as a whole is potentially overheated or undervalued. There is no absolute scale and the figures will tend to rise when the economy is growing fast and inflation is low, and fall when the economy is static and inflation is serious. But in recent years a market average P/E of 25 has been historically high, and 15 on the low side. Growth sectors and companies will have higher ratios than slower growing alternatives.

Dividend per share: a company does not necessarily pay out all of its earnings as dividends, so a measure of how much a company pays in dividends per share is handy. The equation is dividend payments to ordinary shareholders divided by the number of ordinary shares.

So, if XYZ plc had decided to pay £100 000 out of last year's profits to ordinary shareholders, it would have a dividend per share of 10 pence (£100 000 divided by 1 million shares).

Dividend yield: the dividend yield expresses how much a company is paying in dividends as a percentage of its current share price. The equation is dividend per share multiplied by 100, and divided by the market price of share. In the XYZ plc example, the dividend yield would be 1.1 per cent (10 pence divided by 900p, converted to a percentage).

Dividend cover: this ratio indicates how many times the company's dividend is 'covered' by the net profit. The equation is tax-paid profits minus preference dividends, divided by the amount of ordinary dividends paid. A higher cover may be a cautious company but it may also be committed to reinvesting profits to accelerate expansion.

In our XYZ plc example, the dividend times covered comes to 9.0 – the post-preferences profit (£900 000) 'covered' the ordinary dividend payout (£100 000) nine times.

Net asset backing (per share): this provides an indication, albeit a fairly conceptual one, of how much value a company has in tangible assets for each ordinary share on issue. The net assets figure – often assessed as ordinary share-holders' funds minus intangible assets – is divided by the number of shares. If XYZ plc had £20 million in assets, its net asset backing per share would be £20, since it has 1 million ordinary shares on issue.

These ratios, in conjunction with other company research, can provide a handy thumbnail profile. However, the investor must be cautious – the following example shows why.

Take two imaginary American chainsaw manufacturing companies, the Texas-based Massacre Machines Inc. and Florida-based Sharktooth Saws Inc., compared in Table 5.2. Assume that both are trading at around $1.20. Massacre has a dividend per share of 12 cents, compared with 5 cents for Sharktooth. Massacre appears more profitable, with an EPS of 15 cents compared with 8 cents for Sharktooth. Also, Massacre's P/E ratio is 8, compared with 15 for Sharktooth. On these figures, Massacre seems the much better investment.

TABLE 5.2 Bottom-up analysis of two chainsaw manufacturers

	Dividend per share	Net asset backing	EPS	P/E ratio
Massacre	12c	$1.25	15c	8
Sharktooth	5c	$2.00	8c	15

However, it is necessary to look at the whole picture, and ask *why* the stocks are trading at the prices they are. The market may in fact be pricing them correctly. Sharktooth's net asset backing per share is $2, compared with $1.25 for Massacre. Sharktooth may, for example, have been engaged on a major programme to produce a revolutionary chainsaw, the Jaws 185. The programme has required a build-up of assets, and the company has channelled profits back into development rather than pay higher dividends. Response to the newly released Jaws 185 has been excellent, and the market expects Sharktooth to make huge profits in coming years. As a result, investors are prepared to pay a much higher P/E ratio.

This demonstrates the point that the ratios reflect *historical* performance. While this is still valuable as a starting base, what really counts is *future* performance. The skill is in looking ahead – and understanding what is going on behind the numbers. This is why most investment analysts focus their dealing recommendations on forecast or projected rather than historical P/E ratios.

To make an investment decision based solely on analyzing numbers would be folly. A fall in the price of a company does not necessarily make it cheap. A rise in yield alone does not make it a better buy. And most importantly, it is a mistake to assume that the market has not considered the full range of information.

Top-down analysis

Whereas company analysis starts at the lowest level and works up, the alternative is to start with the big picture and work down. This involves studying the environment in which the stock market and its industry sectors are likely to operate. Here are some of the major dimensions.

Demand and supply: one of the fundamental tenets of economics is that price is determined by the supply of a good and the demand for it. This principle applies to just about any market. For example, if dozens of new coal mines are opening around the world and thus increasing supply, and the demand for coal is falling because of a switch to nuclear power, the price of coal is likely to fall. This would spell bad news for coal companies. It could, however, be good news for users of coking coal. The same rules apply to other businesses from car factories to local shops and restaurants.

Government policy: a single government decision can have a huge impact on an industry. For example, the UK government's post-war moves to reduce protection of the domestic motor industry led to the massive influx of imports and the eventual demise of almost all the UK-owned companies. However, it is important not to look at a factor like this in isolation. It may be, for instance, that the policy eliminated dead wood, leaving the market open for the leanest, meanest (and foreign-owned) companies to expand.

The appointment of tough new regulators setting progressively harder targets for higher investment and lower prices has had a major impact on the UK's privatized water, electricity and transport companies. Trade union laws, the costs of compliance with government regulations, and progressive reductions in corporation tax have played a big part in raising the profitability and therefore the share prices of UK companies.

Economic or business cycle: as discussed in Chapter 4, the interactions between interest rates, employment, inflation and economic activity are central to investment analysis. A lowering of interest rates, for example, usually encourages economic activity; consumers are more likely to borrow and buy, thus increasing demand for product. Economic growth, as measured by gross domestic product, also has an important link with the stock market. Economic growth is evidence that wealth is increasing, and this means opportunity for investment. *Economic forecasting* – looking at all of these factors, along with productivity, trade balances, world economic trends, and so on – often provides a useful assessment of the future business climate.

Technical analysis: sailing into uncharted waters

Technical analysis is, in the view of the authors, of little value to investors. However, since it attracts a great deal of media attention, any discussion of stock market analysis would be incomplete without a quick look.

The purists among technical analysts believe that everything discussed in this section so far is a distraction to the main game, the charts. They believe that the prices of individual stocks, and the stock market as a whole, can be predicted based on 'support' and 'resistance' levels and patterns in the movement of share prices. They generate graphs, draw lines purporting to show trends, then look for shapes that have particular omens. These omens include descending flags and wedges, island reversals, and head-and-shoulder patterns (particularly ominous). Different chartists use different time frames; some look at days or even hours or minutes, others at decades.

All of the evidence shows that, as a predictive strategy on its own, charting is no more reliable than studying sheep entrails. This is because share prices do not move in consistent patterns but take a 'random walk' based on emerging information. While it is possible to chart the past, the future covers uncharted waters and the investor is sailing blind.

One intriguing study examined the stock recommendations of a chartist over a long period.[2] It found that the chartist basically recommended selling after share prices had gone down for some time, and buying after prices had gone up for some time. After the recommendations were published, stocks with a 'buy' recommendation basically went nowhere – just a slight increase in price in line with the market average. What is more intriguing is that stocks with a 'sell' recommendation did the same: went up slightly. In other words, the investor would have done just as well using a random method to select stocks. The study concluded that there was no 'free lunch' in investment analysis.

Investment strategy

Armed with an overview of stock market mechanics, a knowledge of risk factors, a grasp of the types of analysis, and a healthy distrust for chartists, where does the investor go from here? Sweep the market for undervalued stocks or pick major economic trends? Get the timing right so that, as the stock market saying goes, you hold stocks while they are going up and let everyone else hold them when they are going down? Buy 30 darts and throw them at the share lists?

Before answering these questions, it is worth surveying the latest theories of market behaviour. First is the long-standing 'efficient markets' hypothesis. The theory holds that it is difficult to beat the market because the market is efficient, and the market is efficient because everyone is always trying to beat it. Even more compelling, in its 'weak' form, the hypothesis notes that even if markets are not perfectly efficient, any 'excess' returns are likely to be captured in the form of additional brokerage fees by the relatively small number of brokers or fund managers whose research generates these returns. The efficient markets hypothesis suggests that markets will generally be 'correctly' valued, in that the prices will represent a logical return in relation to risk and other investment options.

One problem with this hypothesis is that it does little to explain the wild swings that are a common feature of markets in recent times. It denies a common phenomenon – extremes of both over-valuation and under-valuation.

Research being undertaken by people such as Mordecai Kurz of Stanford University to analyze investor behaviour sheds some light on these apparent inconsistencies.[3] Kurz's Theory of Rational Beliefs provides a cogent explanation of why investors who are behaving rationally can still cause these extremes. What the theory suggests is that investors can make *correlated mistakes*, in that while they may all be acting individually, they can in combination force markets to overshoot by leaping simultaneously on to the same bandwagon. It is not that these investors are irrational, but that by acting almost simultaneously based on what they think is a rational analysis, the result is a disproportionate buying or selling spree.

A central plank in Kurz's research is the observation that extreme swings away from fair value are more likely when there is much uncertainty about the appropriate model to use to value companies. This occurs at times of great change, such as at the beginning of the new millennium. At a time of epochal change, who is truly confident in valuing internet stocks, shopping centres, telecommunications companies and a raft of others that are being fundamentally affected by sweeping changes in technology?

At such times, investors are more likely to make correlated mistakes, perhaps by paying excessive attention to outdated ideas and playing 'follow the leader'. While it may be rational for an individual to do this, when a herd does it, it causes extreme swings in markets. The more rapid flow of information, and easier and cheaper access to it, makes such correlated mistakes more likely, as does the existence of new, leveraged transnational players such as hedge funds.

Researchers, including Horace Wood Brock's SED group, have used Kurz's theory to help explain particular events when financial markets appeared to deviate from what a traditional economic model would have predicted. SED, however, argues that Kurz's theory is a useful way to enhance the traditional models rather than a replacement for them.

In essence, Kurz's theory means that investors have to be aware that financial markets are volatile not just because fundamentals can change but also because collectively, investors may react to those changes in extreme ways. It also draws even more attention to the fact that the world economy is dynamic rather than static, and that markets are dictated by the balance of investors' beliefs.

Kurz's theory has several implications. It provides a logical structure for looking at a well-known phenomenon: sometimes investment markets do get out of line with their fundamental value. Undervaluations and overvaluations are only absolutely obvious in hindsight. However, Kurz's theory suggests there may be some advantage in trying to identify a 'fair value range', tilting the portfolio when investment markets are perceived to move outside it. Such an approach is discussed more fully in Chapter 9.

More immediately, the Theory of Rational Beliefs is a reminder that the quality of risk in the stock market can vary far more than the efficient markets hypothesis would imply. The bottom line for the investor is to monitor stock market valuations closely, and to beware of distortions. Although this will be imprecise, it will help to keep a portfolio's overall risk level within the desired bounds.

The market portfolio

Despite the limitations, a logical starting point for the private investor is to consider 'buying the market', or constructing the 'efficient market portfolio'. The investor may then consider 'tilting' this portfolio based on information that the investor believes is not already 'priced in'. There is also scope to go further and deliberately engage in specific bets backing the investor's individual judgement.

'Buying the market' involves a fair amount of technical information – among other things forecasting returns, risk and correlations for all the shares in the economy, and working out the optimal mix. But it is possible to come reasonably close to constructing a representative market portfolio without getting bogged down in technicalities.

This need not involve every company, simply a representative sample. As noted in Chapter 3, a selection of about 30 stocks can provide a portfolio that largely reflects the market. The key, though, is to ensure that this portfolio is properly diversified and is an 'unbiased' representation of industry subsectors. Such a portfolio will most likely represent the best trade-off between risk, return and correlation.

Indexing as a strategy

Combined with the difficulty that even professional fund managers have in con-sistently beating the market, portfolio theory has made 'indexing' an increasingly popular strategy. An index portfolio is one that seeks to replicate the portfolio of a market index, such as the FTSE 100 or FTSE All-Share Index (comprising the 800 or so largest listed companies in the UK) or the US S&P 500 Index, comprising the 500 largest listed companies in the US.

Index portfolios can be bought through a great number of index tracker funds, usually with lower management fees than those of actively managed funds. To the extent that they provide access to a broadly diversified portfolio cheaply, index funds can play a valuable role in building a share portfolio and capturing the longer-term growth of the stock market.

However, investors need to be cautious about growing hype that suggests that indexing is a simple panacea. It is not. One potential problem with indexing is that tracker funds themselves underperform the market they are set to track because the index itself ignores the dealing costs and management charges which all managed funds, including index tracker funds, incur. Tracker funds are also obliged to follow the index blindly and ignore all special situations. This can be a serious disadvantage if individual stocks in the index are under- or over-performing the index for cyclical reasons. In some cases the index itself may be unrepresentative because each company's weight in the index depends on its relative size, as measured by market capitalization. This means that even though an index may comprise a number of stocks, its value and hence its fluctuations may be dominated by a handful of large companies. The distortions that this may cause are often worse in smaller markets such as Finland, Sweden, Spain or New Zealand, in each of which one company accounts for more than 25 per cent of the entire market capitalization. In such countries, many companies that in aggregate contribute substantially to wealth creation – such as small and medium-sized businesses, or the health sector – are not well represented in the stock market.

In the UK, the FT index of the top 100 shares did not contain a single IT company until 1999. By definition it excludes 'smaller capital' companies which significantly outperformed large companies after several years of consistent underperformance. Even in the large US market, periods of highly concentrated returns can distort indices, and hence index funds. For example, the biggest 50 companies in the S&P 500 went from comprising 47 per cent of the S&P's value at the start of the decade to 56 per cent by September 1999. Services were also grossly under-represented in the S&P, and the financial and technology sectors were underweighted compared with their relative import-ance to the US economy.

As the index becomes more concentrated, its risk also rises. More broadly diversified portfolios represent better quality risk, with the prospect that any performance penalty would in due course be reversed. So, while index funds can play a useful role, it is unwise to trust blindly in their efficacy. The investor needs to get beneath the surface, understand a fund's construction, assess the quality and value of the underlying index, and look for potential biases that may expose the investor to risks that will not be compensated.

Trying to beat the market portfolio

The market portfolio is, in terms of risk and return, an efficient portfolio. The question, then, is whether it is worth trying to do *better*. It is certainly difficult to do, however, and most managed funds do not consistently beat the market.

The reason goes back to what we identified as the main influence on price movements: information. The efficient markets hypothesis implies that share prices reflect the consensus among share traders about past and expected profits, debt levels, management and so on. As new information becomes available, the share price adjusts to reflect it. The only way to beat the market, therefore, is to get the information before everyone else. The difficulty of doing so consistently is self-evident. Stock exchange rules require companies to publish all sensitive information about trading conditions, profits and possible takeovers at the earliest possible moment. The latest opinions and forecasts by analysts employed by stockbroking firms also quickly spread throughout the market, giving even their clients little time to act on the information. Even rumours and speculative rushes to buy or sell very quickly become common knowledge.

This is why the investment analysis industry exists. With enough expertise and facilities to scour the market, undervalued stocks can be found, especially among smaller companies and in emerging markets. The problem is that to do so takes money: analysts' salaries, computers, and so on. Some trusts have smart managers with excellent research facilities that enable them to get a slight edge over the competition. But the *information cost* of getting this edge reaches a point at which additional effort is no longer justified. The point at which the marginal utility of acquiring additional data is neutralized provides an equilibrium of sorts – and the benefit to the investor is largely nullified.

This leads to a further important point from the efficient markets hypothesis. Some funds may achieve a higher return than the market average over a period but, on a *risk-adjusted* basis, may be no better off. While it is hard to beat the market, it is easy to take on more risk by weighting the portfolio towards high-Beta stocks. Such portfolios will indeed do better when the market is rising, but when it falls, the results can be alarming. One study found:

> During the couple of years up to October 1987, some fund managers achieved extremely high returns, but with the severe downturn in the share market in October 1987 it was these same managers who were hardest hit. The conservative managers, those who had invested in low-risk portfolios, were less severely affected by the share market downturn.[4]

Although a logical approach is to start with a market-based portfolio, it is still worth looking at individual stocks with the techniques discussed in this chapter. This is because, while a portfolio of about 30 stocks can eliminate most of the diversifiable risk, those 30 stocks still have to represent the broad market. So an investor may buy into a company not because it seems undervalued, but because its risk and return characteristics fit in well with the investor's diversification strategy.

Tilting, timing and the market portfolio

With a market portfolio as the base, the investor may be able to 'tilt' the portfolio to 'beat the market' for various reasons. We look at tilts in more detail in Chapter 8, but here we look at the tilt based on information.

An investor who believes that he or she has some special information or insight that is not reflected in share prices can act on it by tilting the portfolio in that direction. For example, suppose a professor of international relations happened to be writing a paper on Iraqi foreign policy and came to a view, based on interviews and other information not widely available, that a major conflict in the Middle East was imminent. The professor might tilt towards oil stocks; if the existing portfolio contained 5 per cent oil stocks, this might be tilted to 10 per cent.

Finally, market timing is also important in 'beating the market'. It is very difficult to get the timing right consistently, for the same reasons that it is hard to pick undervalued stocks. At any point in time, the market has already largely factored in the body of opinion on whether it is a good time to buy or sell. It is possible, however, to use indicators such as P/E ratios to get a feel for the 'temperament' of the market at any one time. This may provide some guide as to whether to get in or out. In Chapter 9, we discuss such approaches in relation to shifting a portfolio among the asset classes.

The bottom line is that the stock market, in the short term, is relatively risky as asset classes go, and very hard to predict. Any realistic equity investment strategy must accept that there will be periods – sometimes extended – in which the value of a portfolio will decline. A strategy based on sound principles, however, will help to ensure that the portfolio does well when the market picks up and, over the long term, provides a good return.

International dimensions

The quest for a 'market portfolio' and effective diversification need not stop at national borders. Conceptually, the most effectively diversified portfolio would be the 'world market portfolio', incorporating stocks from around the world. The UK accounts for only 9.6 per cent of the market capitalization of the main markets that make up the global investment scene. Table 5.3 shows the size and turnover of some of the other developed markets.

TABLE 5.3 Size indicators of UK and select overseas share markets, December 1998

Country	Total market capital £ billion	Annual turnover £ billion	No. of companies	Market value as % of GDP
United Kingdom	576	712	2921	200.0
Australia	198	94	1162	83.5
New Zealand	20	12	279	47.8
Japan	1498	518	1898	60.0
United States (NYSE)	4009	na	3114	138.5
Germany	661	1957	3525	40.0

Source: London Stock Exchange and Frankfurt Stock Exchange, Australian Stock Exchange, New Zealand Stock Exchange, Tokyo Stock Exchange, New York Stock Exchange.

As a matter of interest, the table includes a comparison of how each market's capitalization relates to the total size of goods and services produced: gross domestic product (GDP). This ratio very roughly indicates how much of each national economy is in the hands of listed corporations.

Investment funds have simplified the logistics of investing in foreign markets considerably. A range of 'country funds', specializing in individual national stock markets, and regional funds, are available. In addition, some of the truly international equity funds manage fair approximations of a world market portfolio by weighting country distributions against the capitalizations of major international markets.

As discussed in Chapter 3, investing in other countries can offload some of the diversifiable risk in the investor's own economy. Some economies are so fundamentally different from those of the UK and Europe that they have low correlations and provide excellent diversification benefit.

Traditionally, overseas investment was concentrated in the main markets, such as the United States, Japan and Europe. In recent years, the opportunity has arisen to become a little more adventurous. The *Financial Times* lists 56 stock markets around the globe, many of them emerging markets in the developing world. Even China is working to redevelop equity markets, although it remains hesitant about allowing in foreign investment unchecked, and foreign and domestic investors are allocated separate classes of shares.

The smaller and more obscure markets present particular challenges for the investor, such as getting information. Regulations governing foreign investors and taxation are complex at best, prohibitive at worst. Quite often, the capital of major companies is so tightly held by a small number of domestic investors that it is hard for foreign investors to get a significant stake. Also, as discussed in earlier chapters, many of the smaller markets are just plain risky, displaying wild and often inexplicable gyrations.

With these considerations in mind, a logical approach is to adopt a strategy for international share investment similar to that employed for the domestic market: start with a broadly diversified portfolio as the base. Under such a strategy, most investments should be concentrated in the large established markets of the developed world. Beyond this base, the investor might wish to tilt towards some of the emerging markets, or international smaller companies, hoping to capture additional returns while accepting that these sectors will involve much more short-term volatility.

Derivative instruments

Equity markets now offer a wide range of derivative products to private investors, mostly through exchange-traded instruments. Some, such as speculation on share index futures, are extremely risky, and many fortunes have been won or lost overnight. Others, such as options, can be employed in such a way that exposure is limited. Some applications can represent genuine hedging, although these are usually of more relevance to institutional investors. As with all derivatives, these products can become complex, and investors would be wise to seek independent professional advice before using them.

The range of equity-based derivatives expands continually, but here is an overview of the main types.

Options: as discussed in Chapter 4, options are some of the most well-established forms of derivatives. They are available on specific individual shares, and on a share price index. Options provide speculators with a means of making a bet, where the potential loss is limited by paying a premium. A speculator who thinks that the price of a particular stock is going to fall, but is nervous about the open-ended exposure that a futures contract would involve, might pay a premium for an option to sell at a set price in the future. If the bet works and the stock falls, the speculator can purchase shares on the physical market and exercise the option to sell those shares at the higher pre-agreed strike price. If the bet fails and the stock price does not fall, the speculator lets the option lapse and loses only the premium.

As with other equity-based derivatives, options can also be used in combination with physical trading. Say an investor intended to sell a parcel of XYZ plc shares in a year's time. If the investor was nervous about the market, one possibility would be to take out an option to sell, perhaps at the current price, in a year. If the stock falls, the investor exercises the option, preventing a substantial loss. If the stock rises, the investor allows the option to lapse, and the only cost for this 'insurance policy' is the premium.

Warrants: these are essentially long-dated options issued by a third party, usually a large investment house or bank. The purchaser of the warrant pays a premium for the right to buy a certain number of shares at a point in the future. Warrants themselves are tradable, creating a big secondary market. The arrangement offers the warrant holder a geared exposure to the stock concerned. For the writer of the warrant, it offers a means of generating income via premiums, and the writer can decide whether to accept the risk or cover it by purchasing physical shares or by other means.

Share price index futures: most major financial markets in the world have some form of futures and options markets based on share price indices, especially the FTSE 100 index, the S&P 500 share index, the Nikkei 225, the CAC 40 in France, and the DAX in Germany. The principle is much the same as that for commodity futures. Traders take out contracts based on a stock market index. For example, on Liffe the contract specification, at the time of writing, was £10 for each point of the FTSE 100 index, or £63 000 with the index at 6300. The American style and European style markets each have up to six monthly contracts open at any one time and contracts are settled in cash by calculating the difference between the index price entered into in the contract, and the actual index value on the settlement day.

There is also a FTSE 100 index options market based on eight different projected index levels straddling the current level of the index itself, and five different time frames giving scope for a wide range of strategies from bullish to bearish over the short to medium term.

A large portion of share index trading is purely speculative, with considerable day trading in which speculators get out of their positions by the end of each day. Effectively, they are betting against each other as to whether the market is going up or down, and doing so with highly leveraged positions.

However, there are also a number of options for hedging, or at least risk management. For example, an investment fund might decide that a particular section of the stock market – say banks – represents particularly good value. However, the fund manager might feel that the overall stock market was a bit overheated, and not be too sure whether or when a correction might occur. The manager essentially wants to capture the extra potential of the banks, while limiting overall exposure to market risk. A solution may be to put, say, £10 million into bank shares, and take out a contract to sell £5 million worth of share index futures in a few months' time.

If the market took a dive, the fund would suffer losses on the bank shares in line with the overall decline, but that loss would be largely offset by a profit on the futures contract. If the market rose, the fund would lose on the futures contract, but if the manager's prediction is right, the bank shares should benefit disproportionately from the general upturn. The point is that if the fund's primary premise is correct – that bank shares will do better than the overall market – the fund will reap this benefit either way. The futures contract separates and neutralizes market-wide risk, and exploits the industry-specific element to maximum effect.

Individual share futures: the London Stock Exchange, at the time of writing, offered contracts on the shares of 11 companies, essentially large public corporations with well-traded share registers. Typically, they involve a contract for a parcel of 1000 shares. These operate much like index futures, except that most of them involve physical delivery, so that they serve as a way of buying or selling actual parcels of shares in the future. These are attractive for speculators, especially as a means of short-selling – betting that prices of a stock are going to fall, and the actual shares can be bought more cheaply when the time comes to deliver on the futures contract.

Individual share futures can also offer avenues for sophisticated investment strategies that combine physical and futures trading. Take an investor, for example, who had a large parcel of Barclays Bank shares. The investor thought that their long-term prospects were good but expected a short-term hiccup which would see the price fall for three months before bouncing back. One possibility would be to sell the shares, put the money into cash, and buy the shares back three months later. An alternative, which could potentially involve fewer transaction costs and tax, would be to take out a contract for settlement in three months' time to sell an equivalent number of shares on the futures exchange. If the expectation proved correct, the futures contract would generate a profit on the downturn, while maintaining the physical portfolio. If the bet was wrong and the price of Barclays Bank shares went up in the three months to settlement, the investor would lose out but would have the option of using the physical share parcel to fulfil the futures contract.

Spread betting

This is not strictly a derivative, but is becoming increasingly popular, especially in the fields of finance, sport and politics. Bookmakers such as the IG Index, Ladbrokes and Coral quote a range or spread of possible results on either side of the most likely outcome, and invite 'clients' to bet whether for example the FTSE 100 share index will close above or below the spread on the due date. If the actual result is within the spread, all bets are lost. If it is outside the spread, the wider the margin the larger the wins for successful gamblers and the bigger the losses incurred by unsuccessful ones. This makes spread betting potentially very risky, but profits are tax-free.

Tax considerations

More than for any other asset class, a sound understanding of how returns are taxed is valuable to getting the best out of equities. The two elements of return from shares – capital gain on the share price, and income from dividends – are taxed in different ways. And a number of idiosyncrasies can significantly affect after-tax gains. The operation of the tax system in the UK was covered in Chapter 2.

The key points to emphasize with shares are that dividends to all intents and purposes do not attract further tax liability, except in the case of investors in the 40 per cent tax bracket who are liable to pay tax at the rate of 25 per cent on the dividend received.

Capital gains are taxed only on realization and gains of up to £7200 a year (in 2000–01) can be taken tax-free. This, together with the tapering benefits described in Chapter 2, the fact that shares listed on AIM held for four years are taxed only at 10 per cent, and the ability to sell shares in small parcels, means that the average investor is unlikely to be troubled significantly by capital gains tax on their stock market investments.

All UK resident investors aged 18 and above can also invest up to £5000 a year in shares through individual savings accounts, holding either shares in individual companies, investment trusts or unit trusts, which are described more fully in Chapter 7. Funds held in an ISA are exempt from income tax and capital gains tax.

Readers considering significant share investment should however seek further current information and professional advice on tax strategy.

The tax advantages associated with share investment, plus the fact that in the long run they offer the best returns of all the asset classes, mean that most strategic investors with a long time frame will want to make them a significant part of their portfolio. Shrewd investors will then use the approaches outlined in this chapter to contain the risks involved in this asset class through effective diversification. The more adventurous in this group will also take some limited tilts because, at the end of the day, stock market investment is also a good way of keeping track of what is going on in politics and the economy and is, consequently, a lot of fun.

Notes

1   Quoted in Richardson, N. (1991) 'Sure thing: the real odds in gambling', *Weekend Australian*, 3–4 August, p. 9.

2   Ball, Ray, Brown, Philip and Finn, Frank J. (1989) 'Published investment recommendations and share prices: are there free lunches in security analysis?', in *Share Markets and Portfolio Theory*, ed. Ray Ball, Philip Brown, Frank J. Finn and R.R. Officer, University of Queensland Press, Brisbane, pp. 434–41.

3   A useful discussion about the Theory of Rational Beliefs can be found in *Strategic Economic Decisions*, February 1997.

4   Officer and Finn (*see* note 2), p. 8.

CHAPTER 6

Property: juggling bricks and mortar

Summary

■ Property comprises half the world's wealth, and most investors see it as tangible and osten-sibly secure. But in fact, as many fortunes may have been lost in property as in any other investment market.

■ The unique nature of individual properties provides more opportunity for skilful investors with time on their hands to do well through serious market research.

■ Property provides space to do things. Since this covers different activities, the residential, retail, industrial and office markets are quite distinct.

■ Property returns tend to lag economic changes, and there are imperfections in the market. This provides more potential for astute investors to benefit from careful selection and timing.

■ More than 100 companies listed on the London Stock Exchange specialize in house building, construction or in the management, development and trading of commercial property.

■ For investors in the UK, direct investment in property has the advantage that interest paid on money borrowed to buy and maintain property can be deducted from rental income in calcu-lating taxable profits. Profits on the investor's own home are exempt from capital gains tax.

■ Property would normally be an important part of the portfolio of an investor seeking long-term growth above inflation.

Introduction: neighbourhood watch

There are two distinct property markets in the UK: the residential property market which forms such an enduring topic of discussion at all those middle-class dinner parties in the heartlands of New Labour; and the commercial property market which deals in shops, offices and factories needed to keep the country's economy housed.

The British public's love affair with bricks and mortar is one of the most enduring expressions of social change since the Second World War. In 1945 only about 30 per cent of all householders owned their home or were in the process of buying it on a mortgage. After the Second World War successive governments were quick to see the political advantages of encouraging home ownership. Tax on residential property was abolished in 1963 and the introduction of tax relief on mortgage interest made loans for home-owners the cheapest form of long-term credit available. Although mortgage rates briefly rose to 15 per cent in the mid-1970s, after allowing for inflation until a decade ago the real cost of housing finance was negligible.

Around 70 per cent of all housing is now owner-occupied and a growing number of individuals are now buying properties for investment. The term landlord, for so long a dirty word in the English vocabulary is becoming respectable again.

One of the enduring attractions of investing in residential property is the chance to back one's instinct and knowledge against the market. Each property is unique, and the opportunity always exists to beat the experts and buy into a growth area. While areas such as London's Belgravia and Mayfair have 'always' been fashionable and pricey, other areas have also emerged as winners in recent years. Forty years ago, Islington was a run-down inner-London suburb, managed by a left-leaning council determined to prevent the gentrification that might attract Conservative voters. Gradually, however, the attractions of good architecture and easy access to the City began a process that has turned the district into a citadel of New Labour.

Notting Hill is another example. Now famous and fashionable, just 40 years ago it was a depressed area of over-crowded and neglected four- and five-storey Victorian houses with shared bathroom and toilet facilities. The area was notorious for the activities of Peter Rachman, the racketeering slum landlord who bought properties cheaply and evicted tenants illegally through campaigns of intimidation. The area also attracted large numbers of immigrants from the West Indies who were unable to find rented accommodation elsewhere in

London. In the 1950s it was the scene of unsavoury race riots. But the establishment of the now world-famous annual Notting Hill carnival parade in 1964 and the popularity of the equally famous antiques market in the Portobello Road have given it a cosmopolitan appeal. That, together with its proximity to the West End of London and its pleasing architecture, attracted private buyers who gentrified the area, forcing prices up. One street of Georgian houses, Elgin Crescent, has the distinction of seeing average prices increase almost 300 fold between 1960 and 2000.

The commercial property market has its own story of rags and riches. The techniques of building houses have changed relatively little over the past century. The great majority of houses are still built of brick with slate roofs, and many homes more than 100 years old are among the most expensive properties in the country. By contrast, the useful life of commercial property is much shorter. Most of the High Street shop premises which dominated retail trade half a century ago are now too small and they are no longer attractive as consumers have moved to the suburbs, public transport is no longer adequate, and the supply of parking space is limited. The most desirable locations are now shopping malls and retail parks in out-of-town locations served by motorways and equipped with extensive parking facilities allowing families to drive and park, visit a variety of stores, and take their purchases home with them.

Factories have also changed out of all recognition. Most buildings designed for traditional industries are no longer suitable for the making of today's high-value goods. The future of the traditional office is also under threat from changes in employment patterns. The average useful life of commercial property will almost certainly continue to decline. The cost of acquiring land and developing new sites has risen steadily but the returns both from rental incomes and capital values have hardly kept pace with inflation.

With hindsight, these developments appear obvious, but there is nothing 'easy' about property investment. While there is no end of information about listed public companies, such a wealth of analysis is not available for the house down the road. Paradoxically, however, this is the key to the attraction of property. The market is less efficient than other asset classes – public information is more thinly spread and subject to less analysis – and this opens up greater opportunities for adding value through personal research.

Property prices are however more predictable and less volatile than share prices. Property has further attractions in terms of tax treatment, especially for medium-term investment. Finally, property is an invaluable diversifier, in part because of its tendency to lag after asset classes in the business cycle. On balance, some exposure to property is a useful part of any portfolio.

Market overview and concepts

Property is the market for space to do things, whether it is raising a family, raising hops, or raising heels at a disco. And all human activity requires space, which is why property accounts for an estimated half of the world's wealth.[1]

In biblical history, the first residential tenancy, and the first eviction of tenants for disobeying a landlord's instructions, took place in the Garden of Eden. However, it is only in relatively recent times that the investor has had the opportunity to gain a stake in all forms of real estate. In the past, property investment meant buying a flat, a house or perhaps a small block of flats. It meant total ownership. In the past three decades, however, the process of securitization has come to the market. It is now possible to buy an interest, in association with other investors, through vehicles such as property bonds, time-share arrangements, property companies, and in some countries even property futures. Securitization means that all types of property, ranging from student lodgings to five-star hotels, are potential investment options in addition to shares in many quoted real estate companies and house builders.

Whether or not the investor chooses the securitized route into property investment, it is important to understand the dynamics of the market. This can provide either the basis for direct investment or the means for assessing property securities.

The property market process

While the property market is huge, all aspects revolve around the concept of providing space to do things. The demand for space creates a complex market with a number of players and several stages of added value. Consider the city office block. The completed building provides space for various service industries to run their businesses. The rent provides an incentive to own the building, which in turn creates a demand for someone to build it. The building will require a financier, builders and land. Also involved, in all likelihood, are agents who act as middlemen, and professional managers who run the building for the owner.

For conceptual purposes, we can divide up the market as follows.

- *Site acquisition:* a site is purchased for a particular purpose. Participants who simply buy the site and sell it without making improvements may be described as *speculators*, although they may consolidate more than one property into a site big enough for a particular purpose.

- *Pre-development:* there is often an intermediate phase in which the raw site is taken to the point where it is ready for development. This may involve physical preparation (such as levelling land and providing water and electricity mains), or taking it through legal channels (such as development and building approval, subdivision or rezoning). Participants in this process may be called *land developers.*

- *Development:* the site is turned into the finished product for residential, commercial or other use. The people or businesses that take on the risk – buying the site and paying for the construction – are known as *developers.* A developer will usually hire a building contractor (or, in a slight variation, a project manager) to organize construction. The contractor, in turn, will hire subcontractors to do the work.

- *Ownership:* developers usually get a project to the point where it can be occupied, then sell it and move on. During the development phase, the entity that buys the completed project is known as the *end owner*.

- *Rental:* the owner need not occupy a property, and may instead lease it out. The entity that occupies the space and pays rent for the privilege is the *tenant*. In some cases, one entity will pay the owner a fee in return for a long-term head lease over a property and rent out space to one or more tenants in a sublease arrangement.

As this section shows, the property market is dynamic, and there are several avenues for involvement: as a speculator, land developer, owner, financier, builder, manager, and so on. The creation of new investment vehicles means that the private investor can, indirectly, be any one of these. It is important to distinguish one from another because they have different risk/return characteristics.

The different types of property, and the ways into them, are discussed next.

Types of investment

There are three dimensions to look at when considering property: the different market functions (discussed in the previous section), the sort of property, and the investment vehicle. Here we discuss the major asset class subsectors (or the main categories of property), then look at the principal investment structures.

Market subsectors

The UK property market can be subdivided into six main categories:

- *residential* (space to live): flats and houses, second homes, and holiday homes;

- *office* (space to work and do business): property mostly associated with town centres, ranging from shop-front offices to skyscrapers;

- *retail* (space to sell things): all types of retail outlets, from restaurants and corner shops to huge shopping centres such as Lakeside in Essex and Blue Water in Kent;

- *industrial* (space to make and move things): usually property that involves noise and sweat, such as factories, warehouses, ports, and so on;

- *rural* (space to grow things): land and fixed capital for every agricultural activity, from grazing to horticulture;

- *leisure and tourism* (space to have fun): facilities such as golf courses, hotels and theme parks.

There are also other types of property that do not fit neatly into these categories, such as retirement villages, private hospitals and care homes for the elderly, and high-tech business parks. The point of classifying property is that each subsector can be identified with a particular aspect of the economy. Office, retail and industrial property is often categorized as commercial property, to distinguish it from residential property.

Investment vehicles

There are a number of different ways to invest in property.

- *Direct investment:* this is the most familiar investment avenue. It involves buying a whole property or developing a site with one's own funds.

Investors can also form a partnership, a joint investment vehicle in which two or more people pool funds to get a stake in property that may otherwise be outside their reach.

- *Time share:* most holidaymakers are only too familiar with the 'time share' concept, often promoted by persistent kids who use promises of free sangria to lure holidaymakers into signing up for a stake in a tacky development in Tenerife. This has become a big international business. Investors who purchase a time-share unit are entitled to use the apartment for a particular week every year, but management charges may rise steadily and properties can be hard to resell.

- *Property bonds and trusts:* the key function of property bonds and trusts, as with all unit trusts, is to pool funds from a large number of investors to purchase major assets. Relatively few property unit trusts have been established in the UK and most are available only for pension funds and professional investors, including stockbrokers investing funds for clients. At the time of writing, only three trusts were available to private investors. A number of insurance companies offer property bonds, which invest direct in property assets, lock in relatively high yields and also offer the prospect of capital gains, but these are regarded as long-term investments and are subject to penalties for early surrender. The structure and operation of managed investments is discussed in detail in Chapter 7.

- *House-building companies:* around 170 000 homes are built each year in the UK, mostly by specialized house builders, the largest of which are listed on the stock exchange. They include Barratt Developments, Berkeley, Bovis, Bryant, Tarmac, Taylor Woodrow, Wilson Bowden and Wilson Connolly. They undertake the whole development process, from buying land that may or may not already have outline planning permission. Most firms try to maintain a land bank containing enough sites to keep them busy for three to four years. Gaining full-scale planning permission can take years, depending on local feeling and the attitude of the government, which has final say on the release of land in the Green Belts. Lead times tend to be long and house building is a highly cyclical business, making the bulk of its profits in the later stages of the economic cycle. In the 1990s this sector underperformed the UK stock market as a whole.

- *Property companies:* around 80 quoted companies specialize in commercial property, including British Land, Land Securities, Canary Wharf, and

Slough Estates. Some are property owners, some builders and developers, some property managers, and others combine several of these functions. Investors can buy shares in these companies just like other companies quoted on the stock market, although they consistently underperformed most other market sectors throughout the 1990s. An increasing number of investment managers now own and operate their own commercial property portfolios, and at the start of the new millennium a number of leading experts believed that many property companies faced the prospect of being taken over and broken up if their financial performance did not improve.

Risk and return

The property market has several unique features that set it apart from other asset classes. There is no single marketplace for property and no central pricing system to record current values. Each property is unique and its value depends heavily on what an individual buyer is willing to pay. Compared with markets for fixed-interest securities and equities, the costs of trading property can also be significantly higher. Direct investment in property also incurs maintenance costs, which other assets do not. On the other hand, interest paid on borrowed money can be offset against profits. For all these reasons, risk and return for property has to be analyzed differently from other asset classes.

Income from property usually takes the form of rent. However, running a portfolio of rental properties involves regular inputs and outputs, plus labour and management, and constitutes a business. Outgoings can cover a number of factors, depending on the property and its stage of development. At the simplest level, this means insurance, upkeep repairs, and any management fees. In a geared investment, it also includes interest payments. For a developer, outgoings include the costs of development such as paying for builders, materials and other inputs. In intermediate developments, such as refurbishment, the refit costs are outgoings.

It follows that there are two key elements of risk in property. One is the usual risk, faced by all asset classes, that the expected capital gain and income may not materialize. The second is the risk that outgoings will exceed expectations.

In a similar fashion to the corporate lifecycle, the stage of development is an important factor in assessing property risk. The earlier on in the process, the more uncertain the outcome – the ability to forecast net return is reduced.

To understand this concept, we take a couple of examples. At one end of the spectrum is the passive investor who buys a completed project with an established income stream. For the small investor, this could be a three-year-old rental flat in an established suburb; for the institutional investor, it could be a three-year-old office building in the City. Costs and income are relatively easy to measure.

Property development, on the other hand, is a more speculative business. The developer has to make assumptions about both the costs and the future total return on the development. For a large-scale developer, it might mean constructing an office building without an end purchaser or guaranteed tenant. The rental capacity is untested, and the value of the finished asset is uncertain. Between project commencement and completion, the property market may change for better or worse. And then there is the uncertainty of costs. The site may prove more difficult than first thought; the cost of building materials may rise; labour problems may occur.

Anecdotal evidence lends weight to the view that property development is risky. In 1975, the property developer William Stern went bankrupt with what was then the largest ever personal debt: more than £100 million. In the late 1980s, a string of high-flying property companies – some of them household names – went into receivership. Clearly, bricks and mortar – and especially glass and concrete – can be risky.

Changing technology, and in particular the impact of the information technology revolution, is also creating an unprecedented degree of uncertainty for property developers. They are faced with the task of designing and building properties that will still have a commercial value in, say, 40 years' time. By 2040, however, information technology will almost certainly have changed the ways and the places in which people live, work and do their shopping. This uncertainty has led to a growing reluctance among tenants to sign long leases committing them to occupy property for more than 15 years.

Another example of the risks of property – particularly in the lead-lag time between investment and completion – can be seen in the great golf course rout. The 1980s saw a rush to build golf courses in South-East England to take advantage of the massive membership and green fees that City traders and high-flying foreign bankers were willing to pay. Almost inevitably, the new courses came on stream just as the recession struck, fashions changed, and the next generation of high-fliers found themselves too busy for golf. Completed courses went into receivership and a number of landowners found they had missed the boat. The value of their land had fallen by 50 per cent or more.

There is one more important aspect of risk and return in the property market. The commercial property market depends on regular valuations conducted by professional valuers. When it comes to profits, what counts is the result, not the valuation, and the valuation system has tended to mask the true volatility of property. In the house price boom of the late 1980s, however, valuers regularly approved high valuations, confident that rising prices would quickly make their estimates look conservative. In the slump of the early 1990s, many valuers sharply reduced valuations to well below the price at which properties changed hands.

If an investor owns bonds or shares, the 'price' is based on actual sales of identical shares or bonds. In property, each building is unique; until it is sold, there is no proof of its value. For all these reasons, measuring risk and return for direct investment in property is problematic. While a few rough indicators are available, they are best looked at in the context of a discussion of overall trends.

Recent trends: residential property

The residential property market includes new homes and the much larger market in existing properties, of which 1.0–1.5 million change hands each year. The price of residential property is driven largely by the demand for home ownership. The market in housing to let is still relatively small. But these markets do share some common features: residential property can be equally suitable for owner-occupation and investment, and all property needs to be well maintained to maximize its value.

House prices do fluctuate but over the second half of the 20th century they proved much less volatile than equities, and until the last decade average property prices matched share prices, and at times outperformed them. From the late 1950s the post-war boom in house building began to slow down. Demand continued to accelerate, house prices began to rise faster than the rate of inflation, and buyers were able to chalk up substantial profits using borrowed money. Figure 6.1 shows that prices rose in all but four of the last 40 years of the 20th century and exceeded inflation in 27 of those years.

Between 1960 and 2000, retail prices in the UK rose tenfold, while the average price of residential property rose from £2300 to almost £100 000, roughly quadrupling in real terms. Average price increases accelerated to a peak of more than 30 per cent a year in 1972–73, and more than 20 per cent in 1978–79 and again in 1988–89. In between peaks, price increases slowed sharply and fell in real terms. But nominal prices continued to rise each year from 1957 to 1990, in the high inflation climate.

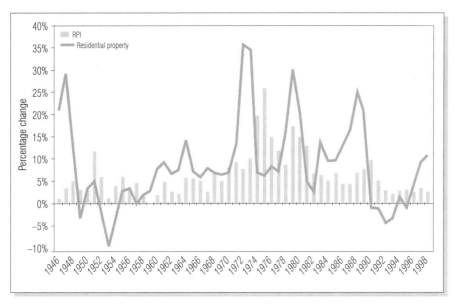

Source: Barclays Global Investors

FIGURE 6.1 UK residential property prices versus RPI, 1946–99

Over the last decade of the century property prices failed to keep pace with share prices and between 1991 and 1995 average prices actually fell, as a result of the recession combined with a drop in the level of inflation. More than 1 million recent buyers found themselves trapped by negative equity, unable even to sell because their homes were worth less than their mortgage debts. As the economy recovered in the second half of the decade, however, prices surged again, carrying the real value of residential property to new peaks. The biggest rises were concentrated in London and South-East England, as well as big cities such as Glasgow, Edinburgh, Manchester and Birmingham. Incomes were rising fastest in these places, and restrictions on building new properties led to shortages in supply.

Property prices in the old industrial cities in the North of England and in isolated rural communities have generally risen more slowly and from a lower base. In some of the most deprived urban areas in the North of England, the market for older, unimproved terraced homes has collapsed, and properties can change hands for nominal sums. But these are exceptions to the general trend.

The reasons for the continuing rise in UK property prices are the subject of earnest debate at those suburban dinner parties, in government-run focus groups, and in the Treasury and the Bank of England. However, the property market is like any other: prices are determined by supply and demand. Although the population is no longer growing rapidly, demand for housing has been inflated by demographic changes, particularly the high divorce rate, the increasing numbers of old people living alone, and by the desire of young adults for a place of their own.

But rising living standards, relatively low interest rates, and government efforts to encourage home ownership through tax incentives have made the biggest contribution. Home owners were able to offset interest on mortgage loans against income tax and, although this concession was diluted and finally phased out in April 2000, capital gains on a taxpayer's main residence remain exempt from tax.

Property prices are also affected by planning controls, which have led to supply shortages in and around some large cities, particularly London, and in much of southern England. This has led to a widening gap between prices in the North and the South, a symptom of a divide that splits society and makes overall management of the economy more difficult.

Largely because of measures to provide tenants with security of tenure and rent controls, which were maintained after the war, the market in privately-owned residential property to rent fell steadily from almost 50 per cent of the housing stock in 1945 to a low of around 10 per cent in 1988, when a new form of shorthold tenancy was introduced. It allows landlords of properties which become vacant to offer leases as short as six months and to raise rents whenever new agreements were signed. This has led to a modest recovery in the market for residential property to let.

Because the rental market is still small and the basic assets are easily interchangeable, the prices of similar owner-occupied and rented properties are unlikely to differ greatly. Rents however change more slowly than prices. When the property market booms, rental yields fall. When the property market is sluggish, buyers become less confident and demand for rented accommodation tends to rise, allowing rental yields to rise.

During the property boom at the end of the 1990s for example the gross yield on unfurnished properties fell within two years from around 12 per cent to 9 per cent outside London and even lower in the capital. After allowing for maintenance and borrowing costs net returns on rented property were probably down to an average of around 5 per cent in London and 7 per cent elsewhere. Because properties vary so much however, averages are often an imperfect guide to would-be investors.

Recent trends: commercial property

The commercial property market includes all other kinds of property, such as shops, offices, factories, farms and leisure facilities. An increasing share of the market is owned by institutional investors, insurance companies, pension funds, and is managed by in-house management teams or farmed out to specialist management companies and investment banks. There are also about 100 listed property companies, plus hundreds of smaller private companies and businesses. The sector consists of three distinct activities: property development, management, and investment.

Developers acquire sites and secure the appropriate planning permission. They then arrange finance, engage subcontractors, and develop properties for sale or to let, preferably to tenants who will sign a lease even before building begins. Leases provide the developer with a guaranteed flow of revenue, which enhances the value of the completed building. Developers usually seek to lease for a minimum of 15 years and preferably 25 years with upward-only rent reviews at regular intervals, usually every five years. Property managers acquire freehold property subject to leases and manage it in the hope of negotiating increased rentals when they come up for review, with the possibility then of selling on at a profit and reinvesting the proceeds.

Most of the smaller property companies operate either as developers, managers or investors, buying and selling developments for their asset value and future rental flows. The larger companies usually operate across the board, developing sites, building up rental income, and also trading sites in the hope of improving their portfolio.

In the past, most industrial and commercial companies of a reasonable size wanted to own their premises. As service industries developed and capital became scarcer, however, ownership and occupation of property often became divorced. Companies found that capital could be better spent on core business strategies, and many premises have been sold to professional investors and leased back. Meanwhile, insurance companies and pension funds found that property could be a useful asset class to have in their portfolios, balancing reductions in income elsewhere at the bottom of the economic cycle and providing a regular return plus the benefits of periodic rent reviews. Until recently, many insurance companies and pension funds would hold around 20 per cent of their assets in commercial property.

Property portfolios are revalued at regular intervals, in some cases annually, and the return on the investment is expressed as a total return, which is the sum of the annual rental income plus a notional figure for the increased capital value of the property. The capital value of a property is usually expressed as a multiple of its annual rental income, and this multiple will tend to rise as the time for a rent review approaches. But the capital value is also a reflection of the value of the annual rental income in relation to other assets such as gilt-edged stocks. So if the yield on gilts falls and the value of the gilt rises, the value of the fixed stream of income from a commercial property will also tend to rise.

The property market is, however, more volatile than the market in gilt-edged stocks. A survey of the annual returns on investments in commercial property, prepared by the specialist Investment Property Databank, and depicted in Figure 6.2, shows that from 1971 to 1998 rental income ranged from 4.3 per cent in 1974 to a high of 9.1 per cent in 1993. Capital values, however, ranged from peak gains of 23–24 per cent in 1972, 1973 and 1988 to falls of 20 per cent in 1974. The early 1990s brought a resounding crash and capital growth turned negative again for three consecutive years, falling by 30 per cent during 1990, 1991 and 1992.

Direct investment by individuals accounts for only a small fraction of the commercial property market. There is, however, a thriving market in the leases of shops, restaurants, garages and buildings that combine commercial uses on the ground floor with residential accommodation upstairs. Many are well within the reach of small investors brave enough to explore the possibilities.

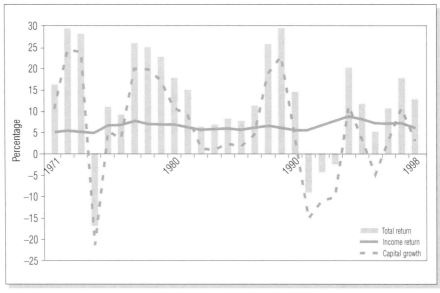

Source: Investment Property Databank

FIGURE 6.2 Commercial property returns, 1971–98

Direct investment in commercial property is particularly attractive for those with self-invested pension plans who can take advantage of tax relief both on money borrowed to buy or improve the property, and also on the initial investment.

Investment opportunities are widely advertised in specialized publications such as *Estates Gazette* and local newspapers, and every sizable town will have at least one estate agency specializing in commercial property. Stamp duty and agents' fees add to the costs, and the market is significantly less liquid than for residential property. Risks and returns can be substantially higher than on other investments, however, and some independent financial advisers make a point of advising wealthier clients to invest part of their pension funds in leases on commercial property.

Investors can offset costs, including the cost of borrowed money, against the rental income. Rents are usually fixed for periods of around five years and subject to upward-only adjustments when they come up for review. However, landlords run the risk of unforeseen major expenditure, of rent reviews coinciding with weak demand, as well as the high risk of shops and restaurants going out of business. Businesses that invest the owners' pension funds in the sites they operate from face a potential 'double whammy' if the business folds.

Larger forms of commercial property are usually beyond the price range of all but a few private investors. They are normally developed, managed and traded by specialized property companies. Many property companies are quoted on the London Stock Exchange and can be bought and sold like other specialized industrial and commercial companies.

Although property companies boomed briefly in the 1960s, in recent years they have underperformed the stock market as a whole. They suffered heavily in the early 1990s, when a number of high profile companies were forced into receivership as the banks that had financed their projects foreclosed on their loans. The victims included Canary Wharf, then a privately owned company that redeveloped the derelict London Docklands. The billion-pound project ran out of money when demand for office space slumped, and it had to be baled out by its bankers. They accepted equity in exchange for non-performing loans, and floated it on the stock exchange in 1998.

Table 6.1 gives some idea of the mediocre performance of this sector in recent years.

TABLE 6.1 Property-related stock market indices, January 1995–December 1999

Index	Annual return	Annual standard deviation
Construction and building materials	8.0%	22.0%
Real estate	9.5%	15.0%

Source: Barclays Global Investors

Behind the price

Although property, unlike bonds or shares, involves issues such as aesthetics, prestige and uniqueness, for the investor the bottom line is still financial: the ability of a property to produce a profit through income or capital gain. It is therefore just as important to have an objective framework to evaluate particular properties and the market as a whole.

Investment – specific factors

Location: it has become a cliché in both the residential and the commercial property markets that everything comes down to three factors: location, location, and location. However, it is a mistake to think of location as a constant. For example, a house may be particularly attractive because it is in a quiet location, with a good view. But planning laws may change to allow a new housing estate or a trunk road to be built or encourage the redevelopment of 'brownfield' sites. The announcement and the subsequent completion of a new transport link, such as the long-delayed Jubilee Line extension across South London, can change the location of properties relative to places of work and shopping. Similarly, an industrial property could become more valuable if a new road or rail link were built, connecting it with a major port.

Physical attributes: after establishing what a property can be used for, the next question is: how well equipped is it to meet the purpose? Residential properties need basic amenities and parking space. An industrial property needs high clearance; a rural property needs peace and quiet; a city office building needs good services. It is important, once again, to look at these factors as dynamic rather than static. Demands may change, such as the need to install computer systems in an office building. The ability of the property to absorb change through refit or refurbishment is an important attribute.

Legal issues: covenants attached to a title, zoning restrictions, easement questions, and specific building regulations can all affect a property's value. This is particularly important for the prospects of the site, such as potential redevelopment. On some properties, the airspace – the right to build higher buildings – is as valuable as the building itself.

Rental prospects: all aspects of a property affect the rent that can be derived, and hence its value. For commercial property, factors include the leaseable area, the technicalities of existing leases and, of particular importance, the security of tenants. A property with a financially strong tenant in a long-term lease is more attractive than one that is vacant.

Useful measures: as with other asset classes, the property fraternity has a toolbox of ratios to enhance qualitative assessment with quantitative analysis. These are used mainly for comparison, with other properties and other markets, and over time. Two are particularly useful. One is the *initial net yield* which, unless otherwise specified, is usually referred to simply as the *yield*. The yield is the annual net income (rent minus outgoings) divided by the purchase price and expressed as a percentage. If a block of flats is offered for £1 million and it generates £100 000 a year in rent, with £25 000 in outgoings, the price will represent an initial net yield of 7.5 per cent. The calculation is:

Gross rent:	£ 100 000
Outgoings:	£ 25 000
Net income (A):	£ 75 000
Purchase price (B):	£1 000 000
Net income (A) as % of purchase price (B):	7.5%

The yield is a measure of return and is used in several ways, including working out a conceptually fair price for a property by comparing its net income with 'market' yields.

The other is the *years/purchase ratio* or, in its mathematically inverse form, the *gross rent multiplier*. This represents the number of years of rent needed to buy the property at its current price. In the above example, the years/purchase would be 10; that is, it would take ten years of a gross rent of £100 000 to equal the offer price of £1 million. This ratio is used in a similar way to the P/E ratio for equities. All else being equal, when the years/purchase ratio is very high for a particular property, either it is overvalued or the overall property market is overheated.

Market sector factors

The most important force in the property market is supply and demand. Market sector factors are all driven by this principle, but can be separated into various categories.

Underlying economics: if an investor owns a factory and rents it to a company that makes widgets, and demand for widgets dries up, the investor has a problem. Worse still, widgets may become obsolete and be replaced with gizmos. If the factory is suitable only for widget production, it will be a big problem; but if it is convertible to gizmo production, it will be manageable.

Similarly, demand for office space is highly cyclical and in a stagnant economy shops and restaurants close, leaving landlords with empty properties that can soon become eyesores. Even residential property prices ebb and flow with demand.

Technological/consumer preference factors: changing technology can dramatically affect demand for property. The modernization of the UK rail network in the late 1980s, combined with rising property prices in inner London, persuaded some families to look for property further out of London. The city's commuting area extended out to places such as Peterborough, Market Harborough, Banbury, Bath, Southampton and even Doncaster, before rising fares began to erode the cost advantages of commuting over long distances. It remains to be seen whether planned measures to discourage the use of cars and encourage high-density development can bring population back to the inner cities. The redevelopment of inner cities has reached critical mass in large cities such as London, Manchester, Birmingham and Glasgow but the inner areas of most smaller cities and towns remain depressed and unattractive.

Technological progress has an even more dramatic effect on commercial property prices. Many shop, factory and office premises built in the last half century have become obsolete long before the end of their normal life expectancy. High Street shops which were suitable for shopping patterns common in the mid 20th century are now too small, and cannot display the range of goods or provide the parking facilities consumers expect. Mills and factories suitable for traditional blue-collar manufacturing industries cannot meet the needs of newer manufacturing industries producing high-tech high value with a largely white-collar labour force.

Offices built before the days of computers often have solid floors and low ceilings which make the installation of air conditioning and the wiring systems needed for modern communications systems impossible or impossibly expensive to install. Increasing congestion on roads and railways and rapid growth of IT systems could eventually encourage working from home and make the traditional large office blocks redundant. The growth of e-commerce could also lead to the replacement of many shops and showrooms by regional warehouses distributing goods ordered on the internet direct to consumers' homes.

Interest rates: when interest rates are low, people are more inclined to buy and build houses; when they rise, the reverse is true. The effect of just half a percentage point or so in the mortgage interest rate can be significant. This is an indicator of why property has good diversification benefits in relation to interest-bearing investment.

Interest rates have an equally important impact on the commercial property market, especially because of the long lead times needed between the decision to develop a site and the completion of the building. Rapid and substantial changes in interest rates can have an immediate impact on sentiment, which makes periodic gluts and shortages of suitable property inevitable.

Demographics: when it comes to residential property, what counts is the number of people in relation to the number of houses and flats. As a result, population movements, both regional and national, tend to influence property prices. London property prices accelerated faster than those in other cities in the 1980s and 1990s due in part to the influx of workers from elsewhere. The make-up of the population is also important. With a declining birth rate and an ageing population, the pattern of housing demand may change radically in coming years. Demand may rise for smaller, convenient houses and flats suitable for retired people.

Planning permission: the biggest single factor influencing property prices in the UK, however, is the shortage of land. Planning permission is in the hands of local authorities but the Environment Ministry has the final say in approving or revoking their decisions. People buying new homes overwhelmingly prefer greenfield sites, where there is often a wider choice of properties available within easy reach of the retreating countryside. This is in spite of the prospects of longer journeys to work.

Builders also prefer greenfield sites. Plots are usually bigger and cheaper, and there are none of the problems with clearing sites which are common on land previously used for industrial purposes. The New Labour government elected in 1997 restricted the release of greenfield land, and increased the proportion of new homes to be built on brownfield sites from 50 per cent to 60 per cent of annual construction.

According to the government's latest planning proposals, however, 900 000 extra new homes need to be built in the UK, at least 250 000 of them in and around London alone by 2015. If these targets are to be met, much more green-field land may be needed.

Investment strategy

The property market, like the stock market, is marked by substantial fluctuations in both prices and levels of activity. And any property investment strategy must address, one way or another, how to work the cycle to advantage, or at least neutralize its potentially damaging effects. There are basically two cycles to look at: the *macro cycle* and the *micro cycle*.

The macro cycle

The property market is, from an efficient markets hypothesis perspective, not very efficient. Information is not always transmitted into investment decisions in a logical and timely fashion. And the lead-lag factor can keep prices up even when the underlying supply/demand trend clearly cannot support them. It is clear that joining the property cycle at the right time can offer the prospect of excellent profits, but getting caught at the wrong time can spell very bad news indeed.

For residential property, analysts can identify a distinct sequence of events in each property cycle. The key indicators are the ratio of property prices to average earnings, the level of mortgage interest rates, and the level of consumer confidence. Over the past 40 years, the ratio of average property prices to average earnings has fluctuated from a low of less than three, to a high of almost five at the height of the boom in 1973. Over the same period, interest rates on standard variable rate mortgages have ranged from 15 per cent to 5 per cent.

Prices can be depressed at the bottom of the economic cycle, when consumer confidence has been hit by high unemployment, and before interest rates have fallen to match the requirements of the real economy. As a result, property prices can fall behind the overall rise in earnings. As the economy recovers, however, earnings start to grow faster than property prices, making property look affordable. As jobs become more secure, buyers gain confidence in their ability to repay mortgage debts. Falling interest rates also make property more affordable by reducing monthly outgoings in relation to income. At the same time, lenders tend to increase the amount they will lend in relation to borrowers' incomes and the value of the property.

As confidence builds, buyers rush to seize opportunities and may create a feeding frenzy, particularly in areas where prices are rising most rapidly. The property price-to-earnings ratio starts to climb, and by the time the economy is overheating and the Bank of England is raising interest rates, property prices can be grossly inflated. Rates rise, the economy slows, and the cycle goes on.

Complicating the cycle, property booms usually precede a rise in the inflation rate, as investors remortgage their homes in order to finance other spending. The Bank of England has struggled for years to isolate the property market from the economy, but deregulation of the mortgage market has only made the task harder. While the recession of the early 1990s – when property prices actually fell for the first time in a generation, leaving many recent buyers with negative equity – sounded a note of caution, recovery led to another residential property boom at the end of the decade.

For the investor, there are two basic approaches in dealing with the macro cycle: try to pick it, or ride it. The first relies primarily on correctly identifying fundamental trends, while the second focuses more on assessing relative value.

The *pick-the-cycle* strategy requires the investor to buy when the market is about to bottom out, and sell when the market is about to peak. For many years now, canny buyers have bought a property, done it up, waited for prices to surge, taken their profits and started again. In earlier chapters, we noted the difficulty of getting 'market timing' right consistently, particularly in equities. In property, this task is still difficult and risky, and the high transaction costs mean that the investor has to make a sizeable capital gain for the strategy to be worthwhile.

Shrewd property investors do however have a couple of things going for them. The first is that property tends to be a lagging, rather than a leading, sector of the economy when it comes to supply and demand. It tends to respond, after a lag, to the key indicators mentioned in this chapter, including interest rates, demographics and economic growth. It also tends to over-respond to such stimuli. The valuation system magnifies this lead-lag effect in market sentiment.

The investor who is able to analyze current economic and demographic trends and act quickly enough can sometimes anticipate a property boom or bust before the general market and enjoy a substantial capital gain. But the penalty for getting it wrong can be a spell of negative equity where the owner cannot move because he cannot repay the mortgage, even if he can still keep up the repayments. The key is to juggle the various factors and forecast demand, interest rates and affordability correctly. One rule of thumb for residential property is that, in a sustainable market, the median house price is about three to four times average earnings. For example, if the average person earns £20000 per year, and house prices average around £60000–£80000, the market is in a sustainable phase. When the median price exceeds four times average earnings, the market is regarded as unsustainable and due for a shake-out. At the height of the property boom in 1989 average prices soared to five times gross earnings in the UK as a whole and six times in London. They fell back in the following recession, but by 2000 the national average was over 3.5 and in London the ratio was again over 4.5, putting housing out of reach of most first-time buyers and low-paid workers with families.

For commercial property one of the useful indicators is the relationship between the income yield from rents and the yield on fixed-interest securities. Although commercial properties have an underlying net asset value, they are usually bought by institutions such as pension funds that have a long-term cash flow requirement to meet. For this reason, they need a portfolio of properties with a relatively long life expectancy. However, they cannot realistically pay prices so high that they depress rental yields below what they could obtain from long-dated fixed-interest securities. Conversely, when the yields on gilt-edged stocks rise, commercial property prices will ease until leases are renewed and rents can be raised to restore the balance.

Many private investors do not try to pick the market at all, and choose instead to ride it. The *ride-the-cycle* strategy relies in part on picking the low point of the cycle, but is less concerned with precise timing. The idea is to identify periods when property is inherently good value, then purchase assets and ride out the subsequent upturns and downturns. Although the investor would, of course, hope to sell on a future upturn, the strategy relies on good yield prospects and the fact that property generally keeps pace with inflation in the long term. Investors who ride the cycle must ensure they can always afford to keep their mortgage going to avoid being repossessed by their lender and losing their investment.

The micro cycle

Land use rarely stays constant. Even in rural areas, agricultural activities vary over time. This trend has an important implication for property investment strategy. In suburban areas, land use zoning is all-important. Land that has received outline planning permission can be worth ten times its value as farmland. If it has received detailed planning permission for housing, its value soars to around 100 times its agricultural value. In urban areas, individual sites tend to go through a cycle of development, stagnation and redevelopment.

There are several strategic implications of this micro cycle. One is that it is important to analyze the current and future land value of a property from the structures on it, and to see how well the current usage fits the land. It may be that the current structure will eventually face 'locational obsolescence' and require refurbishment or redevelopment. Residential property, small shops and commercial premises in run-down urban areas all face this threat. Also, a lot depends on 'picking the micro cycle' in terms of what lies behind the price. An investor who buys a property at the height of a localized boom, but then sees the usage stagnate, can end up losing money.

On the other hand, a developer who can identify a new land use potential for a property entering the stagnation phase can often purchase the site for a relatively good price, redevelop it and make a profit. For example, a developer who bought a dying textile factory and redeveloped it into a modern 'business park' – and got the timing right – could have done well. The textile import businesses that replaced the old textile mills would want just such property: a mixture of office space with storage facilities.

Investors who want to try to pick the micro cycle should invest directly, that is, buy and sell properties themselves or improve them through refurbishment or redevelopment. It is worth emphasizing, however, that while this approach offers significant potential profits, it is very difficult. It is the equivalent of starting one's own airline instead of just buying shares in an airline. Successful direct investment requires extensive knowledge and hard work; it also involves considerable capital, and risk.

International dimensions

Until relatively recently, even big investors faced huge obstacles in bringing foreign property into their portfolios. Direct investment involved all of the usual problems, plus all the complications of foreign property law and ownership limitations. These complexities largely restricted direct foreign investment to the professionals.

Although direct investment still has pitfalls for unwary investors who do not understand market conditions and the legal and tax systems abroad, property securities now appear to be one of the fastest-growing sectors of most foreign securities markets. Apart from property companies, various specialized vehicles have emerged. In Europe, property funds, some listed and others unlisted, have grown into major public investors in property.

In parallel, major international investment and research houses, such as Salomon Brothers, have developed indices to track and compare securitized property investment around the world. These indices have enabled Salomon to produce a series of intriguing reports on international property investment through overseas securities. Some studies carried out in the early 1990s indicated that international property was an excellent diversifier.

One study found that correlations among the property indices of 11 countries were very low. Twenty-two of the 55 correlations were below 0.2 and seven were negative. The study suggested that apart from countries with obviously close economic links, international property markets move quite independently of each other.[2] Another study examined the components of the volatility of various regional property securities markets, and overall equity markets.[3] It found that the property sector in each region moved more independently of other regions than did the overall share market. That is, there is less correlation – and hence more potential diversification benefit – among international property markets than among international share markets generally. Salomon concluded that 'global property could offer diversification benefits when added to an international stock portfolio'.

Derivative instruments

Because of the relatively recent move to securitization in property markets, the application of derivatives to property is in its infancy. There are signs in other countries, however, that this asset class will be the next to which the rocket scientists will apply their skills.

For example, in March 1999 investment house Warburg Dillon Read introduced an instalment warrant based on five Australian-listed property trusts. The warrants allow investors to gain leverage over a package of units in these trusts. An investor puts up about half the value of the package, but gains effective control over the full package. The investor pays interest to WDR pending exercise of the option to take up delivery of the underlying units. Then the investor has the choice of going ahead with the option or selling the warrant through the share market. As a leveraged investment, the warrants offer the same sort of enhancement of risk and return as other derivatives.

It would appear likely that as the property market becomes more sophisticated, other imaginative derivative products will be introduced. These should provide an even wider range of opportunities for getting into this asset class other than the traditional approach of buying bricks and mortar.

Tax considerations

The tax treatment of property is different from the taxation of other forms of investment, and the treatment of owner-occupied property is different from the treatment of homes to let and from commercial property. Tax relief on mortgage interest for owner-occupiers was finally phased out in April 2000, but the notional rent saved by being an owner-occupier is not regarded as taxable income and all capital gains on an owner's home or principal residence are exempt from tax.

By contrast, the net rental income and capital gains from other property assets are subject to tax like other investments, but investors can deduct the full cost of routine maintenance (but not improvements) from the gross rent received, as well as up to 10 per cent of gross rent to cover wear and tear if the accommodation is let furnished.

In addition, the interest on loans to buy residential and commercial property to let is tax deductible. This gives investment in property a distinct advantage over other forms of investment, including shares and bonds where the cost of borrowed money is not allowable against tax.

The gradual withdrawal of tax relief on mortgage interest is a direct response to the growing concerns of the government and the Bank of England over the effect of rising property values on inflation. The graph of house price rises and inflation clearly shows that rising house prices precede general rises in inflation. Although they may have a common cause, it seems quite likely that rising house prices make increases in the retail price index worse.

Rising house prices are also seen as a potential threat to the 'real economy' because of the need to raise interest rates to slow down the pace of house price rises. In the absence of other controls, rising interest rates drive up the cost of business finance and make sterling more attractive, driving up the exchange rate and reducing the competitiveness of British goods and services in the home market as well as abroad.

For all these reasons, in recent Budgets the Chancellor has increased stamp duty on property transactions, including both residential and commercial deals, in an attempt to discourage a merry-go-round of rising property prices.

Despite these various disincentives, property remains a more tax-effective avenue for medium- to long-term investment than many other options. It is a good diversifier, whether purchased as a direct investment or through securitized investments.

Notes

1 Among various studies on world wealth, R.G. Ibbotson and C.L. Fall calculated total world wealth at $21 486.7 billion, of which US real estate was the largest component at 19.8 per cent; other real estate came to 32.7 per cent, for a combined real estate share of 52.5 per cent ('The world wealth portfolio', *Journal of Portfolio Management*, Winter, 1983).

2 Salomon Brothers (1990) 'Global real estate securities: index performance and diversified portfolios', 23 February.

3 Salomon Brothers (1990) 'Global share performance by geographic region', 21 August.

PART THREE

Theory into practice

CHAPTER 7

Managed investments

Summary

- For the majority of people, the best way into property, equities and interest-bearing markets is through managed funds.

- Managed investments do not, in general, beat the market. Their primary value is in pooling funds from private investors to achieve economies of scale and diversification.

- Managed investments include investment trusts, unit trusts, and open-ended investment companies. The prices of all these funds are quoted daily in the media.

- Insurance bonds and pension funds are essentially variations on the theme of managed investments, but they are less transparent and less liquid.

- Contributions to a pension fund are tax-free but money invested in a pension fund cannot be touched before retirement.

- Investments in an individual savings account are made from taxed income but are then exempt from income tax and capital gains tax.

- Investors must use the same methods in evaluating managed funds as with individual investments, assessing the investment process, the portfolio of assets, the fund manager's style and the past returns.

- Of these, the aspect that most people focus on – past returns – is the least useful. Investors must look at the factors which will make for future, rather than past, performance.

Introduction: accessing the sum of the parts

In implementing an investment strategy, everyone faces the same question: which investment vehicle, or vehicles? Direct investment – buying securities oneself – is just one avenue. Managed investments offer a variety of alternative vehicles to access the asset classes. For many investors, pooled funds provide the most realistic way to implement a sophisticated and diversified strategy and get access to sectors, such as small companies, technology, or overseas markets, that investors could not individually afford.

Pooled funds are often viewed as a soft option compared with direct investment – someone else does all the work. But while in some senses this is true, getting the best out of funds requires all of the skills described so far in *Fortune Strategy*. Investors have to choose between managed investments in cash deposits, in fixed-interest securities, in property, in shares, or balanced funds which are an amalgam of all four asset classes. Choosing the right fund also involves specific knowledge of the different types of managed investments, how to assess them, and how to use them to achieve personal investment objectives. Remember, managed investments are tools in implementing an investment strategy – not a substitute for it.

A good starting point in assessing managed investment is to ask why you should give someone your funds to invest, and pay them for the privilege. In the past decade most actively managed funds have done less well than index-tracker funds which simply track the average performance of stock markets and charge lower management fees. Yet millions of people worldwide pour billions of pounds into managed investments every year. This is because – regardless of whether they track or try to outperform the indices – pooled investments offer several inherent advantages.

Managed investments offer the private investor the best way into diversified portfolios. There is no way that an investor with £100 000, let alone £10 000, can achieve a truly balanced portfolio through direct investment. These amounts of money cannot buy the collection of bonds, properties and shares that will provide adequate domestic and international diversification. The dealing costs alone of a small but diversified portfolio would offset many of the advantages of diversification.

Managed funds provide private investors with access to markets and strategies that rely on economies of scale. The commercial money market will not even talk to an investor who has less than £1 million, but private investors can access this market through cash and money market unit trusts. Corporate bond funds offer small investors access to portfolios of up to 50 different corporate bonds in order to spread the risks of investing heavily in a bond issued by a company that can no longer pay its way.

As discussed in Chapter 6, there is only a handful of unit trusts investing directly in property that small investors can buy, and their place is taken by property (real estate) companies, most of which develop, manage and trade properties on behalf of their shareholders. In recent years they have not been very successful and their shares have traded at big discounts to the value of their assets. Most trusts, however, are equity trusts, offering small investors a stake in a wide range of companies, which they could not hope to hold directly.

Similarly, a small investor seeking to run an active, diversified international share portfolio directly would find dealing more difficult and more expensive and he would have to take account of currency risks as well as normal investment risks. International equity trusts, however, can run an active book in which broking costs represent only a fraction of the portfolio.

There is, of course, no free lunch: tracker funds charge an annual management fee equivalent on average to around 0.5 per cent of the value of the investment; actively managed funds charge on average around 1 per cent; and the charges on specialist funds can reach 2 per cent or more. Dealing costs add another layer of charges, which are often unpublicized. Unit trusts and most open-ended investment companies also charge some form of entry and/or exit fee. However, the fees go a long way. Just to create and manage a portfolio that replicates the market is a huge task. It involves tracking and analyzing markets, and dealing with the mechanics of owning and transferring titles to large numbers of securities and incurring trading costs.

Adjusting the portfolio is particularly important in changing economic conditions. The best managers may occasionally foresee key economic changes, but all managers should at least be able to react quickly and effectively to changes that occur. This is difficult for private investors, unless they devote their lives to tracking markets.

While the fund concept has several attractions for the private investor, it is just as important to scrutinize individual managed investments as it is to assess direct investments. To assess an equity unit trust, for example, the investor has to understand equities, and be able to determine the fund's risk/return profile.

There is no *best* fund. Past performance is no guide to the future, and different funds suit different purposes and needs, although some serve those purposes and needs better than others. Yet while managed investment vehicles have advantages of scale, there is nothing magical about them. Their managers are no more than groups of people making decisions about how to invest, in the hope of getting it right. It is therefore important to determine whether the managers would know a dog if they fell over one. This chapter provides the tools for finding out.

The fund concept

The managed funds industry developed through various applications of the idea that pooled funds could be invested for the common good. Life insurance, which evolved in the 18th century, spread the risk of being killed in the process of advancing the industrial revolution. Friendly societies, which provided medical and other forms of social insurance, were designed to assist members in hard times. Pension funds developed to provide workers with an income to retire in comfort.

All forms of managed investment basically come down to a structure for giving someone else your money to invest. What makes one type of vehicle different from another is the legal framework in which it operates, particularly the tax framework.

Trusts

There are several types of trust, including private and discretionary trusts, which are mostly used for reducing inheritance tax liabilities, but here we examine the most common structures in the investment industry: the investment trust, the unit trust, and the open-ended investment company or 'oeic'.

Investment trusts

Investment trusts offer investors the opportunity to pool their funds and spread the risks of investment without the complication of insurance policies or pension rules. Investment trusts are actually companies set up for the purpose of making money through investing in the shares of other companies rather than manufacturing goods or providing services. Shares in an investment trust are offered to investors in an initial public offering and then are bought and sold on the stock exchange through the management groups or brokers. Investors can turn their assets back into cash by selling their shares in the trust to other investors. The price of their shares depends on what buyers and sellers believe they are worth in relation to the trust's assets and earnings potential.

The first investment trust was set up by Foreign & Colonial as long ago as 1868. Its stated objectives were 'to give the investor of moderate means the same advantages as the large capitalists, in diminishing the risk in investing by spreading the investment over a number of stocks'. Today there are more than 300 different trusts run by almost 100 different management companies, most of which run a number of different trusts.

The management of an investment trust have wide discretion to invest in shares to achieve the trust's objectives. Because they are not obliged to redeem shares that investors have bought, the management of an investment trust can have all assets fully invested at all times and invest a proportion of their funds in unquoted companies. They can also gear up the shareholders' capital by borrowing money to increase their buying power. Gearing, discussed in Chapter 2, is a way of putting the investor's hands on more assets. It increases the risk involved in investment by extending the scope for both profits and losses. Gearing also provides potential tax advantages. For example, trusts can reduce taxable income by borrowing and deducting the interest charges, and investing the additional funds with a view to making significant capital gains.

If the demand for an investment trust exceeds supply, the price of the trust's own shares may go to a premium over the net value of the assets (NAV). But for a variety of reasons, including growing competition from unit trusts, the shares of most investment trusts in recent years have stood at a discount to the value of the shares they hold. Over the past 30 years average discounts have ranged from a high of 33 per cent below the value of the assets held during 1974, to a low of just 3 per cent in 1993, but have widened again in the past few years.

Critics often claim discounts are a sign of poor performance by managers, but most managers claim the discounts are a bonus, allowing investors to buy assets at a discount to the market price of the assets themselves and to enjoy the full value of the dividends. This gives the investment trust shares a higher yield than the underlying assets would provide investors who bought them direct on the stock market.

Variations in the average size of the discounts mean that the prices and yields on investment trusts are likely to be more volatile than direct investments in the underlying assets would be, but over the long term, the effects are not significant. Over the past few years investment trusts managers have tried to reduce the size of the discounts by offering free warrants to investors in newly issued investment trusts. These can subsequently be converted into full shares, and increase demand for shares in the process. In addition, investment trust companies are buying back their own shares and promoting fresh sales.

But the persistence of discounts has also led to recurring pressures on investment trust managers to wind up voluntarily the trust and return the asset value to shareholders, or to unitize the trust, converting it into a unit trust and eliminating the discounts in the process. Alternatively, managers of more aggressive trusts mount takeover bids for rival trusts where discounts are large.

Split capital trusts

The different treatment of income and capital for tax purposes means that some investors actively need one but not the other. Split capital investment trusts have been created specially to cater for these needs and are increasingly popular. These trusts have a finite life, usually from five to ten years. They offer two, sometimes three different types of share, each with distinct advantages and disadvantages.

Some split capital trusts offer both income shares, which collect the dividends on the investments, and capital shares, which receive all the capital gains. Others combine the income and capital shares as ordinary shares and also offer zero-dividend preference shares. Some trusts offer all three types of share.

Zero-dividend preference shares receive no dividends from the underlying investments and are issued at a substantial discount to the price at which they will be redeemed at a specific future date, which guarantees a predictable future return that can be counted as capital gain. If the trust performs badly, the zero-dividend shares have first claim on the assets and will pay out in full, provided the funds have not fallen below the 'hurdle' rate, a target which each trust sets itself. The return is not guaranteed but so far all zeros have been paid in full even if the trust's assets fall during the trust's life.

Ordinary shares also have a hurdle rate which they must achieve to ensure they are redeemed in full. Income shares are medium risk and do well if the trust achieves rising dividends, while capital shares have the highest risk. If the trust's overall performance is poor, they will suffer heavily, but if it is very good, the capital shares will benefit most. Each trust sets its own hurdle rates, which are essential information for potential investors.

Unit trusts and open-ended investment companies (oeics)

The unit trust, which began in England in 1931, is a similar concept to the investment trust, but investors buy and sell units instead of shares. Ownership of the trust and, in a beneficial sense, the assets of the trust, are divided into units. Each unit is entitled to a certain share of the income and capital growth produced by the trust's assets. Figure 7.1 shows the basic structure.

Units are bought and sold through the trust's manager, either directly in response to an advertisement or through an intermediary such as an investment adviser. Most trusts are dual priced, which means the managers publish an 'offer' price at which they will sell units to new investors and a lower 'bid' price at which they will buy back units from investors who want to sell. The difference or 'spread' can be up to 5 per cent and covers the managers' dealing costs. A small but growing number of trusts are, however, 'single priced', allowing buyers and sellers to trade at the same price, while managers charge buyers a separate initial charge. Sometimes they also make an exit charge to sellers.

Unit trusts are 'open-ended'. This means that if there are more buyers than sellers, the managers must create new units and invest the proceeds, and if there are more sellers than buyers, the managers must redeem the excess units and sell investments to pay off their investors. Regulations require managers to price their units in line with the underlying value of their investments and eliminate any possibility of premiums or discounts on the value of the trust's investments. Managers are also not allowed to borrow to gear up their investments.

This simplicity of structure has made unit trusts more popular and allowed them to overtake the investment trust movement. By the start of the new millennium there were more than 100 different unit trust management companies in the UK offering more than 2000 different unit trusts.

Open-ended investment companies were introduced in 1997. Unlike unit trusts, which cannot be sold outside the UK, oeics can be marketed throughout the European Union. In spite of their cumbersome name they have quickly become popular, and many unit trusts have converted or will be converting into oeics. Like investment trusts they are companies, whose shares are always bought and sold at single prices but an initial charge is taken out of the sum invested which managers must publicize. Like unit trusts, they are open-ended, which means managers must trade investments to cope with inflows and withdrawals and there are no discounts to worry about.

Trust specializations

The large numbers of investment trusts, unit trusts and oeics on offer, and the wide choice of different managers, means there is a vast array to choose from. Some trusts specialize in managing cash funds that invest in a number of

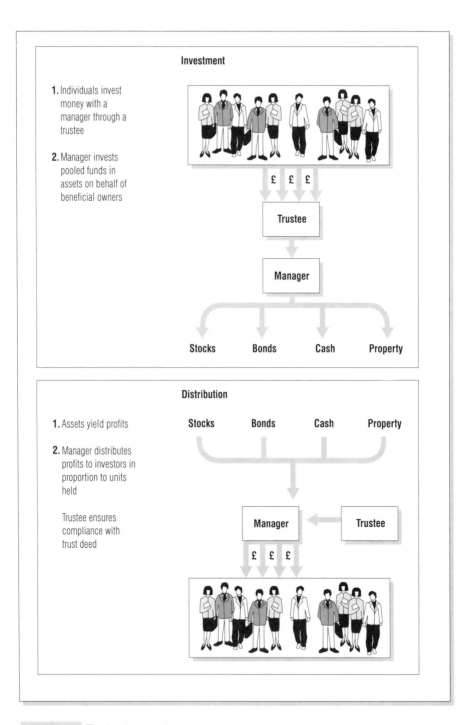

FIGURE 7.1 The trust concept

accounts with banks and building societies and take advantage of the higher rates of interest available on deposits of £1 million or more. Some are money market funds that invest in tradable assets such as Treasury bills, bank bills and certificates of deposit which will mature within a year or less. Like cash funds they can earn higher rates of interest than any individual investor could hope to achieve and have the additional advantage that the assets can be sold and the proceeds reinvested if market conditions change.

An increasing number of unit trusts are specialist bond funds, and invest in gilts and corporate bonds, preference shares and convertibles. These pay fixed rates of interest or dividends and can be kept until they are repaid at their maturity date, or can be easily traded if other opportunities present themselves. Corporate bond funds are popular as investments in tax-free ISAs because they offer a spread of investments and a high yield which makes the most of the ISAs' tax-free status.

The great majority of trusts, however, invest in equities. An increasing number simply track a chosen market by investing in all the shares which are included in one or other of the best-known market indices, including the FTSE 100 share index or the FTSE All-share index in the UK, the S&P 500 index in the US, or the Eurotop 300 European shares index. There are also global tracker funds offering investors a stake in all major markets.

But the majority of equity-based trusts actively manage their investment portfolio to meet specialized investment targets. Some trusts simply describe themselves as income trusts or growth trusts. Others specialize in specific sectors of the market, such as smaller companies or technology stocks, or in international stock markets, for example in Europe, the US, Japan, the Pacific region or emerging markets.

Virtually all managed investments look for profits from both income and capital growth. However, many funds favour one or the other. *Income* trusts invest mainly in established companies that over the years are expected to pay solid dividends even if they are not in fast-growing sectors of the economy. *Growth* trusts look more at the prospects of a rise in a company's share price over time, and are therefore inclined towards younger companies. Apart from being more 'aggressive', growth trusts offer a potential tax attraction for high-income earners by concentrating return as capital gain rather than regular income.

Sector-specific versus balanced trusts

Trusts established with the stated objective of investing in only one asset class, or a subsector, are known as *sector-specific* or *specialized* trusts. Those that include all the asset classes in an effort to provide more broadly based portfolios are known as *diversified* or *balanced* trusts.

Many of the trusts based in offshore centres such as Dublin, the Channel Islands and Luxembourg are umbrella funds, which have a number of sub-funds. A manager may have a property fund, a bond fund, a cash fund, an index-based share fund, an actively managed share fund, and a range of international funds, all under the same trust. Open-ended investment companies also have the same structure.

Figure 7.2 shows the model. An investor can put money into one or several of these sector funds and switch from one to the other. The manager will often also have a 'fund of funds' that can invest in each of the other funds to achieve a diversified portfolio.

The umbrella structure offers managers greater flexibility and opportunities to reduce costs, for example by publishing a single annual report covering all its sub-funds instead of separate reports for each trust. But from the point of view of investors, there are few obvious differences between conventional unit trusts and umbrella funds. Unit trust managers increasingly allow investors to switch from one trust to another in the same management group, at little or no cost.

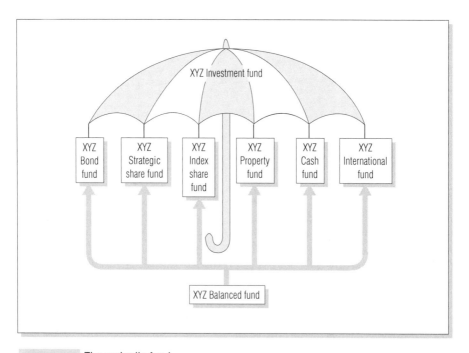

FIGURE 7.2 The umbrella fund

But in all cases a switch is regarded by the Inland Revenue as a taxable event, which may create a liability to pay capital gains tax.

Venture capital trusts (VCTs) and enterprise investment schemes (EISs)

These are the ultimate managed investment play: specialized investment trusts with additional tax advantages, set up to encourage investment in small companies that are unquoted or listed only on the AIM market, and could not otherwise hope to attract risk capital from private investors. VCTs and EISs are managed by professional investment teams who select a range of companies to invest in. They can make an initial charge up to 5 per cent, plus annual charges of up to 3 per cent, and take a slice of the profit when the fund matures. But investors who hold VCT and EIS shares enjoy significant tax benefits, which are summarized in the next section.

Taxation of unit trusts, investment trusts and open-ended investment companies

Special tax rules apply to managed funds based in the UK. The underlying principle is that they should be as neutral as possible, so that investors receive after tax as near as possible – no more and no less – than they would by investing direct in the same assets. The fund managers receive dividends on UK shares that have already been taxed and just like basic-rate taxpayers they have no further internal liability to tax on dividends. Income from foreign shares and bonds is liable to corporation tax at a special rate of 20 per cent, but any withholding tax paid abroad can be deducted from the UK tax liability. Interest received on holdings of cash deposits, bills, UK corporate bonds and gilt-edged stocks is received gross (without deduction of tax).

Investment trusts, unit trusts and oeics are required to distribute all income to their investors. Managed funds are exempt from capital gains tax on profits made within the fund, provided that they are not regarded as trading funds. In the hands of investors, however, all distributed income and any realized capital gains from selling the units in the managed funds are treated in the same way as income and gains from direct investments. This means income from a cash or bond fund is subject to a withholding tax of 20 per cent, after which basic-rate taxpayers have no further liability to income tax, but top-rate taxpayers will be liable to a further 20 per cent tax on income received.

Dividends from an equity fund are paid out net with no further liability for basic-rate taxpayers, but top-rate taxpayers have an additional liability to pay 25 per cent of their net dividends. Switches from one trust or fund to another count as realizations, even if the proceeds are immediately and fully reinvested.

In the case of VCTs, investors who hold these shares for a minimum of five years can put up to £100 000 a year into a VCT and deduct 20 per cent of the investment from their tax bill. No income tax is payable on dividends and up to £100 000 a year of VCT shares can be sold each year free of capital gains tax. Up to £100 000 worth of capital gains tax incurred elsewhere can also be deferred if it is reinvested in a VCT within one year. Enterprise investment schemes (EISs) invest in single companies but have extra incentives. Investors can get tax relief on up to £150 000 a year, defer CGT on gains made over a three-year period, and investment in an EIS is also exempt from inheritance tax.

Individual savings accounts

These are not investments in their own right but investments in shares, bonds and managed funds bought and held within a tax-free 'wrapper'. From April 2001 investors can buy one maxi-ISA, investing up to £5000 in shares and bonds, or up to three mini-ISAs, investing up to £3000 in shares, £1000 in cash and £1000 in insurance products respectively. Income and capital gains from investments in an ISA are exempt from both income and capital gains tax. Within the fund, interest, dividends and gains are treated in the same way as similar funds outside the ISA wrapper, but until April 2004 fund managers can also reclaim the 10 per cent tax credit on net dividends they receive on shares, and pass on the benefit to investors.

From that date equity fund managers will receive only dividend income that has already paid corporation tax, and basic-rate taxpayers who invest in an equity-based ISA will receive no greater benefit than they would receive investing outside the ISA. Top-rate taxpayers will, however, have no additional liability to income tax on dividends and both basic-rate and top-rate taxpayers will remain exempt from any capital gains tax in all circumstances. ISA cash and bond funds will also continue to receive gross income that can be passed on tax-free to all taxpayers.

Insurance bonds

Insurance bonds are lump sum investments, and are offered by a range of life assurance companies, most of whom also offer unit trusts. Unlike unit trusts, investment trusts and oeics, insurance bonds offer an element of life assurance, and all income and gains after deducting annual management charges are rolled up within the fund instead of being distributed as dividends.

Like their managed fund rivals, insurance bonds are available in a range of investments, including cash funds, bond funds and a range of specialized equity funds. A number of companies additionally offer specialized property funds, which can invest in physical properties as well as shares in real estate companies. Insurance bonds come in two main forms: with-profits bonds and utilized bonds. With-profit bonds receive annual bonuses which are 'smoothed' to even out variations in annual returns. For this reason they appeal traditionally to more cautious investors who have no interest in monitoring the performance of their investment. Investors cannot easily monitor their performance until they are redeemed and a final valuation has been applied at the discretion of the managers. Investors will also normally be penalized by a reduced valuation for early redemption. Unitized bonds are considered more volatile but have the advantage of allowing investors to monitor the day-to-day performance of their investments and are not subject to surrender penalties.

The tax treatment of insurance bonds is different from other managed funds in some respects. They receive UK share dividends net of tax, which leaves them with no further liability, but they are liable to pay tax at 20 per cent on income received from interest-bearing investments, rental income and offshore dividends. They are also liable to pay tax at a basic rate of 10 per cent on capital gains, but uniquely they are still allowed to index gains against inflation, and tax payments are calculated annually over a period of years rather than when the gains are actually realized.

The tax treatment of insurance bonds when they are redeemed also differs from other managed funds. Investors are allowed to withdraw up to 5 per cent of their initial investment tax-free for up to 20 years. Any unused allowance can be carried forward from year to year. Additional withdrawals, as well as the profit realized when the bond is cashed or when it matures are treated as income which may be taxable. High taxpayers, though, effectively only have to pay tax at 18 per cent since a credit is given for tax already paid by the insurance company, and standard-rate taxpayers pay no more tax.

As a tax structure through which to invest, insurance bonds are mainly attractive to top-rate taxpayers who wish to invest in a portfolio with a relatively high income yield – from interest-bearing, property or share investments. The ability to roll up the income each year within the bond at a lower rate of tax would, compounded over time, confer a significant benefit. If the investor only needs to draw on the funds after retirement when they may be on a lower tax bracket, tax on the accumulated gain can also be minimized. Insurance bonds are less effective as a structure for investing in high-growth investments which pay minimal income, or for low taxpayers.

Endowment policies

These are also pooled investments managed by insurance companies but unlike insurance bonds, which are single-premium investments, endowment policies are financed by regular premium payments over a period of at least ten years. Premiums are invested in a range of assets, equities, bonds, property and cash, and income and profits accumulate within the fund.

Most are with-profits funds but unit-linked endowments are available. Endowment policies are normally 'front-end loaded' which means most charges are concentrated in the first few years of the policy's life, in order to pay the commission fees the insurance company traditionally pays to financial advisers, mortgage brokers and estate agents who introduce the business. With-profits endowments benefit from the addition of annual bonuses, which are added at the discretion of the insurance company, plus a single terminal bonus added when the policy matures. The relative importance of the terminal bonus depends on the overall investment performance over the life of the policy and varies from company to company. It can, however, be worth up to 40 per cent of the accumulated annual bonuses.

Inevitably this means policies surrendered in the early years may be worth less than the contributions already made, and policies surrendered before they mature will lose the benefit of the terminal bonuses. It is now possible, however, to sell policies to a specialist dealer in 'second-hand' endowment policies rather than simply surrender the policy to the insurance company.

Internally, endowment policies are taxed in the same way as insurance bonds. Investors are not normally liable to tax on the proceeds of endowment policies provided that they hold them for at least ten years.

Endowment policies were particularly popular during the era when investment returns were enhanced by inflation while the mortgage debt remained static, and the tax rules allowed interest on home mortgages to be fully tax deductible. Rather than paying off the mortgage gradually over time, borrowers would instead take out an endowment policy. The returns on such a policy were likely to be well in excess of the additional interest paid over the life of the mortgage and this represented a more effective way to save enough money to repay the mortgage in full when the policy reached its maturity date.

The phasing out of mortgage interest deductibility, combined with the introduction of a new generation of more tax-effective savings vehicles such as ISAs, has seen a significant decline in the popularity of endowment policies and a number of insurance companies have stopped selling them altogether.

Overall, the lack of transparency associated with the traditional endowment policy and insurance bond and relatively high costs mean that the investor may be better off to take out term insurance separately to repay the mortgage if the policy holder dies, and invest the rest in alternative, more transparent structures such as pension funds, oeics or ISAs.

Friendly societies

UK friendly societies traditionally provided savings clubs and burial clubs for the working classes and before the creation of the welfare state they provided income-protection policies. Then, in much the same fashion as life offices, they decided to provide a managed investment product under their special tax structure. Policy holders can invest up to £25 a month in tax-exempt with-profits policies, with life assurance if the policy holder dies. This is in addition to the £1000 a year investors can put into tax-free insurance-linked ISAs.

Pension funds

The rising cost of providing pensions to guarantee a comfortable retirement income for the growing number of pensioners has become one of the most serious social problems facing all Western countries. Figure 7.3 shows the problem graphically. Men and women are retiring earlier and living longer, while the birth rate has fallen to the point where the numbers of new employees coming into the workforce and paying taxes is set to drop while the proportion of pensioners is expected to rise, in some cases quite dramatically. If workers continue to rely primarily on a government-funded pension for retirement, the cost will absorb an ever-increasing share of government revenue.

In the UK, government efforts to alert workers to the growing threat of poverty in old age has raised public consciousness of the problem. The UK is years ahead of most European countries in persuading individuals to start contributing to a private sector pension. In France, Germany and above all

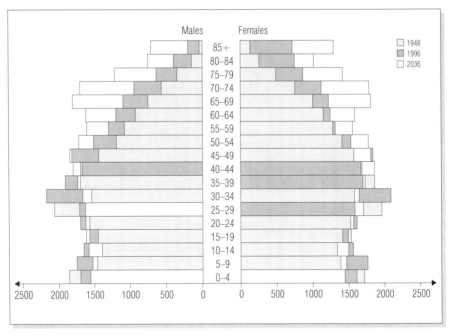

Source: Office of National Statistics

FIGURE 7.3 The UK's changing demographics

Italy, little progress has yet been made and the bulk of pension payments in the next two decades will have to come out of tax revenues. But the UK government's efforts have also led to a number of own-goals that have complicated the process.

The state pension

In the UK, everyone who has paid National Insurance contributions, which are equivalent to 10 per cent of basic earnings up to £27 820 a year in 2000–01, is entitled to a state pension. Since 1978 employees have also qualified for an additional state earnings-related state pension or Serps, which was intended to provide everyone earning up to the average earnings level a second pension also funded out of National Insurance contributions and supplemented out of taxation. Since 1981, however, the state pension has been revised each year in line with the retail price index rather than linked as previously to the earnings index. Over the past two decades prices have risen by an average of 4 per cent a year while earnings have risen by an average of 6 per cent. As a result the basic flat-rate pension has already shrunk from around 21 per cent of average earnings to around 16 per cent and on present trends will be worth barely 10 per cent of average earnings by 2020.

In 1986 the government began to tinker with the supplementary Serps so that it will pay out less to everyone who reaches retirement from 2002 onwards, and the retirement age for women will be raised gradually from 60 to 65 over a period beginning in 2009 and ending in 2020.

In an attempt to persuade as many people as possible to join a personal pension plan the government also offered rebates on contributions to the National Insurance fund to everyone who opted out of Serps and started a personal pension. Unfortunately, over-enthusiastic pension salesmen also persuaded many members of public sector and private company pension schemes to opt out of existing schemes offering guaranteed pensions linked to final salaries, and to join personal pension schemes which provided no such guarantees and usually did not enjoy the benefit of contributions from the employer.

The result was the selling of inappropriate pension plans to unsuspecting and ill-informed individuals, including miners, nurses and other low-paid and vulnerable groups. The government ordered insurance companies and financial advisers who had inappropriately sold pensions to investigate the individual losses and offer compensation, but the resulting publicity has deterred many people who should have taken out personal pension plans from doing so.

Public sector pensions

Most civil servants and other public sector workers are entitled to an extra pension on retirement, based on a multiple of their final salary on retirement and the number of years of service. Employees contribute a set percentage of their salaries, but the employers make no immediate contributions, public sector pensions are unfunded and the pensions themselves are paid out of taxation.

Company pension schemes

Many private employers offer pension schemes. Employers and employees each contribute a percentage of annual earnings into a company fund, which is managed by trustees to generate an income when the employee reaches retirement age. Choosing how to invest the contributions is the responsibility of the managers and trustees and not the employee.

Like public sector pensions, the majority of company pension plans have traditionally been defined benefit schemes, so called because the employee knows in advance the formula on which his or her pension will be calculated. Defined benefit schemes pay a pension based on a multiple of years of service and final salary. So an employee retiring at age 60 on a final salary of £24 000 after 30 years' service might be entitled to a pension of 30/80ths of £24 000, or £9000 a year.

Defined benefit schemes give employees the certainty of a pension that will be related to the salary they earn at the end of their working lives. The task of generating enough income in the fund to meet pension payments when they fall due is entirely the responsibility of the fund manager and the employer and not the employee. They are particularly attractive to employees who enjoy a long career with a single employer and reach a high salary level at retirement. They are less attractive to employees whose earnings peak early and those who change jobs frequently because they are liable to reach retirement with a number of company pensions. The earlier ones will be based on the salary they were earning when they moved, and the pension from the last employer will relate only to the last few years of work. In total they will usually be worth much less than a single pension from a single employer.

For example, a worker who spends ten years at each of three employers where he earns final salaries of £10 000, £20 000 and £30 000 might qualify for three pensions, each of 10/80ths of his salary on departure. They would be worth £1250, £2500 and £3750 respectively, a total of £7500. Even though he ended his career earning more than the employee with 30 years' service to one employer in the previous example, he ended up with a lower pension. Most pension schemes offer a lump sum or transfer value to departing employees who want to transfer the accumulated value of their fund to the next employer's fund, but most funds will charge a departing employee a transfer charge in order to protect the entitlements of those who remain.

As job security has declined, the prospects of anyone now starting work retiring from an employer in the private sector with a pension based on a lifetime of unbroken service have dropped almost to vanishing point. But as the rate of inflation has reduced, making it more difficult to achieve a high rate of return on the contributions, many employers also face the possibility of having to make additional contributions to finance the guaranteed benefits. A growing number of private employers are now closing defined benefit schemes to new employees and substituting defined contribution schemes. These are similar to personal pension schemes where the pension on retirement will be determined solely by the skill with which the contributions have been invested, usually by a professional and independent fund manager.

Personal pension schemes

Many employers, especially in small firms that have accounted for the bulk of the increase in employment over the past two decades, still do not offer company schemes. Their employees have been obliged to rely solely on the state pension when they reach retirement age or to join a personal pension scheme. The growing numbers of self-employed workers also have to take out a personal pension plan to provide for their retirement. In 1970 the government introduced tax relief on pension contributions for self-employed workers and individuals whose employers did not offer a company scheme. At the time of writing, it is not possible to contribute to a company scheme and a personal pension scheme at the same time.

Personal pension plans are contracts between the individual and the insurance company that undertakes to provide a pension in return for contributions to the fund. By definition they are defined contribution schemes and the pensions they provide are based on the value of the fund built up out of invested contributions and not on final salary and length of service.

Personal pensions are portable, which means they are not affected if the employee changes jobs, making them more suitable for employees who move frequently from one job to another. Enlightened employers can contribute to a personal pension plan for employees but they are not obliged to do so. But the fact that the final pension is based on the success of the invested contributions means members of the schemes have a very real interest in how and where the contributions are invested.

Wealthy individuals can choose a self-invested personal pension plan or SIPP, tailor-made by their financial advisers, and can invest in a wide range of assets including specific properties, but they are by definition more expensive to run.

The great majority of individuals will be part of a pooled pension fund. But the choice of which personal pension plan to join and how the funds are invested is still vitally important. Many specialist publications publish regular lists of the best-performing pension funds, but the old rule remains true: past performances are not always a guide to the future.

The investments are selected by the fund's managers and supervised by trustees. Most personal pension providers do however offer a range of different funds and allow members to select what type of funds their personal pension contributions invest in. These include cash funds and bond funds, which are suitable for cautious members and those approaching retirement, as well as with-profits funds investing in a range of assets at the discretion of the fund managers, and unit-linked pensions, which are most suitable for younger and more adventurous fund members.

Individuals are normally asked about their attitude to risk, but until very recently most pensioners were unaware of the options and left the choice entirely to the discretion of the pension manager. Readers of *Fortune Strategy* will hopefully be better equipped to make more active choices in the future.

Stakeholder pensions

From 2001 the government has introduced a new simplifed form of personal pensions, with simple rules and maximum management charges of 1 per cent a year, in an attempt to persuade anyone earning as little as £9000 a year to start a private pension plan. Their progress will be keenly watched.

Tax incentives

Pension funds are allowed to accumulate dividends and capital gains free of tax. Unlike all other forms of investment, contributions to a pension fund are also free of income tax. What this means in practice is that regular contributions either to an employer's company pension plan or to a personal pension plan or stakeholder pension are deducted from the contributor's earned income before any tax is charged. Alternatively, if individuals choose to make a lump-sum contribution out of income that has already been taxed, they can offset the tax paid against other tax liabilities and if warranted claim a tax rebate.

Either way, the contribution qualifies for tax relief at the individual investor's highest rate of tax. A standard-rate taxpayer who contributes £1000 out of earned income to a pension fund receives £1000 worth of credit although the money would have been worth only £780 after tax. Anyone who is liable to income tax at 40 per cent receives £1000 worth of credit to his or her fund although the money would have been worth only £600 as disposable income after tax.

In order to limit the potential loss of tax revenues, however, the government restricts the proportion of income that can be invested in a pension fund. For employees it is a flat 15 per cent of earned income. For the self-employed and contributors to a personal pension, the percentage starts at 17.5 per cent below the age 35 and rises in stages until in the year they reach 61 they can put 40 per cent of earned income into a pension fund. Most company schemes allow members to contribute a fixed percentage – anything from 3 to 7 per cent – to the company scheme, but employees can top up their contributions to the maximum allowed by taking out additional voluntary contributions or AVCs which go into a defined contribution scheme.

The ability to save tax on contributions to an approved pension fund is unique and highly attractive, especially to investors who have already taken care of other competing claims on their income and have bought their own home and raised and educated their children. But there are some disadvantages in investing in pension funds, and some bolder financial experts claim that investments in shares and managed funds, especially in individual savings accounts that offer exemption from income and capital gains tax, are equally likely to produce long-term financial returns and have the additional advantage of flexibility.

If necessary, investments can always be cashed to meet financial emergencies. Pension funds, however, cannot be tapped for money until the individual reaches pensionable age. This can be as low as 30 for professional footballers, 40 for airline pilots. But for the majority of members of a company scheme the earliest age at which they can retire is usually 50. Employees who leave before the normal retirement age of 65 for men and 60 for women will usually receive a substantially reduced pension. This reflects the fact that they will leave with less service and lower final salaries than those who last the course. Younger pensioners will also have a greater life expectancy and will expect to draw a pension for more years than those who work to normal retirement.

Annuities

Although defined benefit schemes pay guaranteed pensions, all other pension funds must sooner or later be used to buy an annuity, which is an income for life. Under UK law an individual who reaches retirement age can draw up to 25 per cent of the value of their pension fund at the time of retirement as tax-free cash. But at the time of writing the remaining portion of the pension fund must be used to buy an annual pension or annuity. Most of the leading insurance companies offer annuities and rates vary slightly from one company to another. Pensioners are not obliged to buy an annuity from the company that manages their pension fund, and can shop around for the best terms on offer, although only one pensioner in seven currently does so. Once a pensioner has bought an annuity he or she can draw an income for life but cannot renegotiate the terms or recover their capital.

Annuities can be arranged for one person or for a couple. They can be chosen to pay a fixed sum for life, or rise each year according to a prearranged formula or in line with inflation. They can be guaranteed for a minimum of five years after retirement or they can die with the pensioner. Naturally, guaranteed annuities, inflation-linked annuities and pensions which provide for spouses pay smaller sums to start with to compensate for the prospect of paying more, for longer, later.

But all conventional annuities which guarantee a fixed level of payment suffer a serious disadvantage. They are paid out of the income obtained from investing the lump sum at retirement in long-term gilts with an average life of around 15 years. For a pensioner, buying an annuity is in fact much the same as investing in a single asset class, and specifically in fixed-interest stocks which as we have seen have proved most vulnerable to inflation. Anyone who buys an annuity surrenders his or her capital in return for an annual income. On current annuity rates, a man retiring at the age of 65 will have to live for around 14 years to recoup the lost capital, and if inflation increases above the rate current at the time the annuity is bought, the income may never be enough to recover the real value of the capital which has been surrendered.

In the early 1990s the yield on long-dated gilts was in excess of 10 per cent and pensioners who retired at that time will enjoy the benefit for the rest of their lives. But as inflation has fallen, so have interest rates and the yield on gilt-edged stock, and annuity rates on new pensions have almost halved in a decade. The situation has been made worse by the strength of the UK economy which increased the tax base and left the Treasury with a tax surplus. That in turn means that the supply of new gilt-edged stocks has fallen sharply, leading to a scarcity of bonds for annuity providers to invest in. After tax the yield on gilts had fallen to its lowest levels in 30 years. Although pension funds benefited from the rise in the value of investments, providing pensioners on retirement with a larger 'pot' of money, the obligation to buy an annuity attracted growing criticism from both individuals and their advisers.

Pensioners who stop working are not obliged to take their pension immediately. They can, if they wish, leave the cash in their fund to accumulate, or arrange to transfer it into an 'income draw-down fund', from which they can draw an income without losing control of their fund. If they die before buying an annuity, the capital in the fund then becomes part of their estate. But draw-down plans are expensive to set up and worthwhile only for pensioners with lump sums of at least £100 000 to invest.

Pensioners can, however, get a better annuity by delaying the date at which they start to take the annuity. A man of 65 could expect around 15 per cent more than a man of 60 because the pension provider knows full well that the pension will die with the pensioner or at least with his surviving spouse. But there is no guarantee that it is worth waiting for the general level of annuity rates to rise. They could just as easily fall further. In any case, pensioners under current rules must surrender the capital in their pension fund and buy an annuity when they reach the age of 75.

A number of insurance companies offer investors an annuity linked to stock market performance rather than the yield on gilt-edged stocks. The pensioner loses the certainty of a guaranteed income each year but gains an exposure to share-based investments which have proved the best investment performers over the longer term. Unit-linked annuities pay annual pensions based on the returns on unit trusts. Another alternative is a with-profits annuity that invites pensioners to choose a target level of growth in equity prices, say 4 per cent a year. If actual returns exceeded the target, the annuity would increase in the following year, but it could also fall if returns were below target. The lower the target, the easier it is to beat but the smaller the starting annuity in year one.

Figure 7.4 shows how six of the main types of annuities performed from 1989 to 1999, based on an initial investment of £100 000. The starting points and the subsequent performances for subsequent years have varied, and the

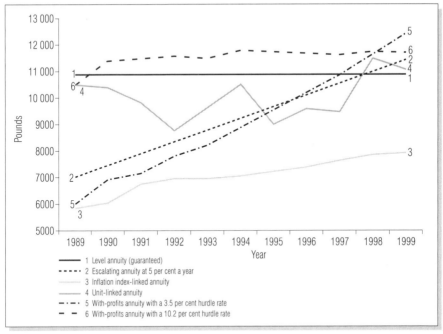

Source: Equitable Life

FIGURE 7.4 Comparison of annual returns of different types of annuities purchased in 1989

results should not be seen as a forecast of future returns however. The purpose is to show some of the dynamics that can drive the returns of different types of annuities.

The escalating annuity taken out in 1989 was worth only 65 per cent of the level annuity in the first year and took nine years to catch up. The inflation index-linked annuity performed poorly throughout because inflation was less than expected. The unit-linked annuity, overall, did not over this period provide a superior return to the level annuity to compensate for its greater volatility. The with-profits annuities both benefited from the solid performance of the equity market, especially the one with the high initial pay-out and high performance target. While the one with the low initial pay-out and low performance target grew steadily, the high starting yield of gilts meant that it took almost eight years for its annual payout to exceed the payout of the level annuity.

Looking forward, some general points are helpful when selecting annuities.

- In the case of all annuities, those who live longest do best and are subsidized by those annuitants who die early. In this sense it is like life insurance in reverse. An investor with a level annuity will also be better off if inflation falls and will be potentially devastated if it rises well beyond inflationary expectations at the time of buying the annuity.

- More complex annuities that try to ensure a minimum payout to investors' estates in the event of early death, to hedge against inflation, or to capture some of the profits in the event of strong stock market performance, result in a significant reduction in the amount paid by the annuity at the outset. Whether it is worth this price comes down to one's assessment of expected longevity and the likely behaviour of both inflation and the stock market over this period. These are, of course, difficult things to pick, so it is worth considering seeking expert, independent advice. In practice, a spread of different types of annuities may be sensible in many cases.

The link between pensions and annuities makes for a complicated equation when deciding investment strategy. The overall complexity associated with pension funds has led some advisers to argue that the disadvantages outweigh their unique tax advantages. Hence individuals would be better off simply paying tax on their salaries and investing the surplus into a balanced portfolio of directly owned assets, including cash, bonds, shares, property and pooled funds, and make full use of tax-free ISA allowances. But the truth is that anyone who can afford to do so should hedge their bets and do both.

We conclude with the following general points.

- For employees in higher personal income tax brackets who are planning long-term savings, a pension plan to which the employer contributes can be a potentially attractive alternative to receiving an equivalent amount in salary.

- For both the employed and self-employed, the ability to save tax on contributions is particularly advantageous, and this is compounded by the fact that earnings can grow tax-free within a pension plan. However, the ultimate pensions themselves are treated as taxable income. It is worth noting that the average investor outside a pension fund is likely to be subject to minimal tax on capital gains and dividend income, and no tax at all is payable on ISAs.

- Unlike other investments, contributions to a pension fund cannot be withdrawn and used for other purposes.

- The opportunity to draw 25 per cent of a pension fund tax-free on retirement is extremely attractive, but the requirement to use the balance to buy an annuity is very restrictive.

- Personal pension contributions are by definition a long-term investment. The value of the eventual fund on retirement depends crucially on compound growth over a long period of time, up to 40 years. Pension fund providers never tire of reminding potential customers that each year's delay in starting a fund is likely to have a disproportionate impact on the eventual size of the fund.

Assessing managed investments

Managed investments have two components: investments and managers. In one sense, a pooled fund is the sum of assets that it owns at any time. However, the mix of assets will change at the discretion of the manager. This makes the manager, rather than the current assets, the key determinant of future performance.

Selecting managed investments involves working out the types of funds that suit an investor's personal objectives, and selecting managers who will achieve those objectives for an acceptable fee. The goal is to choose an *appropriate* fund; searching for the *best* fund can prove elusive, and ultimately counterproductive.

Each investor has different needs in terms of risk and return, and any strategy will require different asset mixes at different times. Also, the sheer size of world securities markets means that no manager is going to perform best in all markets and under all conditions. However, it is still important to distinguish competent, professional managers from opportunistic optimists.

In this section, we point out the limitations of the so-called published 'performance tables', and look at how to assess the key features of a fund and examine its performance in context. We then highlight some requirements of a professional manager.

The checklist

A starting point for winnowing down the hundreds of managed funds is to work out which ones generally suit the investor's objectives. So, the first questions to ask about any managed fund are: what sort of fund is this supposed to be, and how does it work?

Any good fund manager or investment adviser promoting a particular fund should be able to produce some basic information through a prospectus, seminar or interview. The types of data required include the type of fund, the charges including initial charges and annual management charges, how cheap and easy it is to switch from one fund to another, the size and history of the fund, its purpose, objectives and strategy, whether it is geared or intends to be, its asset-allocation policy, and the track records of the manager and key decision makers.

The assets

From the point of view of investment strategy, the most important characteristic of a fund is its risk/return profile. In assessing a fund, the objective is to see where it fits in the spectrum between 'conservative' (low risk) and 'aggressive' (high risk). An informative starting point is to examine the assets of the fund, checking the risk/return qualities of each asset and the diversification of the overall portfolio.

A conservative equity fund (or equity component of a diversified fund) will be weighted towards shares in well-established, larger companies in reasonably secure industries; the stocks will have low Betas. The portfolio will be spread fairly evenly across a range of industries. An aggressive equity fund will lean towards younger, smaller companies with high Betas, and may at any one time have large concentrations in just a few stocks.

In real-estate shares and funds with significant property holdings, a conservative portfolio will be dominated by high-quality commercial properties in prime, central business district locations or major regional shopping centres. The properties will have an established rental flow but will still be relatively new, and will be owned as passive investments. An aggressive property company may own fringe property, and place greater emphasis on adding value through refurbishment and development.

In interest-bearing investments such as gilt and corporate bond funds, those that have most of their assets in government paper, or at least AA+ rated corporate fixed-interest securities, and a large concentration in cash, may be regarded as conservative. Funds with more of a balance towards longer-term securities and higher credit risks such as junk bonds tend towards the aggressive.

In with-profits funds, the mix among the asset classes is obviously critical. Funds with greater emphasis on cash and bonds tend to be more conservative, while those with a higher concentration of equities will be more aggressive. By definition, a with-profits fund would aim to use the benefits of diversification between the asset classes to reduce overall portfolio risk.

The investment style

The assets of a fund provide a snapshot of its risk/return profile. However, the future performance of the fund depends on how the manager selects assets and runs the portfolio over time. This concept is known as the *investment style*, and again ranges from top-down to bottom-up methods of stock selection and from conservative to aggressive.

A conservative manager will place primary emphasis on measures of fundamental value, such as the premium over net tangible assets and the yield. The conservative manager avoids taking big bets on any one stock, property, sector or market, and tends towards a buy-and-hold rather than a pick-the-cycle strategy.

An aggressive manager, in contrast, will look at taking advantage of special situations, such as takeover potential, and capitalizing on market trends, irrespective of fundamental value. The mix of assets reflects a collection of individual bets; investments are selected from a bottom-up perspective. The trading strategy is active, with considerably more buying and selling. An aggressive manager is more likely than a conservative manager to have a 'star' system, in which choice of assets is in the hands of one or two key people.

Like all human beings, fund managers are influenced by fashion, and markets can be heavily affected by fashion and investment buzz-words. Conservative fund managers have tended to support the value school of investment, picking shares whose price is below the value of the net assets, and recovery stocks. These are companies with a good track record whose shares are temporarily depressed by cyclical trends or by specific factors, to the point where the P/E ratio is historically low, or the dividend yield is well above the market average, and there is a reasonable prospect of the payout not being cut.

Aggressive fund managers are on the look-out for growth companies whose earnings are rising at above-average rates and may well decide to run with glamour stocks. Many subscribe to the 'momentum' school, which recognizes bandwagon effects in the market and seeks to exploit them. The momentum theory was responsible for the enormous rush around the turn of the century to buy information technology, internet and e-commerce stocks which sent prices soaring and sucked huge sums out of less fashionable sectors.

Performance

The biggest single pitfall in selecting managed investments is the myth of past performance. The key issue for an investor is: what is the *future* return of a fund likely to be? Many investors try to answer this question by reviewing the 'performance' tables published in newspapers and investment magazines. While they do have some specific uses, on their own such tables have limitations.

Almost all published returns are based on measurements over two points in time – a start date and an end date. In other words, they show only the return that somebody who invested exactly on that start date and withdrew exactly on that end date would have received. They tell you nothing about what may have happened *in between* those dates. Even where the time between the two dates is long, it is not possible to say anything about whether the returns over the entire period were generally good or poor.

For example, Figure 7.5 shows that the return for an Australian investor who invested in a particular balanced strategy managed by ipac securities limited from 1 July 1996 to 30 June 1999 was 11.06 per cent per annum. However, someone who invested on 1 October 1997 was looking at a return of only 0.42 per cent over the course of the next year because of the impact of the emerging markets crisis on world financial markets. Someone investing on 1 July 1998 would have received a return one year later of 8.72 per cent.

What this exercise shows is that information on point-to-point performance, in isolation, is of little use. It is essential to look at the assets, goals and investment style of the manager to work out where over time the fund is likely to go. In this case, the fund is a diversified, medium-risk portfolio which is likely to be fairly resilient and bounce back after short-term fluctuations – as proved the case after the emerging markets crisis.

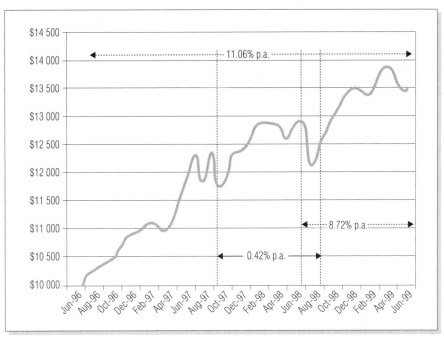

Source: Based on an investment of A$10 000 in an ipac securities' inflation plus 4 strategy

FIGURE 7.5   Value of an investment of A$10 000 from July 1996 to June 1999

The point about looking at past performance is to evaluate what was actually going on during the period in question and see what happened in relation to the fund's stated objectives. As discussed in earlier chapters, it may well be that one fund does better than others during good times, but it may be an aggressive fund with assets that have high Betas. Conversely, a fund may do much worse than others in bad times, for the same reasons. The more general issue is that past performance alone is a poor predictor of the future.

Several studies have demonstrated this point. One by John Evans of the consulting firm PGE examined the returns that would have been achieved if an Australian superannuation investor had placed an annual contribution with the fund manager who, in the previous year, had produced the highest return. If the investor had used this strategy over a five-year period, the overall return would have ranked in the bottom quartile – the worst quarter – of performance of managed superannuation funds.[1] UK studies show similar results.

This study illustrates a fact well known to research companies analyzing funds managers: that relatively high returns over a period usually reflect higher risk, not greater skill. Sometimes market conditions and circumstances allow these higher-risk strategies to persist, but sooner or later they experience periods of substantial loss.

Another trap in assessing past returns relates to the size and age of the fund. Small, new funds may often produce spectacular returns in a short period, but only because they have a narrow portfolio and have been lucky with a few winners.

To evaluate a fund manager's likely results in the future, then, we need to analyze *performance* and not confuse it with past returns. Analyzing performance involves looking at the factors underlying the returns and determining how sustainable they will be in the future. This does not mean ignoring the past. Rather, it involves looking at the past as one of a range of other factors to gauge the *trueness* of the fund to its purpose. And above all, it involves understanding the quality and size of the risks that the manager has taken, and evaluating returns in this context. Managers who use a high-quality risk process are likely to apply the four key investment principles.

They will have the resources to undertake fundamental research to assess the true *quality* of the assets in which they are investing. Low-quality risk managers, in contrast, are more likely to invest in what is fashionable (that is, going up in price), regardless of fundamentals.

High-quality managers will be concerned about ensuring that the assets being purchased are well priced in relation to their prospects and hence represent good *value*. And they will have the resources to generate a *diversity* of well-valued, fundamentally sound investments for the portfolio.

The low-quality manager does not have the resources required to assess value with any reasonable degree of accuracy. A concentration of the portfolio in a small number of investments also represents a low-quality risk, even more so if the manager has a limited ability to value those investments. Finally, the high-quality manager relies on *time*, not timing.

In assessing funds for quality, three further comparisons are useful.

Compare returns with stated objectives: a fund should, over time, have a risk/return profile that is roughly in line with its stated objectives. This can work both ways. A fund that describes itself as seeking high returns for investors with high risk tolerances would not be fulfilling its objectives if it produced consistently poor returns compared with the market average. On the other hand, a fund describing itself as conservative, which enjoyed returns far in excess of the market average, could be questionable. Such a fund might be taking on more risk than it makes out, and could be due for a fall.

An interesting case on the performance issue concerned Peter Young, manager with Morgan Grenfell Asset Management, who during the mid-1990s developed a reputation for being a hot-shot based purely on his performance numbers. Young was a manager of European Growth and European Capital Growth Fund, with a very aggressive strategy of investing in small companies. Young's reputation and the apparently high performance of the funds attracted a flood of money, and in 1996 he was named Fund Manager of the Year by *Investment Week* magazine. The same year, Young was sacked amid allegations that funds under his management had secretly been channelled through Luxembourg shelf companies into highly speculative offshore ventures. Young was charged in 1998 with conspiracy to defraud and of conspiring to conceal material.

At the time of writing he had made his second appearance before a magistrate where, the *Daily Telegraph* reported, he was 'wearing a coral top and vampish tight-fitting red skirt, sporting a shoulder-length classic bob and high-heeled buckled shoes'.

The affair sparked a run on the funds and the only thing that prevented the investors from suffering severe losses was the fact that Deutsche Bank, Morgan Grenfell's ultimate parent, to its credit, stepped in and spent around £400 million by means of compensation and fund injection.

This example highlights the importance of looking behind the performance numbers and truly understanding the risks being taken and the sustainability of the strategy. Something which looks too good to be true probably is.

In a more subtle sense, the returns of a fund should, over time, correspond to the investment strategy, i.e. the ups and downs of a fund should be consistent with the stated strategy of the manager. And, as we will see in the next section, when it comes to using managed funds as strategic tools, consistency is vital.

Compare returns with the efficient frontier: when comparing the performance of different funds, it is essential to compare them on a risk-adjusted basis. A good fund is not necessarily one that produces the highest return. Rather, it is a fund on the efficient frontier: it provides the highest return for a given level of risk, or the lowest risk for a given level of return. An aggressive fund should do better than a conservative fund in good times, but the conservative fund should be more resilient when the markets turn down. In the medium to long term, however, an aggressive fund must demonstrate better returns than a conservative fund to justify the higher risk.

Compare returns with the benchmark: a fund should perform well compared with a relevant benchmark. For broadly based equity funds, this may be the FT

All-Share index. For a fund specializing in smaller companies, it may be the SmallCap index. The identification of a relevant benchmark is handy in identifying which pond a manager is fishing in. Comparing a fund with a benchmark is useful in seeing how the manager has performed against a passive investment approach. If the manager claims to have done better than the benchmark, it is worth asking: how? What tilts and risks did the manager take in deviating from the benchmark portfolio?

Assess fees against the value added: as discussed in the introduction to this chapter, a large part of the advantage of a managed investment is in providing economies of scale, establishing and maintaining the portfolio, and dealing with the mechanics of custodial arrangements. These functions are certainly worth a management fee of 1 per cent or so. But beyond this level, a manager has to add value to the funds under management to justify the fee, especially when fund yields are themselves only 1–2 per cent.

One way of looking at this question is to ask: what is the manager doing that is better than throwing 30 darts at a list of securities? As discussed above, this need not necessarily be producing above-average returns. The manager of an index fund that succeeds in tracking the appropriate index is adding value. A conservative fund manager who succeeds in keeping risk low for a reasonable return is also adding value. Such managers could justifiably charge fees of, perhaps, 1 per cent. A manager who demands a fee of 2–3 per cent has to be adding a fair bit of value to the portfolio to justify it.

It is here that comparing the performance of a fund with the market average has some use. Compare two imaginary equity funds, ABC and XYZ. ABC charges a 1 per cent management fee just to track the index. XYZ charges a 2 per cent fee to run an aggressive, stock-picking equity portfolio. To justify the higher management fee, XYZ will have to produce a return over time that is at least 1 per cent above the index. While this example is simplistic, it provides another perspective on the efficient markets hypothesis: superior information can sometimes enable an investor to beat the market, but this superior performance has to be compared with the cost involved in acquiring that information.

Strategic issues: triple-level diversification

The most important level of diversification is among the asset classes, and here the variety and flexibility of managed investments are of great advantage. An investor who wishes to diversify over all asset classes in a single investment can put money into one of many with-profit funds, each of which will offer a slightly different asset mix and risk/return profile. An investor who wants to have greater direct control over the mix of asset classes can invest in a collection of funds that each covers a single asset class. It is then simple to increase or decrease the weightings by buying or selling units in property funds, equity funds, cash funds and bond funds. As discussed, most management groups offer the ability to 'switch' investments between sector funds for a low fee or, in many cases, no fee – a particularly useful mechanism.

There is, however, another dimension to selecting the right mix of funds, which gets back to the difference between direct investment and management. Apart from the underlying assets at any one time, the performance of a fund is determined by the manager and the manager's investment style. A fully diversified mix of funds, therefore, would be diversified at three levels: over assets, over investment styles, and over managers.

International dimensions

While pooled funds have made domestic diversification easier for individuals, they have revolutionized the ability to diversify internationally. Managed funds have made the most impenetrable markets accessible to the private investor, further expanding the diversification 'toolbox'.

A manager may have separate French, German, British, Italian, Spanish and Swiss funds, and also a European fund that has invested in each of these areas. Alternatively, a manager may have an international bond fund, an international property securities fund, an international currency (cash) fund and an international equities fund. From these, the manager may construct an international balanced fund.

There are, however, complexities associated with international investment through managed funds. The investor can basically do one of two things: buy units in a domestic-based fund, which invests overseas, or invest in an overseas fund. However, a British investor who wanted to put money into the US share market may find it difficult if not impossible to invest in US-based 'mutual funds' that invest in the US market. Most of them will only deal with investors resident in the US.

Next, we look at how the investor can combine all the elements that we have talked about in the book so far into a sensible investment plan.

Note

1   Evans, John, circa 1990 unpublished study, Palmer, Gould and Evans, Sydney.

CHAPTER 8

Designing the portfolio

Summary

▪ The purpose of investment is to give investors a better chance of getting what they want out of life. The first step, therefore, is for individuals to work out their particular needs and aspirations.

▪ Setting goals means thinking carefully about lifestyle priorities, because few investors can have it all. There are trade-offs between risk, return and time.

▪ Investors need a certain level of return to achieve their objectives. So the next task is to identify the long-term asset allocation that will maximize the chances of producing that return, at the least possible risk.

▪ Portfolio managers use computerized models to help in strategic asset allocation, but the principles can be applied without such number-crunching to develop a sensible investment strategy.

▪ Above all, the most important tools in portfolio construction are good judgement and common sense, to provide an overall strategy that can adapt to changing times without undue risk.

Introduction: investing in the big picture

There is no magic formula that suits all investors because each person has a unique set of ambitions, needs and emotions. Similarly, there is no *best* investment, *best* portfolio, or *best* trade-off. The only *best* investment strategy is one that meets the particular lifestyle goals and needs of the individual.

The strategy, then, is simply a means to an end (although it can obviously provide enjoyment and interest along the way). Financial return allows investors to have a greater choice about the life that they want to live. And an efficient portfolio produces the highest return for the risk that the investor needs to take to achieve lifestyle goals.

Designing a lifestyle financial plan involves four main stages, which are closely intertwined:

- establishing realistic lifestyle goals;

- identifying the total level of return (above inflation) required to achieve those goals;

- harnessing the power of investment markets by efficiently allocating assets between the four asset classes. This will maximize the chances of producing that return *reliably*, at the lowest possible risk;

- assessing the level of risk required to achieve those goals and making further trade-offs between risk, return and time if necessary.

The final step, of course, is to implement the strategy. In this chapter, we explore these phases and look at some examples of how the process can work in practice.

Lifestyle financial planning

A coach who is working with a world-class athlete for the first time does not immediately discuss which vitamins should be taken, or which exercises should be performed. First, the coach and athlete set some realistic objectives – if the athlete is truly special, perhaps a bronze medal in the World Championships in four years' time, followed by Olympic gold six years down the track. The coach then assesses the athlete's abilities, age, fitness and physique and designs a plan that maximizes the athlete's chances of achieving these goals.

If the athlete suffers an injury along the way, that plan will probably need to be updated. Perhaps the athlete will develop more quickly than envisaged, in which case the timetable may be shortened and new goals set.

In the same way, the starting point of any investment strategy is also the end point – the personal ambitions of the individual. Not even the best financial adviser can design an effective plan without clear objectives to work with. This would be like the coach training an athlete for some vague possible success, some time in the future.

Conventional statements such as 'maximize return, minimize risk' do not, however, qualify as objectives. This would be equivalent to the athlete aiming to run at great speed with minimal exertion, while ignoring the most important questions: how fast, and for what purpose?

Investment affects material well being but also less tangible things in people's lives, such as the sense of security, confidence or control. Lifestyle goals may include anything from pursuing further education to building a new home, paying for a wedding, or simply achieving a level of income that allows for regular nights out and weekends away.

In defining these goals, almost all investors will have to make trade-offs: between enjoying money now, and saving for later; between retiring earlier or later; and between security and high return. Again, these decisions will be influenced by a range of factors that are specific to each individual. These include the following.

Assets and income: few investors start from scratch; they may have bank accounts, maybe some property, some form of pension fund, perhaps a few shares. It is useful to classify these according to the asset classes: cash, fixed interest, equities, and property. The approximate values of these assets, any income they generate, and the degree to which they are fixed or saleable should be assessed. All significant income should also be calculated, including salary, royalties, pensions, income from self-employment, and so on. It is then worth projecting into the future, to get an idea of income in years to come.

Liabilities and outgoings: this includes the usual things needed for daily life, from food and housing to petrol or clothes, and other less obvious requirements. Debts, ranging from mortgages to credit cards, form one sort of liability, in terms of both interest costs and paying off the capital. The current or future cost of supporting dependants may also need to be provided for, as may health or life insurance. Most investors also allow for children's higher education and providing for retirement income.

Cashflow wants: wants can range from a top-of-the-range sports car to holidays or home improvements. It is important, however, to distinguish between needs and wants because the only way to fulfil some goals may be by taking on additional risk.

Tax: this is not the most critical investment issue, but tax considerations can help to determine which investment strategies will be most effective. At its simplest level, this may involve establishing whether the individual's income, after deductions, is below the tax-free threshold. For taxpayers, it is then a matter of identifying the appropriate tax bracket and any special factors that will increase or decrease this liability now or in the future. We have already discussed the tax advantages of contributing to a pension fund, and investing in individual savings accounts, National Savings Certificates and venture capital trusts.

Time horizon: it is also essential to establish at least a loose time sequence. This may involve assessing roughly when certain sources of income will come on and off line in the years ahead; when the investor's income needs and wants will arise; and, more generally, when the investor expects to do things such as have children or retire. This does not mean ordering life from cradle to grave according to a rigid timetable. A sound investment strategy will be flexible enough to adjust to changing circumstances and goals.

Once lifestyle goals and priorities have been decided, the investor will require a certain level of return over time in order to achieve them. Fortunately, as we have discussed, investment markets have been fairly reliable over time, and a well-balanced strategy can harness their power and deliver the necessary return reliably. This will take time, however, and it will take patience and discipline.

Because inflation erodes buying power over time, the required return is best expressed as a margin above inflation, otherwise known as the real return. Over short periods of time real returns can be negative, and investors may have to accept that as part of the risk, but the whole point of investing is to secure positive real returns over time Real return alone is only part of the story, however. It is also essential to focus on the *total return* that a portfolio will generate from income and, where appropriate, from capital gains, rather than simply annual income. During the high-inflation 1970s and 1980s, it was common practice to worry about income first, and pursue capital gains with whatever was left. But while this may have provided an immediate income to spend, it usually meant accepting a lower *total return* and a lower standard of living later on.

Last but not least, the investor needs to aim at securing a total return after paying due taxes. As we have seen, income and capital gains are taxed in different ways. In practice most people require their investments to generate some cash flow for them to live on. Rather than sacrificing return by focusing on income-providing investments, it may be more sensible to generate a higher total return and draw down on capital to fund cash flow requirements as necessary. By focusing on total return, the investor can generate a far greater pie from which to cut a slice.

After establishing the required total return, the next step is to allocate assets so that the investor achieves that return with the least possible amount of risk. In the next section, we consider how the investor can do this effectively.

At the same time, the required return and asset allocation determine the degree of risk that the investor needs to take to achieve his or her lifestyle goals. Both technical and emotional issues arise with this decision. The technical issues include security of income, age, underlying assets and commitments. The emotional issues relate to the individual's temperament. Some people prefer to live fast and will accept higher risk in the hope of gaining more return. Others may have a deep aversion to any possibility of losing money.

The point is for the investor to understand the potential results of taking on more or less risk in the planning phase. As a general rule, the lower the risk, the more secure the investment but the lower the expected return in the long run. The higher the risk, the greater the chance that the return may be more or less than expected – particularly in the short term – but the greater the expected return in the long run.

If the investor is unwilling to accept the necessary level of risk to achieve his or her lifestyle objectives, further trade-offs will be needed. It is important that the investor knows the impact of each decision on the lifestyle that they wish to lead.

The series of steps outlined here – set lifestyle goals, establish required return, allocate assets and assess risk – differs from the traditional financial planning approach. The traditional method is to take the investor's 'risk profile' at the outset, then determine the types of assets that the investor will feel comfortable with and, finally, estimate the level of return that the investor will receive. This then determines the lifestyle that the investor should be able to lead.

The problem with this approach is that it starts with – and therefore depends on – the investor's perception of risk. And, not surprisingly, investors have utterly different ideas about what risk is, and what it means to their lives. The process also fails to pay enough attention to the lifestyle trade-offs that will need to be made, depending on the risk level that the investor will accept. And this is why, even today, a significant proportion of savings is still invested in cash or conservative investments which carry no risk of capital loss, no prospects of capital gains, and no protection against inflation. Investors with such a strategy are unlikely to enjoy the type of lifestyle that they may otherwise be able to pursue. And, just as importantly, they are unlikely to enjoy the sense of control that can come from having a set of goals, and a clear strategy to achieve them.

Lifestyle financial planning involves working out what these goals are, and then taking actions today (for example, sacrificing some of today's consumption) to achieve them. By taking sensible investment risks and managing them well, the astute investor is able to achieve more of each of their short-, medium- and long-term goals. In doing so, they are able to choose a better life.

We now look at the technical aspects of putting together an investment strategy.

Asset allocation 1: technical approaches

The most important decision an investor will make is how to distribute funds among the four asset classes. The investor can achieve a considerable part of the potential benefit from investment markets just by making this decision well. Making good decisions is not the same thing as trying to pick the market, in terms of either individual assets or market timing.

In this section, we look at technical approaches that involve computer calculations. In the next, we describe common-sense approaches that achieve the same objectives.

Finding the best mix of assets involves three key variables: risk, return, and correlation. The ultimate goal, having determined the degree of risk required, is to find the optimal portfolio on the efficient frontier.

Many investment advisers tell clients to diversify their portfolios to reduce risk, and 'spread the money around' to cover shares, property and interest-bearing investments. However, simply dividing up the portfolio among these asset groups in equal proportions, or by some other arbitrary formula, does not necessarily reduce risk and can substantially reduce return. Modern portfolio theory can help to work out the *optimum* mix of asset classes that provides *maximum* return for the risk taken.

Variation in asset allocation within portfolios can produce quite different results over time, as demonstrated in Chapter 3. This shows the potential for superior asset class allocation to produce better results for all investors, whether by reducing risk, increasing returns, or both. Whatever the investor's objectives, a strategically planned portfolio will stand a much better chance of achieving them than a randomly diversified portfolio.

Of course, while this is useful, putting modern portfolio theory into practice involves several more dimensions. First, using risk and return data based on historical performance is not good enough. The investor is putting money into the future, not the past, so it is necessary to incorporate forecasts of future market performance. Second, the tax profile of the investor has to be taken into account if after-tax returns are to be maximized. Third, any special considerations such as the investor's nervousness about putting too much money overseas or a need to hold a certain level of cash should also be incorporated into the asset allocation equation.

This task can be accomplished in several stages, starting with the establishment of historical benchmarks for risk, return and correlation. From there, economic forecasts can be applied against these benchmarks to provide a set of assumptions about future market performance. Next, the optimal basic asset mix to achieve particular return targets at the lowest possible risk can be determined. Finally, the portfolio can be fine-tuned to take into account tax, and any special constraints. We now look at the stages.

Setting the benchmarks

The first step is to acquire historical risk, return and correlation data for the selected range of investment options. In this section, we will use data collected from January 1990 to December 1999 for UK asset classes, plus foreign equities (other foreign asset classes such as bonds and property could be included, but for this exercise the options were kept to the five). This period is reasonably reflective of the modern deregulated UK economy. Table 8.1 presents the data.

TABLE 8.1 Performance of UK and foreign asset classes, January 1990–December 1999

			Correlations				
Asset class	Return	Risk	Shares	Property	Cash	Gilts	International shares
Shares	14.7%	15.2%	1				
Property	8.2%	4.6%	0.1	1			
Cash	8.1%	1.7%	−0.1	−0.6	1		
Gilts	11.7%	8.5%	0.5	−0.1	0.2	1	
International shares	11.4%	18.9%	0.8	0.2	−0.2	0.2	1

Source: Barclays Capital, Equity-Gilt Study, 1999

The next stage is to work out *why* these asset classes performed the way they did – to look 'behind the price' to see what motivated the markets. The years from 1990 to 1999 included a period in which interest rates were relatively high, the stock market took a tumble and later recovered, and the commercial property market fell from a major peak before stabilizing and then recovering modestly. It was also a period of fairly high inflation, followed by several years of low inflation. Having established these factors, the investor can start to assess how they may change in the future.

Assembling the forecast

The next stage of the exercise uses a hypothetical five-year forecast, based on a set of economic assumptions. It assumes that the economy is likely to remain in a period of lower inflation. While interest rates are expected to fall as a result, political uncertainty may still cause them to fluctuate considerably. Lower interest rates generally may be expected to maintain good stock market returns, and a supply shortage may cause returns from property and gilt-edged stocks to rise. Table 8.2 shows the data produced in this forecast.

TABLE 8.2 Hypothetical future performance of asset classes

Asset class	Return (%)	Risk (%)
Shares	13	18
Property	11	17
Cash	6	1
Gilts	7	5
International shares	14	20

The forecast, rather than the historical returns data, will be used in the optimization process. The risk numbers have been altered somewhat. In particular, the overall strong bull market conditions that prevailed for much of the 1990s probably resulted in an understating of the future risk of UK equities. The evidence is that correlations among the asset classes are not subject to great volatility, so we have not amended these.

Using the optimizer

We now have the data for working out the best asset allocation. In this exercise, we look at two investors: one with a short-term horizon who can tolerate only very low risk, and another whose time horizon and goals allow medium risk. We can define the low-risk investor's risk tolerance quantitatively: a standard deviation of about 4 per cent. The medium-risk investor, we decide, can tolerate a maximum standard deviation of around 11 per cent. The objective is to get the best possible return for these levels of risk. We know there will be optimum portfolios for each risk profile, which will have specific mixtures of the asset groups. But how do we find them?

The best portfolio takes into account risk, return and correlation: a complex three-way relationship. The fact that a particular investment has a low correlation and hence provides good diversification benefits may not be sufficient if the return is too low. Conversely, a particular investment may provide a good return and an acceptable risk, but be so closely correlated with the rest of the portfolio as to be virtually useless for diversification.

Economists and finance theorists have developed sophisticated models to work out the optimal portfolio from risk, return and correlation data. Investment firms call them *asset allocation models*. The computer sorts through all possible combinations of assets, and selects the portfolios that make up the efficient frontier. Even for five investment categories, and simplification of allocation options to whole percentage points, the process involves sifting through hundreds of thousands of alternative portfolios.

The exercise described in this chapter came from a real computerized optimization sequence. The computer was asked to find the optimal portfolios for our low-risk and medium-risk investors. Figure 8.1 shows the portfolios.

For the low-risk investor, the computer allocated most of the portfolio to the lowest-risk asset class: cash. A significant proportion, 9 per cent, went into gilts. Given the low correlations between gilts and cash, this would produce a mix of interest-bearing investment with very low risk. To provide a slight lift in the return to the investor, and for diversification benefit, the computer put as much money as it could into higher-return assets until the maximum risk level (or risk threshold) was reached. It allocated 11 per cent to UK shares and 10 per cent to international shares. The estimated volatility of the portfolio was kept down to 4 per cent, but with a respectable expected return of 7.6 per cent.

For the medium-risk investor, the computer came up with a more diverse portfolio. Again, there was a reasonable allocation to cash and bonds, but this time the major weighting went to the higher-risk, higher-return bonds sector. The rest was devoted to higher-risk assets, including international shares, property and domestic equities. With this mix, the computer produced a

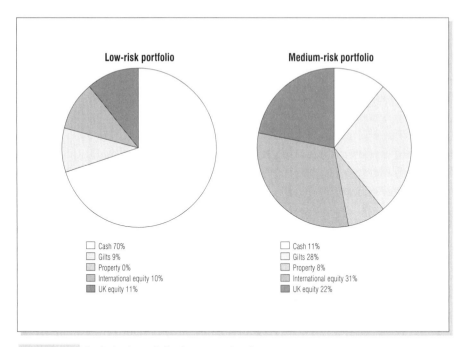

Low-risk portfolio

Medium-risk portfolio

Cash 70%
Gilts 9%
Property 0%
International equity 10%
UK equity 11%

Cash 11%
Gilts 28%
Property 8%
International equity 31%
UK equity 22%

FIGURE 8.1   Optimized portfolio: incorporating forecasts

portfolio with an expected return of 10.5 per cent, with a volatility risk factor of 10.8 per cent.

This is a prime example of how portfolio theory works in practice, and can help to make a well-designed portfolio more than the sum of its parts. The process of optimization can trade off the risk associated with the asset classes against each other, taking advantage of the diversification benefit of low correlations, to produce a far more efficient risk/return result.

We now demonstrate how to use the optimizer to outcomes that are even more fine-tuned.

Taking tax into account

What counts to the investor is the return from a particular asset, or portfolio of assets, after tax. So tax considerations can significantly alter the relative attractiveness of different asset classes. As noted in Chapter 2, at the time of writing the capital gains allowance in the UK is substantially more generous than the allowance on income.

The computer can be used to calculate the after-tax returns of the asset classes. This adjustment will, in turn, affect risk characteristics because the range and volatility of returns have changed. For this exercise, we programmed the computer to assume that our investors are in the top income-tax bracket and had it adjust the forecast risk and return inputs accordingly. In doing so we also assumed that the capital gains realized by both investors in any one year fell within the tax-free threshold for capital gains. This gave investments likely to generate capital gains, such as shares and property, a distinct advantage over mainly income-yielding investments. Table 8.3 shows the results.

We then used these new data, instead of the unadjusted forecasts, for the optimization process, and the optimal portfolios changed again. Figure 8.2 shows the effect.

TABLE 8.3 Hypothetical future performance of asset classes after tax adjustment

Asset class	Return (%)	Risk (%)
Shares	12.1	16.7
Property	8.4	13.6
Cash	3.6	0.9
Gilts	4.2	3.0
International shares	12.9	19.1

The low-risk investor's risk tolerance prevented a big move away from the low-risk, interest-bearing asset classes, which are less tax effective. The computer still put as much as possible into the more tax-effective asset classes, with a significant 13 per cent now devoted to UK shares. However, this investor ended up with a much lower after-tax return of 5.7 per cent.

The medium-risk investor can accept greater exposure to both domestic and international equities, as well as property. The allocation to these asset classes increased substantially, while less was allocated to gilts and cash. This left the investor with a still quite acceptable after-tax expected return of 9.5 per cent.

Adding constraints

While these results are instructive, it is important not to get over-confident about the 'recommended' allocations coming out of a computer optimization program. Their validity depends entirely on the accuracy of the forecasts fed in. Given that even the best forecasts can be subject to a high degree of error, portfolio managers will usually check their portfolios for robustness, as well as for their efficiency in terms of the efficient frontier.

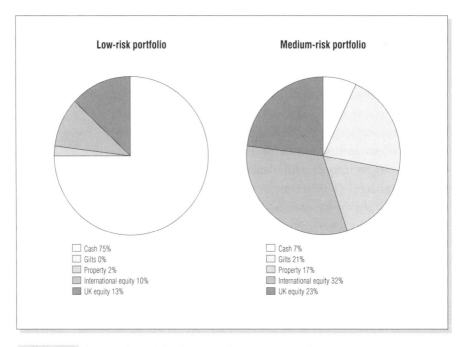

FIGURE 8.2 Optimized portfolio: incorporating forecasts and tax

For example, suppose the computer indicated that an extreme allocation, such as investing most of the portfolio in UK shares, was the optimal allocation. If the forecasts fed in proved overoptimistic in this regard, the results could be very poor indeed. So, although the portfolio may be efficient if the forecast proves correct, it is not robust if the forecast proves wrong.

Fortunately, for every portfolio that sits exactly on the efficient frontier, hundreds and thousands of different asset allocations will be very close in terms of their efficiency, but may be more robust in terms of the results that they produce should the forecast be wrong. Invariably, the more robust portfolios will be more diversified and investors may wish to specify a minimum and maximum exposure to each asset class to ensure that they are not too badly affected by an unexpected event that damages any one asset class.

The limits should reflect the confidence that an investor has in the forecasts. For example, if the investor was highly confident about the quality and value of overseas shares that underpinned the risk and return forecasts, relative to the quality and value of the other asset sectors, a greater exposure to foreign shares may be acceptable.

The scope for using computer optimizers is conceptually boundless. If one were prepared to calculate and input the risk, return and correlation data for any particular set of assets, the optimizer could find the best portfolios among them. However, computer models have no predictive ability of their own. They are an aid to, but not a substitute for, understanding the fundamentals of investment markets and strategy. They do not replace the most critical elements in investment: good judgement and common sense.

Nevertheless, computer models do have a number of specific uses. They provide a consistent format for analyzing the historical risk, return and correlation characteristics of different investments. They provide handy indications of how different balances of portfolio allocation will affect expected risk and return. And they provide a consistent structure for making forecasts and applying those forecasts to portfolio design. They enforce a *discipline* to use the principles of modern portfolio theory in planning investment.

It is this sort of discipline that all investors can and should apply, regardless of whether or not they use a computer. A disciplined approach to portfolio planning involves:

- highlighting the assumptions behind the investment strategy and applying the principles of quality, value, diversity and time in producing forecasts;

- considering investment options on a consistent and measurable basis;

- considering risk and return simultaneously, and for the portfolio as a whole.

The investor who has access to computer asset allocation models will have an additional implement at hand. However, computers are not needed to make good use of portfolio theory. The same principles can be applied by using the knowledge developed in this book.

Asset allocation 2: intuitive approaches

The essence of asset allocation is contained in the risk/return characteristics of the asset classes and how they relate to each other. We will briefly review the key characteristics of each asset class, and of overseas investment.

Cash: the safest asset class, retaining flexibility for the investor at the cost of low returns in the long run. Low correlations with all other asset classes. Return on cash is the benchmark for assessing the risk/return trade-off: higher-risk investments should offer higher potential returns. Cash is also tax-ineffective for high-income earners.

Gilts/bonds: a low-to-medium risk and return asset class, with low correlations with cash and fairly low correlations with shares and property. Tax-ineffective for high-income earners, except in an ISA.

Property: a medium-to-high risk asset class, with low correlations with cash, and low to moderate correlations with bonds and shares. Returns from investment property, while commensurate with risk in the long run, are highly susceptible to cycles, investments may be 'lumpy', and maintenance, management and dealing costs on direct property investments are higher than on other asset classes. The fact that tax relief can be claimed on the interest on borrowed money makes property more suitable for long-term investment.

Shares: a high-risk asset class that in the long run produces high returns. Because of short- and medium-term volatility this asset class lends itself best to long-term investment, but the more lenient tax treatment of capital gains relative to income is a bonus.

Overseas investment: all four asset classes offer opportunities to invest abroad as an alternative to the UK. Potentially high risk in terms of individual investments if currency exposure is totally unhedged. But superior diversification can reduce overall risk in a portfolio, provided that the unhedged currency exposure is moderate. The 'natural hedge' reduces some of the currency risk and at least partial currency hedging can remove the rest. An excellent diversifier, which can substantially enhance returns and, for an overall portfolio, reduce risk. Requires special analysis of tax, risk, correlation, currency, and political factors.

With this knowledge, it is possible to employ an asset allocation strategy that is basically a common-sense version of that produced by the computer exercise in the previous section. The approach is to apply the characteristics of the asset classes against three main criteria of the investor profile: risk/return, tax, and the time horizon.

Risk/return: the general logic of the risk/return trade-off suggests that investors who can take on more risk in the hope of getting a higher return will allocate proportionately more of their portfolio to shares, property, and overseas investments. Conversely, investors who have a higher aversion to risk and are prepared to accept a lower return will put a larger proportion of their funds into cash and bonds in the UK. The medium-risk investor will have a reasonable investment in each class. Between these three positions lie an infinite number of combinations.

Tax: as the computer exercise indicated, investors in high tax brackets should frame their asset allocation strategies in terms of after-tax returns. Because of the tax-advantaged position of property and shares, top-rate taxpayers may tilt their asset mix towards these asset classes and away from cash and bonds. For investors who pay lower-rate tax or no tax, *gross* (before-tax) returns are more relevant. The tax issue arises only if the returns from investment become so large as to create a significant tax liability.

Time horizon: the time horizon of the investor will have a great impact on the relative risk of the asset classes. Investors who want to invest for the long term will find that property and shares are better investments. A long time frame makes short-term volatility less of a concern, and the higher long-run returns of property and equities make them much more attractive than interest-bearing investments. Conversely, investors with a short time frame will require a less volatile portfolio, which will incline them towards bonds and cash.

From these criteria it is possible to draw up a general guide to asset allocation, shown in Table 8.4. This shows the *neutral* weightings for portfolios that deliver different levels of return. These are the target allocations based on the inherent long-term characteristics of the asset classes rather than the particular circumstances of markets at any one time. As an example of how each market sector can be subdivided, the table includes a couple of specialized options for overseas equities investments which are accessible through managed funds: international smaller companies, and global emerging markets.

As discussed in the last section, an investment strategy should respond to current and forecast market conditions. In other words, the most suitable mix of assets may alter over time and this, together with the actual assembling of the portfolio, is discussed next.

Dynamic asset allocation and investment selection

The most efficient portfolio will be that which is best diversified at every rung of the risk ladder, and in relation to prevailing market conditions. The process is demonstrated in Figure 8.3.

After getting the mix of asset classes correct, it is important to diversify away industry risk and firm-specific risk going down the risk ladder, and country risk going up the risk ladder. The efficient markets hypothesis provides guidance on dealing with this issue. Within each asset class the most efficient portfolio is the market portfolio, representing the full range of possible investments or a representative selection. Investors should diverge from the market portfolio only if they believe that they have a particular insight that is not already reflected in the

TABLE 8.4 Portfolio optimization and construction for four investment profiles

	Conservative	Balanced	Growth	High growth
Investment objectives:				
Recommended investment term	3 years	4 years	5 years	7 years
Benchmark net return objective – over minimum investment term	RPI+ 1 to 3% p.a.	RPI+ 3 to 5% p.a.	RPI+ 5 to 7% p.a.	RPI+ 6 to 8% p.a.
Portfolio characteristics (indicative splits):				
Defensive v. growth asset balance	65% v. 35%	30% v. 70%	15% v. 85%	5% v. 95%
Domestic v. international asset balance	80% v. 20%	73% v. 27%	60% v. 40%	50% v. 50%
Asset classes:	_Target_	_Target_	_Target_	_Target_
Cash	30	5	2	2
Gilts	20	15	7	3
Indexed-linked securities	10	8	4	Nil
International fixed interest	5	2	2	Nil
UK shares	15	40	42	43
International shares	15	25	30	36
Property	5	5	5	2
International smaller companies	Nil	Nil	4	6
Global emerging markets	Nil	Nil	4	8
Risk characteristics (% p.a.)				
Targeted range of returns with 95% confidence				
Time horizon 1 year	−5.0 to 19.7%	−13.5 to 32.8%	−15.6 to 35.9%	−17.2 to 39.1%
3 years	0.2 to 14.4%	−3.7 to 23.1%	−4.7 to 25.0%	−5.3 to 27.2%
5 years	1.8 to 12.8%	−0.7 to 20.1%	−1.3 to 21.7%	−1.6 to 23.5%
Likelihood of a negative return over the following periods:				
any 1-year period	1 year in 8 = 12%	1 year in 5.5 = 18%	1 year in 5 = 20%	1 year in 4.5 = 22%
any 3-year period	Low	1 period in 13 = 8%	1 period in 11 = 9%	1 period in 10 = 10%

Note: The assumptions underlying the table may no longer be current. No reader should regard the table as a substitute for specific advice.

Source: ipac

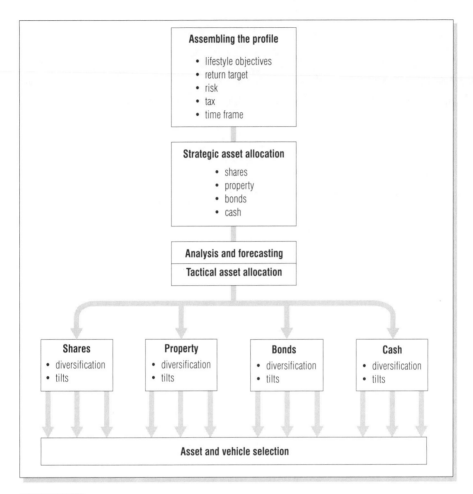

FIGURE 8.3   Process of portfolio design

market. The way to put this principle into practice is to work out the 'neutral' or 'market' allocation, then *tilt* away from this when a particular asset class appears under- or overvalued. Using this approach, the investor can build the portfolio by buying investments in three stages: selecting first the asset classes, then the sub-sectors or industries, and finally the specific investments or managed funds. We look at these stages next.

Neutral asset allocations provide a guide based on long-term asset class characteristics. They should, however, have the flexibility to adapt to changes in market conditions and forecasts, as well as to incorrect valuations.

A good way to structure the decision-making process is to define a range that allows some variation on either side of the neutral allocations. Having established these ranges, investors can fine-tune the asset allocation according to their assumptions about markets.

The reason for discipline and staying within the ranges is that in practice it is hard to pick good value because of market efficiency. And even when markets are inefficient, because of herding behaviour by investors, it is rarely obvious when the market is over- or undervalued. The long-term allocation is what is ultimately most likely to achieve the investor's objectives. Investors should bet against the market – which is what a tilt amounts to – only if they are truly confident. Setting ranges limits the bet, and hence limits the damage if it goes wrong. We look more closely at dynamic allocation in the next chapter.

Subsector (industry) allocation

Having decided on a fine-tuned mix among the asset classes, the investor has to select the mix of subsectors within each class. As outlined in Part Two, for equities this means the various industry sectors; for property it covers primarily residential, commercial, retail and industrial sectors; and for interest-bearing securities it covers several types of instruments, which vary in maturity and credit risk. In each case, the 'neutral' selection will be one that covers a representative range of subsectors within the asset class. From there, the issue is whether to apply tilts to one sub-sector or another.

The most obvious tilt would be carried out if the investor felt that one subsector had a higher relative value than others. An investor may, for example, believe that information technology and in particular e-commerce will outperform the rest of the market in the longer term, or the oil sector is going to shoot ahead because of a particular underlying theme. Others may look for 'value' investments – high-yielding shares that are due for a re-rating, or for recovery stocks in sectors such as mining and construction that are subject to deep cyclical fluctuations.

There is nothing necessarily wrong with acting on intuition. However, making a tilt is tantamount to saying one of two things: that the market is not fully efficient, or that it is efficient but the rest of the market has got the themes wrong. Once again, the most important issue is a proper spread to provide diversification; and unless the investor has confidence in an insight, it is best to avoid tilts.

This principle applies in much the same way to choosing international invest-ments. Unless an investor believes that a particular region or a particular country is going to surge ahead economically, the logical approach is to seek a reasonable geographic mix reflecting foreign market capitalizations and/or economic size. A slightly more sophisticated approach would be to diversify overseas according to the importance of various countries as trading partners with one's own country.

Investment and vehicle selection

The guidelines for choosing individual investments follow those for choosing subsectors. The focus should be on selecting a mix of assets that is sufficiently diversified to remove most of the firm-specific risk. As discussed, studies have shown that about 20–30 stocks selected on a random basis will get rid of most of the market-specific risk of the stock market, for example. The only reason for a tilt in terms of individual assets is, once again, if the investor believes that a particular company, property or managed investment is likely to move ahead more than others – and only the investor knows about it.

An important issue, which should go hand in hand with selection of investments, is choice of vehicle. The investor should look at the universe of managed and direct investments as a huge toolbox: each one can serve a particular function in building the investor's overall strategy.

Take an investor who, in designing a diversified portfolio, decides to allocate £30 000 to the stock market. The investor adheres to the efficient markets hypothesis and believes that the market portfolio is the most efficient portfolio, but wants to be able to try the occasional tilt on individual stocks, based on an insight supposedly not already reflected in the share price. The investor could achieve the objective by allocating £20 000 to a broadly based share fund, and using the remaining £10 000 to punt directly on individual stocks.

As discussed in the previous chapter, the increasing specialization and sheer number of managed investments mean that it is possible to invest in just about any asset class through a managed fund.

We have now discussed the strategy and tactics for taking investors from the point of working out their lifestyle objectives down to selecting assets. In the remainder of this chapter, we look at three hypothetical examples, which show how this process can apply to different sorts of investors. Any similarities to real people and businesses are, of course, accidental.

Example 1: the yuppies

Situation

Late one Saturday night, after cruising home in the Porsche from a superb dinner at their favourite Thamesside restaurant, Jonathan and Kate Overhead have a serious chat. 'I just can't understand where all the money goes,' says Kate, as she sips some specially imported Peruvian liqueur that they discovered on their last adventure holiday in Latin America. 'It's a mystery,' replies Jonathan, as he finishes off a mouthful of best beluga and slips a compact disc into their brand-new, top-of-the-range player.

This conversation is becoming increasingly common in the Overhead household. Jonathan has worked his way up the ladder in a City firm of accountants, and has just been promoted to a junior managerial position on £75 000 a year. Kate runs an interior design business from home, which provides another £25 000 or so, giving the Overheads an annual income of £100 000.

However, the Overheads have found their lifestyle has adapted to their rising income at an alarming rate. Kate used to buy dresses at department store sales, but now finds in her mid-30s that to be a successful interior designer she has to wear designer clothes. Jonathan wears Italian suits. Soon after his promotion, the Overheads moved to a bigger house in a new development of executive homes in one of the leafier parts of the Home Counties. They have £250 000 owing on the mortgage at a fixed rate of 6 per cent. Their two children, eight-year-old Priscilla and ten-year-old Horace, are in private schools. The Overheads expect the fees to increase in coming years and to send the children to university.

Jonathan, in his late 30s, works incredibly hard and compensates for his absence with extravagant gifts and frequent weekend trips to Paris for his family. Kate likes her faster lifestyle but has started to worry about the future, and about Jonathan, who has lost that 'zing' he had in his 20s.

Kate estimates that they have saved nothing over the past two years. Until now, they have thought that Jonathan's pension plan would be enough – his company contributes an extra 5 per cent of his salary to the fund. However, the family doctor has said that, at this rate, Jonathan will burn out long before 65 and will probably have to retire at 55 or die in the job.

Except for the family home and the pension fund, the Overheads have no investments apart from holdings in a salmon farm which they were talked into making over a few whiskies after a Burns Night supper three years ago. Unfortunately, just as the salmon were approaching maturity, a pack of hungry seals found a hole in the net and gobbled the lot.

However, there is a bright spot. Jonathan Overhead's middle name is Slick. And a lawyer has phoned Jonathan to say that his great-uncle Horace, the founder of Slick Oil which was one of the early beneficiaries of the North Sea oil bonanza, has died and left Jonathan £350 000 – just because he called his son Horace.

Analysis

Jonathan and Kate's position is typical of that of many professionals whose salaries have soared on promotion to executive or partnership ranks. The rapid change in expectations and material lifestyle, plus Jonathan's feelings of guilt over the time he spends away from the family and his subsequent overspending, are beginning to exceed their income growth. Investment advisers often find that people with a combined income of £30 000–£40 000 save more than families with three or four times that income. And it is often people with the Overheads' profile for whom retirement presents the greatest financial trauma.

The Overheads' main problem, apart from adding more 'zing', will be maintaining their lifestyle when Jonathan retires, in about 17 years. Generally, for somebody who retires at 65 with a pension fund, the pension pot will have to be about ten times the size of their final salary to maintain their standard of living in retirement. But Jonathan hopes to retire at 55, and will need about double that ratio. The value of his accumulated pension savings from his employer may provide about £300 000 in real terms when he retires. If the rules stay as they are, it will provide a tax-free lump sum and an annuity of £12 000 – only a fraction of the Overheads' needs. Without action, they will either rapidly run out of money or have to scale back their lifestyle drastically.

Fortunately for the Overheads, they have recognized the problem and still have enough high-earning years to deal with it. The £350 000 windfall provides the spur to develop a strategy.

Investment strategy

The immediate issue is how to allocate the £350 000. The first option is to pay off their mortgage, which ties them to non-deductible interest payments of 6 per cent. Paying it off is the equivalent of receiving a 6 per cent return after tax, risk free. It eliminates their debt and frees about £1250 per month to allocate to an ongoing investment strategy. Without a savings plan, the Overheads have shown that they will fritter away their money. However, by adopting a few minor economies they can save another £500 a month, liberating around £1750 in all.

Jonathan arranges a 'salary sacrifice' deal from his employer's newly introduced Flex Plan which offers a choice of additional benefits, and another £500 per month of his salary will be paid into the pension fund, keeping the total contributions within the 15 per cent maximum contribution limit. Kate also takes out a personal pension plan to make tax efficient use of her income.

After careful analysis of Jonathan's job security and other factors, the Overheads decide to take the increased risk of gearing, and remortgage their home to raise £100 000 to invest in a second property, which is put in Kate's name to take advantage of her lower tax rate. The Overheads get an adviser to ensure that the gearing strategy is tax-effective. Out of the gross rent of £650 a month, the Overheads pay off the loan, and receive a tax deduction for the interest. Jonathan also takes out a term life insurance policy and some critical illness insurance to cover the family if he dies or is incapacitated, and the premiums come out of their new investment fund.

Paying off the mortgage left £100 000 as the nucleus of an investment portfolio. After allowing £5000 to pay off credit cards and other debts, they are left with £95 000, plus the £1750 a month they have set aside to invest after increasing their pension provision and allowing for the life insurance premiums.

The Overheads have adequate income and, since they will not need to start drawing down on their investments for nearly 20 years, short-term volatility is not a problem. They can therefore take on a reasonable level of risk, through a growth portfolio. A real return of 7 per cent p.a. (before taking into account the impact of borrowing) will help them to maintain their desired standard of living. So the Overheads adopt the asset allocation shown in Table 8.5, representing the 'high-growth' portfolio in Table 8.4 which concentrates on assets aimed at capital gain – shares and property. They set maximum and minimum ranges for each asset class to ensure discipline. They are comfortable with the fact that, on average, this portfolio has a 1 in 5 chance of producing a negative return in any one year and they may experience a period of several years when returns are low to negative.

TABLE 8.5 Dynamic asset allocation and ranges: the yuppies – high-growth strategy

Asset sector	Target allocation	Dynamic ranges
Cash	2	0–10
Gilts	3	0–10
Index-linked securities	Nil	0–5
International fixed interest	Nil	0–5
UK shares	43	37–50
International shares	36	30–40
Property	2	0–5
International smaller companies	6	0–10
Global emerging markets	8	5–10

The likelihood is that over 17 years (when Jonathan turns 55) the high-growth portfolio will grow to about £600 000 in today's pounds. In contrast, the less volatile 'balanced' portfolio is likely to be worth only £400 000. Even if the aggressive portfolio performs lower than expected, it is very unlikely to underperform the balanced portfolio over 17 years. And if the worst came to the worst, Jonathan could probably extend his working life by a few years, perhaps working as a consultant, to preserve his wealth. As an illustration of the power of compounding, if Jonathan retired five years later, his high-growth portfolio would likely total around £900 000, an additional £300 000.

The Overheads then allocate their portfolio in conjunction with their adviser, based on current and expected market conditions. All income from the portfolio is to be reinvested, maximizing the compounding effect. Since Jonathan cannot find time to play with his son, let alone watch securities markets, the money is invested in a diversified array of managed funds under the eye of an independent financial adviser. Under current rules they can invest up to £5000 a year each in a maxi-ISA investing in equities for growth or corporate bonds for income, all tax-free, so they take advantage of the ISA structure in implementing their portfolio.

Example 2: the lump summers

Situation

Fred and Linda Blunt have looked forward to retirement as a time to enjoy their simple tastes more fully. Fred, 65, is retiring this year from his job as manager of a farm machinery manufacturer in a small town in the Welsh borders.

The Blunts are originally from Birmingham, and Fred's rural sojourn was supposed to last only a few years. However, they fell in love with the scenery and stayed for 15 years. Linda, 60, is a former teacher who enjoys doing a little voluntary work at the local community centre. They sold their home in Birmingham to buy a house with a few acres in a village, and a canal boat they use for weekends and holidays. Of the Blunts' three children, all with families of their own, two live in London and one in Brussels, and all come to visit every so often.

Fred will receive a lump sum of £45 000 and a pension of £10 000 when he retires. Linda's pension adds £4000. Both are index-linked. The Blunts have no debts and have £65 000 in a building society account. They calculate that they will need £10 000 to cover their immediate expenses, which include house repairs, a new car, and a trip around Australia. Fred, who enjoys betting on international shares but never seems to make any money, has £10000 in equities. His portfolio, which he thought was well diversified, has fallen in value by 25 per cent in the past year. It currently comprises shares in a German motor company, a South African synthetic rubber plant, a French power utility, and an Australian aluminium smelter.

The Blunts live comfortably but not lavishly. Their main pleasures are canalboating, walking in the Welsh hills, enjoying a drink at the local club, and the odd garden party. But they need a little extra to visit their children now and then. Their health is good, and they have adequate private health insurance. Overall, they estimate that they require just over £20000 to live on, after tax. In 2000–01 they expect to receive a joint state pension of about £5500 per year (also index linked), which will top up their pension income to about £16000 per year after tax. Their lump sum plus savings will earn another £4000 net, so they are close to their comfort zone but are at risk if interest rates fall, or inflation takes off, or emergencies start eating into their capital. Fred also wants to ensure that Linda will be comfortable if he dies before her.

If any money is left when they die, they are happy for it to go to their children. However, since the children are all financially independent, and barring disasters will inherit the house, inheritance tax planning is not a major issue.

Analysis

The Blunts' position is fairly typical of people who have worked throughout their lives and receive a moderate lump sum on retirement. At one time the state pension may have looked after virtually all their needs. However, the wind-down of the scheme in the 1980s and 1990s means it will now provide only 25 per cent of their income needs. Their pensions will keep pace with inflation but not with average incomes, and their financial wellbeing will depend largely on their investment strategy.

The issue they face sounds simple but actually requires considerable finetuning. Fred's lump sum and their savings must cover their retirement celebrations and their cash flow needs for the rest of their lives after retirement. So although the Blunts are in a fairly good position, they cannot afford any mistakes.

The equation the Blunts have to work out has three main variables: living standards, security, and protection against any resurgence in inflation. They have to strike a balance between maintaining their quality of life and assuring that their lump sum will see them out, while also protecting against unforeseen circumstances.

Once again, risk, tax and time frame are key criteria. It is clear that the Blunts need a steady and immediate cash flow, and cannot take on speculative risk that could produce a permanent loss of capital. Their pension provides some security, but they still need to generate income plus some capital growth from their savings to maintain their lifestyle. Further, based on actuarial life tables, Fred's life expectancy is about 18 years, and Linda's as much as 26. This means that they are not short-term investors; their lump sum has to serve a medium- to long-term time frame. An investment strategy based purely on income-producing securities, such as cash, would probably not keep up with inflation and thus fail to meet the Blunts' lifestyle objectives.

Investment strategy

There are basically two strategies available to the Blunts. The first is to use most of the capital to buy a with-profits insurance bond which will be invested in a mix of assets and will allow them to draw a tax-free income of 5 per cent a year and at the same time preserve their capital for their children. They mighr keep £30 000 in reserve in a predominantly interest-bearing portfolio to meet short-term needs. They might also consider taking out a long-term care policy in case one or both needs to go into a home.

The alternative strategy involves designing their own portfolio. Given that Fred likes to dabble in securities and now has more time to do so, this may be the more attractive option. Considering the Blunts' goals and needs, the portfolio has to provide steady growth but with low to moderate risk, suggesting that spread and balance will be essential. The lump sum has to last for around 20 years, and possibly longer. For this reason, the Blunts need enough exposure to the growth provided by property and shares to protect against inflation and keep the lump sum from running down too quickly.

In this case the Blunts have £100 000 to invest, and they need £5000 in additional cash flow each year, after tax. If they adopt a 'conservative' strategy, as shown in Table 8.4, it is possible that their capital will run out after 15 years, sooner if they face unexpected bills. This is cutting it a bit fine. If they live beyond this, they will have to rely increasingly on state pension payments, involving a significant reduction in their living standards. While the growth exposure and hence volatility of this strategy is relatively low, Fred has been reading about the biotechnology revolution and realizes that the current life expectancy tables may be out of date. He and Linda may well live for another decade or more than expected.

A high-growth strategy would mean that their money would likely last another decade. But Fred and Linda feel uncomfortable with its potential volatility. In particular, the possibility of this strategy occasionally producing negative returns for a period of three or so years worries them. Even though they know that the markets will eventually come back and they will probably be better off in the long run, they decide on a 'balanced' strategy, with the ranges shown in Table 8.6. This will extend the expected life of their capital to about 18 years, while the prospect of a prolonged period of negative returns is 2 per cent lower than that of the high-growth strategy.

TABLE 8.6 Dynamic asset allocation and ranges: the lump summers – balanced strategy

Asset sector	Target allocation	Dynamic ranges
Cash	5	5–15
Gilts	15	10–20
Index-linked securities	8	5–10
International fixed interest	2	0–5
UK shares	40	35–45
International shares	25	20–30
Property	5	0–8
International smaller companies	Nil	Nil
Global emerging markets	Nil	Nil

The outstanding issue is the £10000 that Fred has invested in shares. Because Fred enjoys betting on direct investment, he may as well continue doing so with this amount of money since the overall strategy does not rely on it. If Fred loses the money, it will not destroy the cash flow base, and if he makes money, he will have more to spend in the club.

However, Fred could take a lesson in looking 'behind the price'. Although he believes that his portfolio is diversified, his four investments depend on the same theme: energy. Over the year in which his portfolio fell by 25 per cent, petroleum prices rose by a similar figure. This made consumers reluctant to buy the German motor company's high-performance motors; led to increased input costs for the South African synthetic rubber plant, which uses petroleum derivatives; and directly chopped the profitability of the French power utility, which happens to run on diesel-fired generators; at the same time coal prices rose and greatly increased electricity costs for the Australian aluminium smelter because Australian electricity is mostly produced from coal. Fred's first investment will be to purchase a copy of *Fortune Strategy*.

Example 3: the pension fund

Situation

Phipps Instruments has been a byword for quality and craftsmanship since 1935 when old Harry Phipps senior saw an empty factory beside the railway line an hour's journey out of London and made the snap decision to get off the train at the local station, buy the factory, and set up business in it. Phipps Instruments has made metal fittings and chromium-plated trim for the UK motor industry ever since.

Most of the traditional names in the UK motor industry – Riley, Singer, Austin and Morris – had door handles and window winders, bonnet catches and seat runners made by Phipps. The motor manufacturers themselves were gradually swallowed up into BMC, British Leyland and Rootes, and in turn even they are only memories. But Phipps has survived and thrived thanks to the desire of the new generation of foreign-owned manufacturers – Nissan, Toyota and Honda – to outsource their supplies.

The Phipps have run the factory in an old-style, paternal fashion. Old Mr Phipps and his son Harry junior never had much time for trade unions and restrictive practices, red tape and government interference, but they did set up a pension. The company pension fund has six trustees: three each appointed by management and the employees. The management-appointed trustees comprised Old Mr Phipps, his son and grandson. The fund had £10 million under management. It started with a 3 per cent salary-equivalent contribution from the company, which later rose to 6 per cent, and the workers contributed an average of a further 5 per cent of their salary voluntarily. In all, the fund received about £1 million a year in employer and employee contributions.

And fluctuate it has. The portfolio reflects a collection of *ad hoc* decisions made by the trustees at their monthly meetings, where they invest the £80 000 or so in new contributions in whatever happens to be flavour of the month. In the boom of the mid to late 1980s, this approach worked well. The trustees' stock picks, based on brokers' recommendations and what they had read that morning in the *Daily Telegraph*, were going up in value. And before long, they began to confuse luck with skill.

When the 1987 crash came, the fund was overexposed to equities and under-diversified. It had bought into several entrepreneurial companies and other high-risk stocks. The value of the fund tumbled and, unnerved, the Phipps changed tack. 'Owning stocks is just holding pieces of paper. Let's go for something secure – bricks and mortar,' said Harry junior.

The trustees bought an office block nearby, 'to keep control of things,' said Mr Phipps. Unfortunately, the property market peaked soon after and the recession reduced property prices locally by more than the national average. In 1989, the office block was destroyed by a gas explosion, which rendered the investment a pile of bricks and mortar. This turned out to be reasonably fortunate for the trustees because, although the insurance paid out only 80 per cent of the purchase price, this was still more than its current market value.

By this stage, the trustees were losing their nerve altogether. So the trustees increased the fund's exposure to cash, at what turned out to be the bottom of the equity market. Cash rates fell progressively, and the fund missed out on a spectacular share market surge in late 1992 and into 1993.

At this point Christopher Phipps, the third generation of the family and a graduate of the Harvard Business School, was elected chairman of the fund's board of trustees. At his insistence, the trustees converted the fund into a defined contribution scheme and handed over the management to a professional fund management company.

Analysis

The experience of the Phipps's original pension fund was like that of many privately-run funds, which tended to 'follow the pack' instead of developing an investment plan and sticking to it. Without a coherent strategy, a fund is subject to the whims of the market and stands a good chance of losing out.

The challenge for the trustees of any fund of this type is to define the objectives. The trustees' responsibility is to devise and carry out an investment plan in the best interests of the beneficial owners, in this case the workers. The problem, of course, is that if a company has hundreds of workers, it is impossible to devise a strategy that will suit the lifestyle of every worker perfectly.

The members' needs will vary greatly. Some may be young workers who see a long future ahead of them with the company. For them, short-term volatility is not critical, and they would be best served by a growth-oriented investment strategy concentrated in shares and property. Other workers may plan to spend only a couple of years with the company, or may be about to retire and have specific plans to spend their lump sums. For them, short-term volatility can significantly affect their payouts, so a lower-risk portfolio would be best.

Many trustees try to encompass all of these needs into a single fund, and end up with a middle-of-the road approach. There is, however, an alternative: to offer the members a choice of funds. In the case of Phipps, two or three funds would probably do (although a wider choice is desirable). One could be the conservative fund, whose capital value is relatively secure because it has half its portfolio in cash and bonds. The second fund, the growth fund, would suit members with a long time to go at the factory, who can accept a higher level of risk in anticipation of receiving a higher return. This may be the existing fund, but redesigned and better managed.

Investment strategy

The advantage of having two funds is that the trustees can define two clear sets of objectives, as follows.

Phipps's conservative fund: the objective is to produce a fund with low volatility, but with enough return to keep modestly ahead of inflation. Such a fund will be concentrated in interest-bearing investments, and cannot afford much exposure to currency risk. However, it will still need a modest exposure to equities and property to provide some protection against inflation. The asset allocation and ranges may work out as in Table 8.7. To reduce the currency risk, the fund may use a currency hedge to cover about half of its exposure.

TABLE 8.7 Dynamic asset allocation and ranges – conservative fund

Asset sector	Target allocation	Dynamic ranges
Cash	30	25–35
Gilts	20	15–25
Index-linked securities	10	7–13
International fixed interest	5	0–8
UK shares	15	12–18
International shares	15	12–18
Property	5	3–7
International smaller companies	Nil	Nil
Global emerging markets	Nil	Nil

Phipps's growth fund: the objective is to provide long-term growth to maintain the buying power of members' entitlements over time, and increase its value. However, the risk that the fund can take is moderated by the fact that at any one time there may be some members (such as those about to turn 55) who have a relatively short time frame with respect to the fund. Therefore, a reasonable approach is to adopt a moderate, or moderate-high, risk approach.

The fund may have the target allocation and ranges shown in Table 8.8. Unless some of the trustees have particular knowledge and skills, they are best to use a variety of managed investment vehicles.

Figure 8.4 illustrates the range of likely lump sum benefit payments from each of these two funds for workers with different times to retirement. The payouts take into account contributions to the funds (adjusted for the fact that older members are likely to have higher salaries) as well as the likely investment returns. The bars in the chart show the range of likely payouts based on a 95 per cent degree of certainty. The bottom shaded area shows the return in a 'worst case' scenario; the middle area is the expected return; and the upper, unshaded area is the 'best case' scenario.

TABLE 8.8 Dynamic asset allocation and ranges – growth fund

Asset sector	Target allocation	Dynamic ranges
Cash	2	0–5
Gilts	7	4–12
Index-linked securities	4	0–7
International fixed interest	2	0–5
UK shares	42	35–50
International shares	30	25–40
Property	5	0–10
International smaller companies	4	0–8
Global emerging markets	4	0–8

In the case of workers with 35 years to retirement, the choice is easy. They should opt for the growth option. Even in the worst case, over 35 years the growth fund produces a likely payout of £139 059, almost £18 000 greater than the payout for the conservative fund. And if markets behave normally, the expected payout of £308 112 in the growth fund is almost £130 000 more than the payout of £174 203 in the conservative fund.

On the other hand, in the case of workers with five years to retirement, the situation is not as clear cut. Although the expected payout of £46 000 from the growth fund is greater than the £41 600 from the conservative fund, in a worst-case scenario, the member could be £2400 worse off in the growth fund. On the other hand, someone who wishes to draw on the 25 per cent of the pension fund

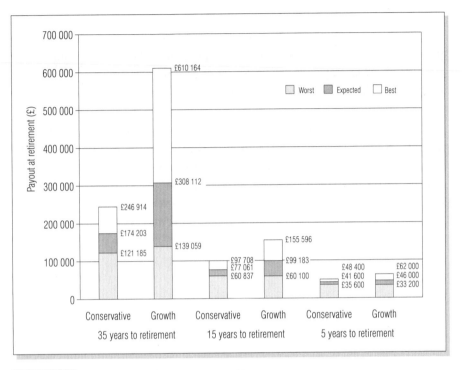

FIGURE 8.4 Benefit payout at retirement age 65

that they can take as a lump sum on retirement for a specific purpose, and is more inclined towards purchasing a fixed-interest-based annuity, may be better off with the conservative option. In fact a mix and match policy may be best for all. The trustees will probably recommend all workers switch an increasing amount of their funds to the conservative fund as they approach retirement age.

Conclusion

While the task of determining the optimum portfolio may seem complex, considerable progress towards this target can be made by applying a few common-sense rules.

Most important is to define the objectives and priorities. As part of this exercise, investors should determine their own time frame for fulfilling goals, and what this implies for access to money. Next, the investor can set the long-term, strategic asset allocation. For investors with a long time frame, the bulk of the portfolio should be invested in shares and property securities, particularly for high taxpayers. The portfolio should include international assets, and should be diversified effectively within each asset class. Those investors who have short time frames, are risk averse, and for whom tax is not a serious issue, should lean towards a portfolio dominated by interest-bearing investments.

These first two steps are the most important. Investors who apply them correctly and have the discipline to stick with them through the day-to-day ups and downs of investment markets will be among the few who achieve their lifestyle goals.

Because markets change, investors need to continually review the assumptions that underpin their asset allocation. From time to time this may require a substantial change in long-term allocations. More often, investors may perceive a particular asset class to be wrongly valued and want to fine-tune their asset allocation accordingly. The difficulty of this should not be underestimated. Moreover, the efficiency of the market means that such fine-tuning efforts are not critical to achieving goals.

However, if dynamic allocation is done, it should be done well. In the final chapter of the book, we examine techniques that may be used to time entry into the asset classes and determine how best to manage the portfolio.

CHAPTER 9

Portfolio management in a changing world

Summary

▤ Most investors dream of making a fortune by 'picking the market'. This goal is an illusion, and those who focus on short-term timing often lose out in the long run.

▤ There are, however, some tactics that can reduce timing risk, such as putting money into the riskier markets in instalments, and rebalancing asset allocations regularly.

▤ For the more adventurous investor, trying to establish fair value may be of more practical benefit than attempting to pick absolute tops and bottoms of markets.

▤ When personal circumstances change, or economies or markets go through a transformation, investors should review their overall strategy and asset allocation.

▤ Greed, fear and trying to be too smart are the real destroyers of wealth. The good news is that investors who stick to comparatively simple strategies can usually get where they want to go, with some fun along the way.

An introductory parable: paralysis by analysis

When middle manager David Rose took early retirement in 1994 he thought he had his financial future all worked out. He had a £100 000 payoff to top off his pension and other savings. After working through his objectives, tax and risk profile, he put £100 000 into a managed fund which invested in a balanced portfolio of domestic and foreign equities, commercial property, domestic bonds and cash.

David Rose had developed his approach after reading the first edition of *Fortune Strategy*. It had been a struggle because his wife Matilda thought that the stock market was too risky, the bond market was too complicated, and anything foreign was unBritish and therefore inherently unreliable. Matilda had wanted to put the whole lump sum in a savings account at the local bank.

Within weeks of making the investment, the Roses' portfolio was falling. Interest rates, which many investors thought would continue to fall, turned upwards both at home and overseas, causing alarm in equity markets. Matters went from bad to worse. The year ended with the financial crisis in Mexico, which devalued and then floated its currency, sending tremors through international markets.

By the start of 1995, the Roses' portfolio had lost more than £10 000 – or nearly £1000 per month. Although David had read about volatility, he was shell-shocked – a situation exacerbated by Matilda's barrage of 'I told you so'.

Around this time, the Roses' neighbours, the Bears, were debating how to invest a lump sum. Alan Bear also had a £100 000 golden handshake to invest. Like David Rose, he planned to invest in a diversified portfolio. Alan's wife, Norma, was inclined to agree, but insisted on getting the timing right. They debated whether to go in immediately or wait until the crisis ended. A talk over the fence, when Matilda told Norma her tale of woe, decided the issue. The Bears decided to keep their entire lump sum in a cash fund, where it had been since Alan retired on 1 January 1994. Figure 9.1 shows the comparative fates of the Roses' and Bears' portfolios.

To everyone's surprise, investment markets turned up sharply in early 1995. By the middle of the year the Roses' portfolio had recovered its losses, and their marital well-being improved with each point the stock market rose. Meanwhile, the Bears agonized over what to do. They subscribed to *The Economist*, and read about US economic problems and the potential long-term effects of the emerging markets crisis, sparked by the Mexico debacle. They decided to keep the lump sum in the managed cash fund until it was clear that the world

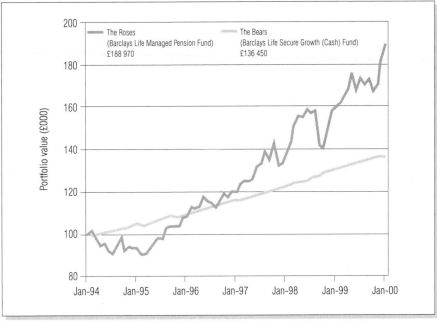

FIGURE 9.1   A tale of two portfolios

economy had bottomed.

The rally on world securities markets continued through 1996. The Roses took a second honeymoon. The Bears decided that the rises could not possibly be sustained. By this time, Norma Bear had started a part-time economics degree. It was clear, the Bears decided, that sooner or later the 'bubble' would burst and markets would take a big fall, allowing them to get in.

As 1996 turned into 1997, markets rose steadily, while the Bears waited for their opportunity to buy in. At the end of 1996, the US Federal Reserve chairman, Alan Greenspan, had warned of the 'irrational exuberance' of the US share market, prompting the Bears to further delay their move into equities until this exuberance had run its course. By this time, Norma Bear had decided that she was becoming quite good at top-down macroeconomic analysis. She concluded that there was no rational reason for the markets to move ahead, the expected Labour victory in the 1997 election would trigger a downturn in the market, and the lump sum stayed in the cash management account. Labour duly won by a landslide, but Chancellor of the Exchequer Gordon Brown proved himself the very model of economic prudence and equities resumed their advance.

By the autumn of 1997, the Roses' portfolio was worth £140000, about £20000 more than that of the Bears. The Roses had also been tucking their full allowances into tax-free personal equity plans and built up quite a useful tax-free nest-egg.

Finally, the crisis long expected by the Bears seemed to take hold in October 1997, prompted by the Asian 'meltdown'. The FTSE suffered a mild correction, and the Bears were getting ready to diversify when the markets started to turn up again. They again held off, believing that this rise was the beginning of a head-and-shoulders technical pattern that would soon see markets in freefall. It never quite happened. Each subsequent crisis, in Indonesia, Russia, and Brazil, brought a dip followed by a strong rebound. The Bears kept getting the timing wrong – waiting for equity markets to fall just that little bit further, but instead finding that the markets rose before they could get in.

Stock markets moved ahead through 1998 and 1999 and the bond market also boomed. By January 2000, the Roses' portfolio was worth nearly £190000. The Bears, holding on for the correction, still had their money in the cash fund, where with reinvested interest it was worth £136000. Declining interest rates, which spurred equity and bond markets upwards, reduced the return on the Bears' other savings so that they could no longer live comfortably on the income. The Roses bought a new car. The Bears cancelled a holiday. Relations over the fence cooled.

Although this parable deals with fictional characters, the numbers and themes are real. The two portfolios depicted in Figure 9.1 chart the actual performances, on an accumulation basis but excluding tax considerations, of two analagous portfolios. The Roses' diversified approach uses as a proxy Barclays Life Managed Pension Fund, a balanced portfolio with a target allocation of just over 50 per cent in domestic and international equities. The Bears' portfolio is based on the Barclays Life Secure Growth (Cash) Fund. Figure 9.1 shows the actual performance of these funds.

The point is that, sooner or later, anyone who intends to be an investor has to bite the bullet and invest. The rational concern in deciding when to invest is whether it is the *best* time – whether investment markets are looking cheap. However, while it is great to get the timing right, in practice it is very difficult. The best time to buy usually proves to be when the markets are most uncertain, as during the crisis in Mexico. By the time markets can be decisively categorized as 'on an upswing', they are generally overvalued.

The danger lies in over-analyzing the markets, and creating a never-ending series of excuses to defer diversified investment. The investor runs the risk of losing the defence against inflation or declining interest rates, and the bet may not pay off. As the Bears found, the net result of deferring diversification may be to do so at a later date but at higher prices, having missed the benefits of economic recovery.

In short, the Bears had no genuine insight that the markets were overvalued. They fell into the trap of greed and fear, instead of adopting a long-term investment strategy appropriate to their objectives. While Norma's studies helped her to understand the business news and what was happening in the world economy, she failed to consider whether prices in financial markets already reflected this news.

This said, it is still important to strike a balance between over-analysis to the point of inaction, and ignoring market fundamentals to the point of making rash decisions.

This final chapter deals with ways of finding that balance, and how to manage a portfolio over time to cope with changing markets and personal goals. But first, we review the myth that investment is about getting the timing right.

The timing myth

In May 1987, one of the authors, Ean Higgins, wrote a major feature article for the now defunct Australian national newspaper *Times on Sunday* about the possibility of a major stock market crash. The story was headlined 'Dancing on the Titanic'.[1] The comments by analysts and fund managers quoted in the article make interesting reading now, in light of the world stock market crash which occurred five months later.

On the bullish side was the head of the AMP Society's investment division, Leigh Hall. He was quoted as saying: 'I have a pretty positive approach to the market.' Asked whether he felt like he was fox-trotting on the *Titanic*, Hall said: 'If we are, this is not the trip it will hit the iceberg.' (In fairness to Hall, it would have been difficult to say much else. For the investment manager of the AMP, a leading Australian financial institution, to have foreshadowed a crash might have produced a self-fulfilling prophecy.)

On the bearish side, the late Sir James Goldsmith decided the UK stock market was riding for a heavy fall and sold a large part of his investment portfolio. He may well have got the timing right, and the market fell 30 per cent in October 1987, but it recovered so fast that the FTSE 100 index ended the year slightly higher than it began. Analysts are frequently wrong about when a market is likely to take off from the bottom. Unanimity is no guarantee either. Even when all the pundits seem to agree, markets often go in the opposite direction.

Figure 9.2 shows how bad news can precede a boom. By mid-1982 the US economy was in a severe recession, thanks to the determination of the Federal Reserve to defeat the inflation which had stalked the economy during the 1970s. High interest rates had caused company profits to plunge, banks to fail and the stock market to slump. Notwithstanding the depressing headlines at the time, the Dow Jones Index took off. Within one week of hitting its low for the year on 12 August 1982, it had recovered all its losses for the year. Within nine months it had risen by more than 80 per cent. In hindsight this was the beginning of the biggest bull market in American history, with the Dow rising 13-fold over the next 13 years.

FIGURE 9.2   Press headlines on eve of Wall Street's biggest ever share boom

This discussion is not intended to make the forecasters look silly, but to show how difficult it is for even the most experienced investment managers to get the timing right. The reason is simple: the only certainty in financial markets is uncertainty. Unforeseen events can make even the most sophisticated economic analysis irrelevant.

A more general point about market timing stems from the efficient markets hypothesis, discussed in previous chapters. To the extent that a market is efficient – and most *are* fairly efficient – all the available information and forecasts are already reflected in prices. So, if everyone was able to predict accurately that a market was going to rise or fall, the market would not be where it is: it would be higher or lower, reflecting those expectations.

When it comes to managing a diversified portfolio, the question of timing is even more complex. The issue is not just getting the timing right for one asset class – which is difficult enough – but getting the timing right for all of them together. To achieve the optimum portfolio in the ideal world, the investor would be constantly juggling allocations of funds among shares, cash, bonds and property, to maintain the best mix in relation to their separate market cycles.

There is no magic formula. But the investor still needs some basis for deciding when to invest in what. We look at an 'active' framework for this later, but even without the more sophisticated active strategies, the investor can use some relatively simple passive techniques to get most of the benefit from markets. These approaches – two of which are outlined next – rely largely on common sense and discipline.

Passive portfolio management 1: pound cost averaging

The principles of diversifying away risk over different assets, markets and asset classes should by now be well understood. What may be less obvious, however, is how the same principles apply to another dimension: time. The risk of adverse market timing can sometimes be reduced by diversifying over time.

One of the toughest choices facing the investor is when to jump in and invest. Of course, if the investor is absolutely sure that markets are at a low, or that they are going to plunge within months, the decision will not be difficult. However, when the investor thinks that markets may be overvalued but is not certain when the downturn will occur, the decision is at its most vexing. This is one situation where diversifying over time may provide a compromise strategy.

Just as there is no reason for an investor to put all available money into a single company, bond or fund, there is no need to invest it all at once. Rather, the investor can put the money into the market in portions, over months or years. The Bears, from the introductory parable, could have gradually diversified their portfolio by putting, say, £500 per month into each of five asset classes (domestic bonds and shares, international bonds and shares, and buying some property with an investment mortgage). This would have provided them with a balanced portfolio over about five years, taking them through at least one market cycle, and spreading their investment over the tops and bottoms.

While this type of strategy may seem simplistic, the mathematics can make it attractive to investors who perceive markets as unstable, with some short-term downside risk. A particular strategy, known as pound cost averaging, means that

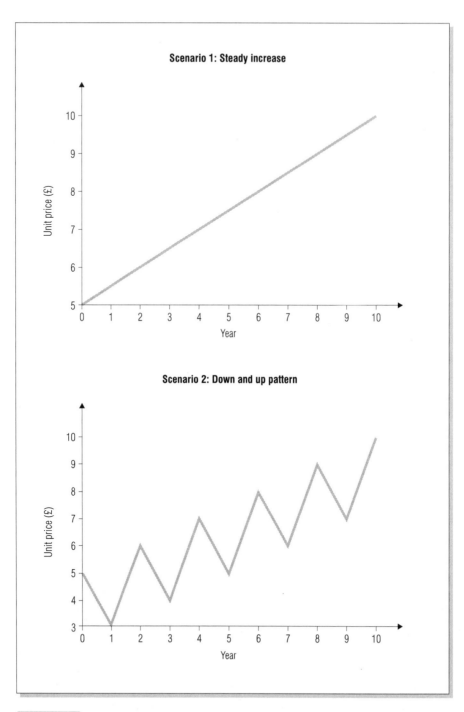

FIGURE 9.3 Pound cost averaging

investors can actually benefit from downward fluctuations in asset prices. This is because when the market is up, an investor's assets are worth more, but when the market is down, the investor is able to buy more for the same regular payment. Pound cost averaging is a particularly effective way of building up holdings of investment trusts, unit trusts and oeics. For many investors with spare income but no capital, it is the only option available but it also works for anyone with a lump sum to invest. Spreading the time of investment can potentially take advantage of this phenomenon.

The following analysis deals with what would happen, with two different market scenarios, to a strategy based on investing £1000 each month for ten years, regardless of market conditions. (The 'market' can apply to any asset class or individual assets.)

Scenario 1 in Figure 9.3 shows a steadily increasing market, where unit prices start at £5 and rise to £10 after ten years – a compound growth rate of about 7 per cent per year. By the end of the decade, the investor's portfolio will be worth £172 500, a 43 per cent gain on the £120 000 invested.

Scenario 2 depicts a market that has the same long-term trend, but is highly volatile in the short term. Unit prices start, once again, at £5 but collapse to £3 in the first year. They then fluctuate, before finishing at £10 at the end of the decade. Unlikely though it may seem, the volatility significantly improves the performance of the portfolio, which at the end of the period will be worth £220 620 – an 83 per cent gain.

The explanation lies in the fact that on the downward plunges the price per unit is lower, so that the investor's £1000 buys more units that month. In the first month, when unit prices are £5, the regular investment buys 200 units. A year later, when unit prices have sunk to £3, the investor's £1000 buys 333 units. Since all units are worth £10 at the end of the period, the low purchase price on the downturns is highly advantageous.

As discussed, the markets that offer the highest returns in the long run tend to be the most volatile. Pound cost averaging can help the investor to benefit from the risk that markets may turn down in the short term. This approach does not eliminate the vagaries of the market, including the risk that individual investments may not turn upwards at all. A market may fluctuate in such a way that pound cost averaging can 'average down' the return that the investor would otherwise have received by investing all at once. If, for example, the price of units averaged £15 in the middle years, those purchases would average down the final return.

It is also worth noting that if the investor had the option of investing the full £120 000 initially, without averaging in, the total value of the portfolio after ten years would have been £236 000. In other words, averaging in will, overall, reduce returns if the overall trend of the market is upwards. However, this is only an extension of the principle of diversification. The reason for diversifying over assets is because of uncertainty about which individual assets will perform well or badly. Diversifying over time reduces exposure to a single upward or downward movement of a market as a whole.

There is also a further benefit from systematic investment over time: it provides *discipline*. Discipline is the investor's weapon against fear and greed. Coupled with the fact that most markets eventually move upwards, it can prove a simple but effective strategy.

The US business magazine *Forbes* provided an interesting example of discipline in action, noting a survey in 1991 of the 7500 local chapters of the National Association of Investment Clubs (NAIC). The NAIC represents amateur investors, and the survey applied to the lifetime of the clubs, which averaged ten years. The survey found that 61.9 per cent of the clubs had bettered the S&P 500 index over the decade, while only 19 per cent of equity mutual funds run by professional investors had managed to do so.

The NAIC's approach was simple: member clubs were required to put some money into the market *each month*. While this was effectively continuous dollar cost averaging, the main reason the NAIC recommended it was to impose discipline. The NAIC advised against trying to time the market, and recommended investing in long-term growth stocks, looking for fundamental value. Commentator Mark Hulbert wrote of this phenomenon:

> Why do the clubs do so well? Neither the clubs' buy-and-hold approach nor
> their growth-stock concentration is all that unusual. I can only guess at the
> answer, but I suspect it lies in the clubs' exceptionally faithful adherence to those
> principles.[2]

In the same way that it is possible to 'average in', the investor can also 'average out', that is, take money out of investment markets gradually over time rather than all in one swoop. An investor with substantial share holdings of shares may be considering a major purchase a couple of years away, such as a new home, but be concerned that the share market will take a downturn before then. As with averaging in, averaging out (into cash) reduces the investor's exposure to a sudden downturn in the markets.

Having decided to invest, the next issue for the portfolio investor is how to juggle allocations – or 'rebalance' – among the various markets over time.

Passive portfolio management 2: rebalancing

The key to managing a portfolio over time is knowing when to take funds from one asset class and put them into another. As discussed in earlier chapters, there are reasons why the asset classes do not move up or down simultaneously. Therefore, at any point in time it will be best to be selling out of the asset class that has been moving up, and using those profits to buy into the asset class that is undervalued.

The next section looks at some active approaches to maximizing the benefit of rebalancing the portfolio. However, an investor who starts with a sound asset-allocation strategy, and sticks to it, will find that the portfolio can do much of the work itself.

Rebalancing enables the investor to stick to the original investment strategy, while potentially gaining automatic benefit from changes in relative value among the asset classes. Say an investor with £100000 to invest has worked through the portfolio design strategy outlined in the last chapter. The investor takes a medium-term view, and decides on a moderate-risk strategy. The investor allocates the £100 000 according to these ratios: £15 000 UK equities, £5000 UK property shares as a proxy for property exposure, £10 000 in international equities, £40 000 in gilts and bonds, and £30 000 in cash. Table 9.1 shows the process.

Some of these asset classes are likely to move up faster than others, and some may go down. As a result, in terms of market value the actual asset allocation ratios will deviate from the original strategy over time.

TABLE 9.1 Rebalancing a portfolio

Date	UK equities	UK property equities	International equities	Gilts	UK cash	Total
Start	£15 000	£5000	£10 000	£40 000	£30 000	£100 000
	15%	5%	10%	40%	30%	
After 12 months	£13 708	£4860	£9003	£46 852	£33 837	£108 260
	13%	4%	8%	43%	31%	
After rebalance	£16 239	£5413	£10 826	£43 304	£32 478	£108 260
	15%	5%	10%	40%	30%	

Suppose that within the first year the value of the UK shares falls to £13708; the property holdings fall to £4860; the international shares falls to £9003, the gilts allocation rises to £46 852, and the cash component increases to £33 837. The total value of the portfolio is now £108 260. However, because of changes in market value, the asset allocation has now become 13 per cent UK equities, 4 per cent property shares, 8 per cent international equities, 43 per cent gilts, and 31 per cent cash.

Suppose the investor wants to get back to the original asset allocation. The portfolio is now overweighted in cash and fixed interest, and underweighted in domestic and international equities and, to a lesser extent, property. The investor can sell off a portion of the overweighted asset classes and use the liberated money to buy more investments in the underweighted asset classes. In this case, the investor sells £3548 worth of investments in fixed interest and takes out £1359 worth of cash, and uses this money to buy more international and domestic shares, and property shares.

The asset allocation, post-rebalance, is then £16 239 in domestic shares, £5413 in property shares, £10 826 in international equities, £43 304 in gilts, and £32 478 in cash. This rebalance has restored the original 15/5/10/40/30 percentage allocation. Portions of those asset classes that have gone up in value – in this case cash and fixed interest – have been sold off for a profit. This profit has been used to buy more of those asset classes that have become cheaper.

Regular rebalancing is extremely handy for keeping to the original investment strategy, and it also insulates the investor from the risk of overexposure to one asset class in the event of a crash. The next exercise further explores the advantages of this approach.

Using various market indices, the exercise asked what would have happened if the investor in the previous example had invested the £100 000 in December 1986 according to the 15/5/10/40/30 allocation, and rebalanced the portfolio in December each year for the following 13 years. Table 9.2 shows the result.

At the end of those years when interest-bearing investments had done particularly well compared with other asset classes, such as 1990, rebalancing would have taken profits out of the interest-bearing portion of the portfolio. It would have redistributed them into equities and property when these asset classes were undervalued after a downturn. As equities and property turned up, the portfolio reaped the benefit from this reallocation. During periods when valuations in these sectors were stretched, the process then put proportionately more money back into interest-bearing investment, in effect taking profits and reinvesting them.

Over the 13-year period, the portfolio would have risen in value from £100 000 to £419 644, representing an average annual compound growth rate of around 12 per cent. It was also a very reliable performer, increasing in value every year except 1994, when the decline was marginal. This is a most respectable performance, particularly considering the portfolio would have taken about ten minutes each year on a pocket calculator to manage.

TABLE 9.2 Rebalancing a diversified portfolio, 1986–99

	UK shares 15%	Real estate 5%	International shares 10%	Gilts 40%	Cash 30%	Total 100%
Dec 86	£15 000	£5 000	£10 000	£40 000	£30 000	£100 000
Dec 87	£19 123	£6 261	£13 960	£44 614	£33 270	£117 228
Reweight	£17 584	£5 861	£11 723	£46 891	£35 168	£117 228
Dec 88	£19 615	£7 491	£12 517	£50 068	£39 043	£128 734
Reweight	£19 310	£6 437	£12 873	£51 494	£38 620	£128 734
Dec 89	£26 278	£6 798	£16 868	£55 724	£44 246	£149 914
Reweight	£22 487	£7 496	£14 991	£59 966	£44 974	£149 914
Dec 90	£20 298	£6 534	£10 154	£65 731	£52 091	£154 407
Reweight	£23 161	£7 720	£15 441	£61 763	£46 322	£154 407
Dec 91	£27 966	£6.690	£19 005	£71 753	£51 696	£177 110
Reweight	£26 566	£8 855	£17 711	£70 844	£53 133	£177 110
Dec 92	£32 005	£7 722	£20 841	£84 062	£58 177	£202 807
Reweight	£30 421	£10 140	£20 281	£81 123	£60 842	£202 807
Dec 93	£39 074	£19 212	£25 522	£98 170	£64 399	£246 377
Reweight	£36 957	£12 319	£24 638	£98 551	£73 913	£246 377
Dec 94	£36 782	£15 712	£25 700	£92 019	£67 884	£238 096
Reweight	£35 714	£11 905	£23 810	£95 238	£71 429	£238 096
Dec 95	£44 218	£12 524	£29 107	£110 887	£76 226	£272 961
Reweight	£40 944	£13 648	£27 296	£109 185	£81 888	£272 961
Dec 96	£47 778	£17 617	£27 889	£117 154	£86 934	£297 371
Reweight	£44 606	£14 869	£29 737	£118 948	£89 211	£297 371
Dec 97	£55 108	£18 432	£35 734	£135 764	£95 358	£340 396
Reweight	£51 059	£17 020	£34 040	£136 158	£102 119	£340 396
Dec 98	£58 087	£13 813	£42 291	£161 934	£110 214	£386 338
Reweight	£57 951	£19 317	£38 634	£154 535	£115 901	£386 338
Dec 99	£71 971	£22 214	£50 585	£153 179	£121 696	£419 644
Reweight	£62 947	£20 982	£41 964	£167 858	£125 893	£419 644

Note

UK shares: FTSE all share – total return index
Real estate: FTSE real estate – total return index
International shares: MSCI world ex UK – total return index (£)
Gilts: FTA government all stocks – total return index
Cash: UK Treasuries: Barclays Global Investors – total return index

This exercise shows how a sound asset-allocation strategy, a good automatic review mechanism, and discipline can achieve many of the goals of investment.

Of these three elements, discipline is often the most difficult. It requires avoiding, on the one hand, *greed* (which discourages an investor from progressively selling out of a rising market) and *fear* (which discourages an investor from buying into a falling market).

We have now seen that a well-designed passive portfolio-management strategy can produce at least satisfactory results. The question is whether a more active strategy can do even better. We address this issue in the next two sections.

Active portfolio management 1: the fair value range

The trick to deciding whether it is a good time to invest in a particular asset class depends on where it is placed in its cycle. Many investors interpret the task as trying to pick the peaks and troughs precisely. There is, however, another way of approaching market timing, which sets more realistic objectives than picking the absolute highs and lows. This approach is to determine a *fair value range* and treat deviations as opportunities to make limited tactical shifts in the portfolio.

The value-oriented approach not only helps to avoid fear and greed in the investor but seeks to gain an advantage from the fear and greed displayed by others in the market as a whole. These principles can be drawn out by comparing two conceptual approaches to the market.

Figure 9.4 shows what tends to happen in practice during a market cycle, such as for equities. The diagram starts at the high point of the cycle, where investors are convinced that the market is still in a boom. As the market starts to come off, *complacency* keeps new investors buying in as brokers assure them that the falls reflect only a temporary downturn and a great buying opportunity. *Wishful thinking* keeps some investors buying; but as the market continues downwards, investors start having real *concern* about whether the decline is transitory or not. Fear sets in, and reaches a point when speculators panic that they could lose everything. They eventually *capitulate* to fear and sell out altogether. Buyers disappear, and stock prices fall to levels below their *fair* value.

The next phase after the crash is a period of *contempt*, when investors decide that the share market is no more than a way to lose a fortune. In time, however, a few buyers start coming into the market as they perceive how fundamentally low stock prices really are. Thus the cycle begins again. *Caution* gradually gives way to *ego*, as speculators believe that their betting ability is being borne out. The market becomes *confident* that the bull market is back, and pushes market prices above their fundamental value. At the top, investors once again reach the

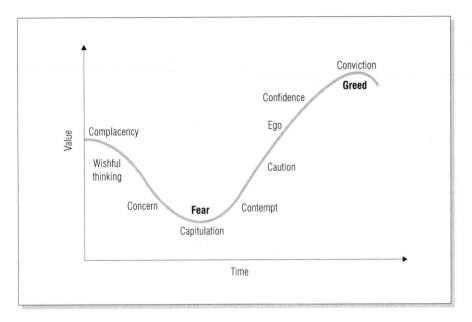

FIGURE 9.4 Market emotion approach

conviction that the boom is here to stay. And this emotion leads to *complacency*, when the market starts its inevitable downward slide.

The value-oriented approach makes use of the psychologically driven exaggerations of the cycle. It is based on the view that most of the time an asset class will trade in a range that more or less reflects its value. This view flows logically from the efficient markets hypothesis. However, this position is modified by the idea that market sentiment, dominated by fear and greed, can play an important role in the prices that people are willing to pay for assets.

From time to time, the prices of assets can become overvalued or under-valued with respect to normal expectations. As noted in earlier chapters, recent research into behavioural finance is suggesting that the herd behaviour that underpins these swings may be increasing. The investor who is capable of assessing quality and value will watch for such 'correlated mistakes', and rebalance the portfolio to take advantage of them.

Figure 9.5 demonstrates the value-oriented approach. When the investor decides that the share market is trading within a fair value range, the 'neutral' asset allocation is maintained. If the investor believes the market is becoming overheated by greed, the exposure to shares will be reduced. When the market,

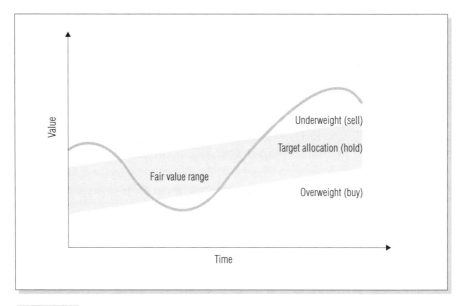

FIGURE 9.5 Market value approach

driven by fear, goes below the fair value range, the weighting to shares will increase. In this way, the investor does not try to pick the absolute timing of the market highs and lows, but takes limited tilts whenever the market moves outside the fair value range.

As discussed in the last chapter, a key tool of the shrewd investor is to establish neutral asset allocations and dynamic ranges around them. In the fair value approach, an investor might have a target allocation of 30 per cent for shares and dynamic ranges of 5 per cent either way. When the market is perceived to be overheated, the investor may bring the share component of the portfolio down to 25 per cent; when the market is seen to be unduly low, the investor may increase the holding to 35 per cent.

The value approach, combined with dynamic allocation, allows the investor to respond to changing markets without losing the discipline of a long-term strategic outlook. It also emphasizes the necessity of devising, and sticking to, dynamic ranges. Such an approach limits the bet made on insights, and helps in becoming a beneficiary rather than a victim of greed or fear. This approach is useful for investors who wish to adopt something more than a totally passive approach.

The question is, of course, how to determine where the fair value range of a particular asset class lies. Part of the approach has been outlined in the strategy sections of the chapters dealing with interest-bearing investments, shares and property. Knowing the investment themes that affect these markets, and examining their historical performance and cycles, can provide a guide to when they represent reasonable value.

There is, however, another dimension that must be taken into account to make the value approach effective. For the investor with a diversified portfolio, all of the markets must be considered together. If the share allocation is going to increase from 30 per cent to 35 per cent, that 5 per cent has to come out of another asset class.

The supreme challenge, therefore, is to apply the value concept simultaneously to shares, property, cash and bonds. This requires huge amounts of information and considerable mental energy. And while many investors may choose to leave such an effort to professional managers, it is worth knowing some of the principles involved so that the investor can judge whether managers know their job. Two key related concepts are involved: comparative value among the asset classes, and the integrated market cycle. We now look briefly at each of these.

Active portfolio management 2: riding the market cycles

Running an active portfolio over several asset classes involves selling some assets in one class to invest in another. What counts, therefore, is not so much the expected performance of each individual asset class in isolation, but the *comparative* performances of the asset classes in relation to each other. Active portfolio management then comes down to assessing the *relative value* of the asset classes.

Ideally, at any one time a portfolio will be neutrally weighted to asset classes that are within their fair value range, underweighted to those above it, and overweighted to those below it. Each of the asset classes has its own cycle, and the key is knowing how these cycles interact.

This is one of the toughest challenges for any investment manager. However, some basic economic themes do incline the asset classes to move in a pattern over time, based on the business cycle, and the interest rate and inflation cycle. At each phase of the cycle, some asset classes become better value than others. Figure 9.6 displays this pattern.

The graph shows, on the one hand, the movement of the business cycle, which represents corporate profitability and confidence. On the other hand is the inflation and interest rate cycle, representing cash rates and the RPI. (For the purposes of the exercise, we assume that interest rates and inflation move in

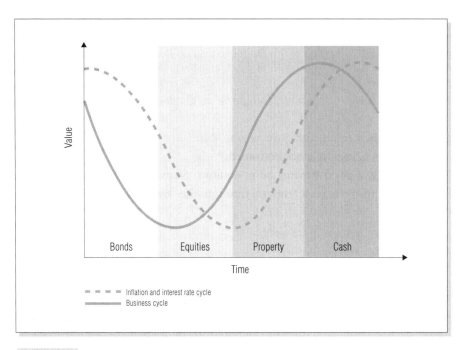

FIGURE 9.6 Integrated cycles approach

unison.) The key to understanding the pattern is the interrelationship between these cycles. A lead-lag gap exists between the business cycle – determined by corporate activity – and the interest rate/inflation cycle – which is determined primarily by monetary policy.

The graph starts at the left with the economy coming off a boom. The government (or central bank, but for convenience we will call it the government) has been using high interest rates to choke inflation, and this policy is starting to take effect. Business expansion and profitability ease back. The government starts to ease monetary policy as inflationary pressures recede, and cash rates fall. However, the government's enthusiasm for its previous high interest rate policy has proved excessive. The business cycle continues its downward trend, unemployment starts to rise, and business investment declines. As the discouraging business indicators start to come in, the government lowers interest rates to stimulate growth.

During this phase, bonds are a particularly attractive investment. An investor who purchases bonds at the start of this phase will lock in a good return and find that their capital value increases as interest rates and inflation decline. This is precisely what happened in the UK in 1997–98. Interest rates came down while inflation remained low. Investors who had put money into bonds during the early part of this period made big profits.

In the next phase, the reduction of interest rates finally starts to bite. The business cycle turns the corner, and profitability, confidence and investment start to improve. Again, there is a lag between the actual business upturn and its appearance in clear statistics, such as growth in GDP, corporate earnings and employment. As a result, the government keeps interest rates down for some time after the business cycle has bottomed.

This phase is a good time to be in equities. Share prices will be relatively cheap as the business cycle moves through the bottom, and will still be reasonable value until the prospective economic upturn is perceived. However, since the market always looks ahead, the window of opportunity for investors may not be long. As soon as the market sees indications that earnings growth will increase, share prices will rise. By the time the higher earnings are actually reported, equities may well be overvalued.

The next phase represents the recovery turning into a boom, as business investment expands, consumption increases, and inflation reappears. The government or central bank, seeing unemployment recede, starts to become more concerned about the economy becoming overheated, and gradually tightens monetary policy. For a while, however, growth in the economy is strong enough to keep propelling corporate earnings. The greed element sets in, and the bull market in equities continues.

This phase is the best time to be in property. As discussed in Chapter 6, the physical property market tends to lag behind the equities market. As the recovery matures, the effect of stronger earnings growth flows through to all sectors of the market. The commercial market enjoys an increased demand for office space, the retail sectors see an upturn as consumer spending rises, and renewed corporate investment sees greater interest in industrial property. Higher wages, enhanced confidence and interest rates – which at the start of the phase are relatively low – contribute to a residential boom.

The final phase is the peak before the crash. The monetary authority, becoming increasingly concerned at the inflationary pressures, further tightens monetary policy and sends interest rates soaring in a bid to 'smooth out' the cycle. Eventually, interest rates hit home, killing the boom. However, the authority, whether it is the government or central bank, does not know when that trigger point has been reached until the statistics start to reflect a slowing in economic activity. It maintains a tight policy, which sees interest rates continue to rise beyond the point at which the business cycle has in fact turned down. This is what happened in the UK in the early 1990s. At some point, the equities market anticipates that corporate earnings will fall away sharply, and shares fall in value.

This is an excellent time to be in cash. Cash interest rates are relatively high and, ironically, it is the riskiest time to be in the other asset classes, since they are at a peak and in danger of collapsing. Successive governments have proclaimed the death of the business cycle, and certainly they are getting better and more committed to ending the cycle of boom and slump, but none has yet conclusively proved its skill, and no government can prevent external inflationary effects such as the tripling of oil prices.

The best way to use the cycles concept is not to pick precise market timing but to use it as a broader application of the fair value range approach. Rather than try to switch dramatically from one asset class to another, the investor can marginally increase or decrease the weightings between them according to their perceived relative value. The advantage of making dynamic decisions at this level, rather than agonizing over individual stocks or properties, is that it is not necessary to worry about everything. Rather, the investor can watch the big picture: the more gradual movements in the financial and economic cycle, and the changes in relative value of the four main asset classes.

Dynamic tilts are, however, still of secondary importance to the long-term investment strategy. The asset allocation will probably remain the key determinant of portfolio performance over time. And by just sticking to the neutral allocation, the investor can be fairly confident of achieving objectives over time spans of 5–10 years. Tilting is only really worthwhile when an investor believes that he or she has a particular insight that is not already 'priced in' to the market.

The concept of riding the market cycles is very attractive, and in hindsight it is simple to fit the conceptual pattern to actual economic and market indicators. The problem, again, is that it is very hard to do so reliably in practice. The precise timing of each phase varies from one cycle to the next. At any particular point, there is a mass of conflicting statistics, which require considerable skill to interpret correctly. Unforeseeable factors, such as changes of government or major developments overseas, can also throw the pattern out of kilter.

Tilting the portfolio to time the market is not free of its own risks; specifically, if the tilt fails, the investor can miss out on the benefits of the strategic allocation. A study by US finance group SEI Capital Resources found that investors who tried to pick the market cycle between shares and cash over a 90-year period would need to have got it right 69 per cent of the time just to beat a buy-and-hold strategy of a shares-only portfolio.[3] Essentially, this was because investors who missed a bull year in the stock market by an incorrect pick on cash would be so far down that they would need to make several correct picks on cash to make up.

With this in mind, it is always worth exercising caution before tilting the portfolio to take advantage of perceived insights. What appears to be a major gap in relative values may actually reflect a fundamental change that has already been incorporated into asset prices. An investor should always ask whether an 'insight' is too good to be true. At any one time, an asset class may appear to be better value based on historical performance, but in fact be correctly valued, based on forecasts. For example, equities, based on earnings yields, may sometimes look expensive compared with bonds, but the market may be anticipating a rise in corporate earnings or higher-than-expected productivity rises.

Also, sometimes what looks like a temporary cyclical anomaly is in fact a tidal shift in the economy or investment environment. In the next section we look at such fundamental changes, and how to incorporate them into investment strategy.

The strategic review

So far we have looked at tactical issues in portfolio management. However, fundamental changes in economies, investment markets, or in the investor's personal situation can call for more than a tactical tilt. Any one of these factors may have changed so much that a *strategic review* is necessary. The objective of such a review is to assess whether the neutral asset allocations and ranges themselves must be adjusted.

The design of the strategic asset allocation process, described in Chapter 8, focused on certain inputs: the investor's profile after establishing specific objectives; the 'rules of the game' in terms of tax and investment; and the economic environment. In a strategic review, the investor goes back to stage one to assess whether these inputs have changed, and adjusts the portfolio accordingly.

Investor's objectives and profile

In Chapter 8, we described the investor's lifestyle goals and needs as the starting point of any sound investment strategy. Portfolio design is directed at balancing time, risk and return to best achieve these objectives. We also looked at a range of information that is required in devising the investor's strategy: assets and income;

income needs; income wants; the tax profile; risk tolerance; and time horizon.

Any of these criteria may change. An individual may receive an inheritance, or face an unexpected financial commitment such as a legal battle or illness. An investor may get divorced or remarry. A tax profile may change as a person enters or leaves the workforce. Risk tolerance, and time horizons, may also change as the investor sets new priorities for his or her life.

A strategic review should identify these sorts of changes, and adjust asset allocations to suit the new set of goals and needs. Changed circumstances may mean that the investor is unable to tolerate the same level of risk, so target allocations for interest-bearing investments might be increased. Conversely, the investor may move into a higher tax bracket, which could dictate a shift in the target allocations in favour of property and shares.

Rules of the game

Changes in the 'rules of the game' – particularly alterations in tax laws – can make some types of investment much more attractive than others. Apart from tax, other legislative changes can shift the playing field. For example, the successful introduction of stakeholder pensions would mean, for some investors, that a greater portion of their long-term retirement needs were met. Such investors might want to alter their savings strategy for their discretionary investment and put more into individual savings accounts.

The rules of the game can also change overseas, which can open or close opportunities for foreign investment. The frequency of these changes means that investors who do not keep abreast of them and incorporate them into strategic reviews may be missing out on new opportunities.

Economic environment

'Quantum leaps' in the economy can also require a strategic change in asset allocations. An example of such a 'leap' was the move to a low-inflation, low-interest rate environment in the UK in the 1990s. This tidal change, under-pinned now by a major technological revolution, is likely to affect investment strategy for most of the first decade of the new millennium.

These changes called for significant shifts in asset allocations. While cash became less attractive for all investors, the challenge was to decide which asset classes to switch into. More generally, the investment scene in the late 1990s became more focused on the true quality of assets and the risk/return trade-off. Such a shift simply emphasizes the need for investors to be well versed in analyzing and valuing the fundamentals, looking for long-term growth rather than speculative short-term gain.

The three dimensions of change discussed above are best considered together, since they may offset or amplify each other. Professional portfolio managers usually have standing orders for periodic strategic reviews, perhaps once every quarter. For private investors, such a review may be necessary once every year or so, or whenever a major change warrants it.

Investment vehicles

It is also worthwhile, perhaps at the same time as a strategic review, to re-examine investment vehicles periodically. Changes in tax laws, apart from altering the relative attractiveness of asset classes, may also make some vehicles more or less tax-effective. It is also appropriate to review the performances of each vehicle.

As discussed in Chapter 7, fund managers have different investment strategies and styles. Some may be better suited to one type of economic environment than another. While the strategy of diversifying across managers is designed to deal with this issue, it is still worth assessing whether a particular manager is doing a good job in *any* economic situation. This will help the investor to know when to move from one fund manager to another. It is essential to take the attitude that the people who run investment vehicles – from a small unit trust to a giant life office – are the investor's servants, hired for a fee to manage one's money. If the service is poor or the fee is too high for the value added, it may be time to find a different manager.

A few key questions will assist in deciding whether to persevere or move.

- Has the manager added value against the benchmark for the asset class?

- What were the reasons, and how does this relate to the strengths or weaknesses identified by the investor (or an adviser) at the time of going into the fund?

- If the manager did add value, are there any contributing factors that may disappear, such as the departure of a 'star' or changes in the economic structure that suited the manager's strength?

- If the manager did not add value, how likely is it that this will be rectified over a reasonable period, and why?

- Above all, what risks did the manager take?

Strategic reviews are one way of helping to keep the investor's eyes on the big picture – one of the most rewarding abilities in investment. We expand on this theme in the final section.

Conclusion: wealth without tears

The investment scene that investors in the UK and Europe face in the new millennium is the most exciting for more than a century. Deregulation of domestic and international markets has created a vast array of easily accessible investment opportunities. New technologies offer prospects for a major leap forward in wealth creation.

This revolution coincides with the greatest changes in the geopolitical map of the world in half a century. While there was a lot of bad news around the world at the start of the new millennium, there was also much cause for optimism. While difficulties continued, the transition of the former communist bloc to independent free market states passed the point of no return. The world had weathered the Asian meltdown and the technology stock 'crashette' and emerged from them more mature. While local conflicts continue, the global struggle between power blocs has receded. As the deputy editor of *The Economist*, Nicholas Colchester, once told a Melbourne audience: 'The multi-world does not exist any more.'[4] These changes, he said, offer the chance for a new golden age of international trade and investment:

> So there should now be a new dawn – a return to that golden, pre-ideological time of the late 19th century, when the mature world was trading with, and investing in, the developing world.

The teething problems in the transformation of politics, economics and technology, at home and abroad, are not yet over. The economies of both the UK and its neighbours are likely to experience distress from time to time as they adapt to the modern world.

Overseas, world politics is likely to remain fluid for some time as the new world order is cemented. The experts say the 21st century will see China join the United States as an economic super-power if it can solve the problems caused by its huge and inefficient structure of state industries and accommodate demands for greater democracy. Europe may have to choose whether it wants to compete outright on all world markets or maintain its social and welfare policies built up over the second half of the 20th century. The UK may have to decide whether it wants to continue as an outpost of US enterprise culture 'in Europe but not controlled by Europe', and risk the possibility of finding itself marginalized.

Investment in the future may involve looking at wealth creation in a radically different way. While traditional European manufacturing industries may be dying, the European Union is a dynamic market, expanding in area, population and wealth and well placed to export services to the emerging markets. Free trade deals under the World Trade Organization are seeing many barriers to trade in services removed, and could offer a significant opportunity.

The internet seems certain to have a bigger and certainly a faster impact on the future than the internal combustion engine. New jobs are being created in industries that did not exist before as the explosion of business conducted on the internet has created a market not only for computers but for website designers, software writers, online gambling vendors, credit card transaction programmers, and so on.

This technology is being passed to developing economies more rapidly than any previous wave of progress, islands of poverty are being eroded, and investment opportunities are opening up more widely than ever before. Very few generations of investors have had the privilege of witnessing a time of epochal change. And the biggest obstacle to taking advantage of the opportunities and dealing sensibly with the challenges that this such change presents will be the behaviour of the individual investor.

Prospective investors are likely to approach this revolution in one of two ways. Some will have a narrow view and see only the short-term problems. These investors will be confused and fearful of the investment scene, and are likely to make the sorts of mistakes discussed in this book. They may, in their search for 'safe' investments, expose themselves to the dangers of renewed inflation or a narrow asset allocation. They will probably miss out on major wealth-creation avenues both at home and abroad. And they will generally not enjoy investment.

Other investors will view the changing investment scene at home and abroad as a treasure chest of opportunities. They will apply the techniques and philosophies outlined in this book. While restricting risk to their own tolerable limits, they will not let this concern prevent them from taking advantage of emerging markets. And they will have fun.

Using the basic rules outlined in this book, successful investment is not difficult. It involves common sense and keeping it simple. Above all, investors who adopt these principles will look forward to enjoying the life that they want to live in the third millennium.

Notes

1   Higgins, Ean (1987) 'Stock market '88: dancing on the *Titanic*', *Times on Sunday*, 24 May, p. 23.

2   Hulbert, Mark (1991) 'Keeping it simple,' *Forbes*, 25 November.

3   SEI Capital Resources (1992) 'The asset allocation decision', position paper, April.

4   Colchester, Nicholas (1991) 'The changing nature of trade', public address in Melbourne, 8 October.

Index